MULE BONE

MULE BONE

A COMEDY OF NEGRO LIFE

LANGSTON HUGHES AND
ZORA NEALE HURSTON

Edited with Introductions by George Houston Bass
and Henry Louis Gates, Jr.
and the complete story of the *Mule Bone* Controversy

HarperPerennial
A Division of HarperCollins*Publishers*

FIRST EDITION

Designed by Cassandra J. Pappas

Library of Congress Cataloging-in-Publication Data

Hughes, Langston, 1902–1967.
  Mule bone : a comedy of Negro life / by Langston Hughes and Zora
Neale Hurston ; edited with introductions by George Houston Bass
and Henry Louis Gates, Jr., and the complete story of the mule bone
controversy.—1st ed.
    p. cm.
  ISBN 0-06-055301-4
  ISBN 0-06-096885-0 (pbk.)
  I. Hurston, Zora Neale. II. Bass, George Houston. III. Gates,
Henry Louis. IV. Title.
PS3515.U274M85 1991
812'.52—dc20   90-55835

91 92 93 94 95 CC/FG 10 9 8 7 6 5 4 3 2 1
91 92 93 94 95 CC/FG 10 9 8 7 6 5 4 3 2 1 (pbk.)

For
George Houston Bass,
In Memoriam
1938–1990

CONTENTS

ACKNOWLEDGMENTS

T he editors would like to thank the estates of Langston Hughes and Zora Neale Hurston for permission to publish their play, and Robert Hemenway and Arnold Rampersad for permission to publish excerpts of their biographies of Hurston and Hughes. We would also like to thank the staffs at the Beinecke Rare Book and Manuscript Library at Yale and the Moorland-Spingarn Research Center at Howard for their advice and expertise in locating drafts of the play and relevant correspondence. Without this assistance, this publication would not have been possible.

PREFACE

Mule Bone is a three-act play, jointly written in 1930 by Langston Hughes and Zora Neale Hurston. Because of a dispute between the authors, the origins of which remain mysterious, the play was never performed during the authors' lifetimes. Indeed, only its third and final act was published, and this not until 1964. Drafts of the play were accessible only to scholars, through the Alain Locke Papers at the Moorland-Spingarn Research Center at Howard University and through the Langston Hughes Papers at the Beinecke Rare Book and Manuscript Library at Yale. But the quarrel surrounding the play's authorship has made it an object of great curiosity in Afro-American literary history.

I first heard of the play when reading Langston Hughes's autobiography, *The Big Sea* (1940); there, Hughes describes his perception of the affair in a chapter entitled "Literary Quarrel." Two careful and perceptive scholars, Robert Hemenway and Arnold Rampersad, present meticulous accounts of the controversy in their biographies of Hurston and Hughes.

These three accounts we reprint here, along with much of the archival sources upon which their accounts are based.

It is apparent to the editors that *Mule Bone* was written jointly by Hughes and Hurston, and that their quarrel not only interrupted a productive friendship, it also killed a most promising collaborative team in the theatre, which in turn stifled the development of an African-American theatre based upon black vernacular forms. We can only wonder at the directions that black theatre might have taken in America had *Mule Bone* been produced and published. However, it was not.

The first production of *Mule Bone* is scheduled, at this writing, for February 1991, at the Lincoln Center Theatre, thanks to Gregory Mosher, the Artistic Director; George Bass, executor of the Hughes Estate; and Clifford Hurston, executor of the Hurston Estate. The play has been copyrighted in the names of the authors.

Two days before the editing of this volume was completed, George Houston Bass died quite unexpectedly. Mr. Bass, a professor of Afro-American Studies and founder and Artistic Director of the Rites and Reason Theatre at Brown University, and Langston Hughes's secretary and confidant, had been especially excited about both this edition of *Mule Bone* and about its Lincoln Center premiere, exactly sixty-one years after it was written. Bringing this "lost" work of the Harlem Renaissance to the stage had preoccupied the last two years of his life. Mr. Bass and I designed together every aspect of this volume.

George Bass loved the theatre, as he loved all of literature, and life itself. He had recently edited the complete poems of Langston Hughes and was planning to edit Hughes's collected papers. His devotion to Hughes was total and unflinching. No author's legacy has been better served by an executor than Bass has served Hughes.

It is altogether fitting, then, that this edition of *Mule Bone* and its Lincoln Center premiere are dedicated to George Houston Bass.

H.L.G., Jr.
September 20, 1990

MULE BONE

ANOTHER BONE OF CONTENTION:

Reclaiming Our Gift of Laughter

George Houston Bass

In her writing of Afro-American folklore, Zora Neale Hurston has cited the art of laughter as one of black folk's gifts to American culture. Langston Hughes also recognized laughter as one of the great strengths of the Afro-American people. Hurston and Hughes, who combined their creative skills and appreciation for laughter in writing their play *Mule Bone,* are widely recognized masters of the art of "laughing to keep from crying" and of the blues sensibility which is so central to the comic imagination of Afro-American tradition. Hurston mastered the language and lore of southern black American landscape and Hughes claimed black folk sounds and rhythms of the urban north. Their appreciation for the

1

oral tradition of Afro-American people and their understanding of black folk's use of laughter as a coping mechanism for personal and group survival have made them primary sources of instruction for students of Afro-American history and culture.

Hurston and Hughes adapted *Mule Bone* from a folktale, "The Bone of Contention," which Hurston had collected from her all-black hometown of Eatonville, Florida. The playscript was written during the early months of 1930, a period when images of black people in popular American culture were still shaped by notions of primitivism, exoticism, and minstrelsy. Unlike the contrived images of black folk-life presented in such plays as *The Emperor Jones, Porgy,* and *Green Pastures,* the authors of *Mule Bone* envisioned their play as an "authentic" portrayal of black comic characters and the rich uses of language and laughter southern black folk had invented as a way of creatively coping with the harshness of being black in America. Unfortunately, the play was never produced in the authors' lifetimes and in a real sense *Mule Bone* is an unfinished work. The cover page of the draft of the playscript in the Hughes papers at Yale University bears a handwritten note by Langston Hughes that reads, "This play was never done because the authors fell out."

In the spring of 1988, almost sixty years after the script was written, Greg Mosher, Artistic Director of Lincoln Center Theatre, expressed an interest in producing the first known public performance of *Mule Bone.* It was thought that the staging of an unproduced script by two of the most gifted black writers of the twentieth century could make a significant contribution to the American theatre. But, on close reading of the script, it became very clear that a production of the 1930 draft of the text could become quite problematic in terms of the current cultural, social, and political sensibilities of the American public. Rites and Reason Theatre became a collaborator in the task of developing the playscript left by Hurston and Hughes into a viable performance work for a popular theatre audience sixty years after the script was created.

One of the principal issues and creative challenges that has surfaced in the development of the script concerns the use of broad black comic types in the play which can be easily viewed in terms of the stigmas and offensive stereotypes of minstrel shows and the plantation tradition of American literature. A genuine appreciation for the richness of black folk culture and for the genius of Zora Neale Hurston and Langston Hughes has allowed us to look beyond the problematic aspects of the text and try to recognize the poetic insights and dramatic possibilities that could have been the thematic focus of the "Negro folk comedy" Hurston and Hughes wanted to create.

The expansion of moral and aesthetic consciousness that has occurred in American society since 1960 has produced a social climate that does not allow one to laugh easily at broad comic interpretations of black people. Many of the comic characters, comic devices, and forms of laughter that were sources of renewal and release within the black community before 1960 are now inhibited by the politics of race and gender. Forms of parody and self-parody which were once a way of dealing with the stress and pain of a bad situation and finding a way to change it are now quite often viewed as assaults and insults.

The millions of black folk who have endured cruel and dehumanizing situations as they inched their way through the years of slavery and Jim Crow laws to the years of the Civil Rights Movement and beyond knew how to use laughter as a tool for regeneration, transformation, and re-creation. They left folk tales, family stories, songs, rhymes, toasts, and jokes that document their great ability and skill in laughing at very ugly conditions. Obviously, they viewed the world quite differently from the black persons who in recent years found little humor and no cause for laughter in George Wolfe's *The Colored Museum* and in Spike Lee's films.

In *Mule Bone*, Zora Neale Hurston and Langston Hughes have made very deliberate use of laughter and broad comic characters and devices from Afro-American tradition. The art of "lying" and telling tall tales as well as the art of "signifying" and "putting down" one's friends and neighbors in defining and refining one's sense of self and community are demonstrated by more than two dozen characters from Eatonville who know how to laugh away the overwhelming pains and burdens of hard times. The sense-meaning of their laughter holds the meaning and significance of the playscript Hurston and Hughes have left to us.

A TRAGEDY OF
NEGRO LIFE

Henry Louis Gates, Jr.

This play was never done because the authors fell out.

—LANGSTON HUGHES, 1931

And fall out, unfortunately, they did, thereby creating the most notorious literary quarrel in African-American cultural history, and one of the most thoroughly documented collaborations in black American literature. Langston Hughes published an account entitled "Literary Quarrel" as the penultimate chapter—indeed, almost as a coda or an afterthought—in his autobiography, *The Big Sea* (1940). Robert Hemenway, Zora Neale Hurston's biographer, published a chapter in his biography entitled "Mule Bone," and Arnold Rampersad, Hughes's biographer, presents an equally detailed account in volume one of his *The Life of Langston Hughes.* Only Zora Neale Hurston, of the two principals, did not make public her views of the episode. But she did leave several letters (as did Hughes) in which she explains some of her behavior and feelings. In addition, Hurston left the manuscript of the short story, "The Bone of

Contention," upon which the play was based. These documents—letters, the short story, Hughes's account, and two accounts from careful and judicious scholars—as well as a draft of the text of the play, *Mule Bone: A Comedy of Negro Life,* comprise the full record of the curious history of this brilliant collaboration between two extraordinarily talented African-American writers. We have assembled this archival and published data here to provide contemporary readers with the fullest possible account of a complex and bizarre incident that will forever remain impossible to understand completely, beclouded in inexplicable motivation.

In a sense, this is a casebook of a crucial—and ugly—chapter in the history of the Harlem Renaissance, that extraordinarily rich period in American cultural history that witnessed the birth of jazz, the coming to fruition of the classic blues, and the first systematic attempt to generate an entire literary and cultural movement by black Americans. The Harlem Renaissance, also called "The New Negro Renaissance," is generally thought to have begun in the early 1920s and ended early on in the Great Depression, about the time when Hughes and Hurston had their dispute. The origins of the Renaissance are, of course, complex and have been written about extensively. It is clear, however, that the production of a rich and various black art, especially the written arts and the theatre, could very well help to reshape the public image of black people within American society and facilitate thereby their long struggle for civil rights, a struggle that commenced almost as soon as the last battle of the Civil War ended. As James Weldon Johnson put it in the "Preface" to his *Book of American Negro Poetry* (1922):

> A people may be great through many means, but
> there is one by which its greatness is recognized and
> acknowledged. The final measure of the greatness
> of all peoples is the amount and standard of the

literature and art they produced. The world does not know that a people is great until that people produces great literature and art. No people that has produced great literature and art has ever been looked upon by the world as distinctly inferior.

If, then, African-Americans created a recognizable and valued canon of literature, its effect would have enormous political ramifications: "The status of the Negro in the United States," Johnson concluded, "is more a question of national mental attitude toward the race than of actual conditions. And nothing will do more to change that mental attitude and raise his status than a demonstration of intellectual parity by the Negro through the production of literature and art."

Johnson, by 1922 one of the venerable figures of the black literary and theatrical traditions, effectively issued a call to arms for the creation of a literary movement. Soon, political organizations such as the National Association for the Advancement of Colored People (NAACP) and the National Urban League, through their magazines, *The Crisis* and *Opportunity*, began to sponsor literary competitions, judged by prominent members of the American literati, with the winners receiving cash prizes, publication in the journals, and often book contracts. At the prompting of Charles Johnson, the editor of *Opportunity*, Hurston submitted two short stories—"Spunk" and "Black Death"—and two plays—*Color Struck* and *Spears*—for consideration in *Opportunity*'s annual literary contests in 1925 and 1926. While "Spunk" and *Color Struck* won second-place prizes, *Spears* and "Black Death" won honorable mention. Two other short stories, "Drenched in Light" and "Muttsy" would be published in *Opportunity*, along with "Spunk." It was at the 1925 annual awards dinner that she met another award winner, Langston Hughes, who took third prize jointly with Countee Cullen and first prize for his great poem, "The Weary Blues." It was a momentous occasion, attended by "the greatest gathering of black and white literati ever assembled in one room," as Arnold Rampersad notes, and included among its judges Eugene O'Neill, John Farrar, Witter Bynner, Alexander Woolcott, and Robert Benchley. Hughes was quite taken with Hurston, Rampersad tells us: She " 'is a clever girl, isn't she?' he soon wrote to a friend; 'I would like to know her.' " Eventually, he would know her all too well.

II

Between 1925 and their collaboration on the writing of *Mule Bone* between March and June 1930, Hughes and Hurston came to know each other well. As Rampersad reports, by mid-summer of 1926, the two were planning a black jazz and blues opera. Hemenway calls it "an opera that would be the first authentic rendering of black folklife, presenting folk songs, dances, and tales that Hurston would collect." By the end of that summer, the two (along with Wallace Thurman, John P. Davis, Gwen Bennett, Bruce Nugent, and Aaron Douglass, all members of what was jokingly called "The Niggerati") decided to found a magazine, called *Fire!!,* the title taken from a Hughes poem. The following year, in July 1927, Hughes and Hurston met quite by accident in Mobile, Alabama, and decided to drive together to Manhattan in her car, "Sassy Susie." "I knew it would be fun travelling with her," Rampersad reports Hughes writing. "It was." The trip lasted about a month, with the two sharing notes on hoodoo, folktales, and the blues along the way, and even meeting Bessie Smith, the great classic blues singer. Shortly after this trip, Hughes introduced Hurston to his patron, Charlotte van der Veer Quick Mason, who would contribute about $75,000 to Harlem Renaissance writers, including $15,000 to Hurston. While Hughes received $150 per month, Hurston received $200. Ironically, their subsidies would end just about the time of their feud over *Mule Bone;* although Hurston's contract ended March 30, 1931, she received "irregular" payments until September 1932; Hughes and she fell out late in 1930, just before his confrontation with Hurston in Cleveland.

A more natural combination for a collaboration among the writers of the Harlem Renaissance, one can scarcely imagine—especially in the theatre! Hurston wrote to Hughes often during the early period of her research in the South, collecting black folklore as part of her doctoral research in anthropology at Columbia under Franz Boas; Hemenway describes her correspondence as "frequent and conspiratorial," providing "an unintentional documentary of the expedition." In April 1928, she shared with Hughes her plans for a culturally authentic African-American theatre, one constructed upon a foundation of the black vernacular: "Did I tell you before I left about the new, the *real* Negro theatre I plan? Well, I shall, or rather we shall act out the folk tales, however short, with the abrupt angularity and naivete of the primitive 'bama Nigger. Quote that with native settings. What do you think?" They would share the burdens and the glory: "Of course, you know I didn't dream of that theatre as a one man stunt. I had you helping 50–50 from the start. In fact, I am perfectly willing to be 40 to your 60 since you are always so much more practical than I. But I know it is going to be *glorious!* A really new departure in the drama." Despite their enthusiasm for this idea, however, Mrs. Mason ("Godmother") disapproved; as Hurston wrote to Alain Locke, the veritable dean of the Harlem Renaissance and another beneficiary of Mrs. Mason's patronage: "Godmother was very anxious that I should say to you that the plans—rather the hazy dreams of the theatre I talked to you about should never be mentioned again. She trusts her three children [Hurston, Hughes, and Locke] to never let those words pass their lips again until the gods decree that they shall materialize."

Not only did the two share the dream of a vernacular

theatre and opera, but both had established themselves as creative writers and critics by underscoring the value of black folk culture, both of itself and as the basis for formal artistic traditions. By 1930, when, at last, the two would write *Mule Bone,* Hughes had published two brilliant, widely acclaimed, experimental books of poetry that utilized the blues and jazz as both form and content. And Hurston, though yet to publish a novel, had published sixteen short stories, plays, and essays, in prestigious journals such as *Opportunity, Messenger,* and the *Journal of Negro History,* and was pursuing a Ph.D. thesis in anthropology which was to be built around her extensive collection of Afro-American myths. With Hurston's mastery of the vernacular and compelling sense of story, and Hughes's impressive sense of poetic and theatrical structure, it would have been difficult to imagine a more ideal team to construct "a real Negro theatre." For, at ages twenty-eight and twenty-nine respectively,* Hughes and Hurston bore every promise of reshaping completely the direction of the development of African-American literature away from the blind imitation of American literature and toward a bold and vibrant synthesis of formal American literature and African-American vernacular.

III

The enormous potential of this collaborative effort was never realized, we know, because, as Hughes wrote on his manuscript copy of the text, "the authors fell out." Exactly *why* they "fell out" is not completely clear, despite the valiant attempts of Hemenway and Rampersad to reconstruct the curious series of events that led to such disastrous consequences. While we do know that Hughes and Hurston wrote acts one and

---

*Hurston, the scholar Cheryl Wall discovered, shaved ten years from her age. Actually, in 1930, she would have been thirty-nine, not twenty-nine, as she claimed.

three together, and, as Hemenway reports, "at least one scene of the second act," it is impossible to ascertain who wrote what. Hurston had conceived the plot, based as it was on her short story, "The Bone of Contention" (published here for the first time). Hughes would write that he "plotted out and typed the play based on her story," and that Hurston "authenticated and flavored the dialogue and added highly humorous details." Rampersad's estimate is probably the most accurate: "Hurston's contribution was almost certainly the greater to a play set in an all-black town in the backwoods South (she drew here on her childhood memories), with an abundance of tall tales, wicked quips, and farcical styles of which she was absolute master and Langston not much more than a sometimes student. . . . Whatever dramatic distinction the play would have, Hurston certainly brought to it." But, just as surely, it was Hughes who shaped the material into a play, into comic drama, with a plot, a dramatic structure, and a beginning, middle, and end. While Hurston had published a play, and Hughes had not yet completed his first play, Hughes was the superior dramatist. Neither, however, would ever achieve the results that they did, in close collaboration, with *Mule Bone.*

While we cannot explain Hurston's motivation for denying Hughes's collaboration, which caused the dispute and the ending of their friendship, we can re-create the strange series of events through the following chronology, which is based on the accounts of Hemenway and Rampersad, printed in this book:

Late February–early March 1930: Hughes meets Theresa Helburn of the Dramatists Guild at a party; Helburn complains about the lack of real comedies about blacks.

April–May 1930: Hughes and Hurston write the first draft of "Mule Bone" in Westfield, New Jersey. Complete acts one and three and at least scene one of act two, dictating to Louise Thompson.

May 1930: Hughes's relation with patron, Mrs. Mason, begins to collapse.

June 1930: Hurston returns to the South, ostensibly to complete the trial scene of act two.

September 1930: Hurston returns, apparently without the scene completed.

October 1930: Hurston files for copyright of *Mule Bone* as sole author.

December 1930–January 1931: Hughes ends relationship with "Godmother," Mrs. Mason.

January 1931: Hughes returns to his mother's home in Cleveland, has tonsillectomy.

Winter 1930–31: Hurston gives Carl Van Vechten copy of play. Van Vechten sends it to Barrett Clark, reader for the Theatre Guild. Clark, an employee of Samuel French, the theatrical producer, contacts Rowena Jelliffe and sends script.

January 15, 1931: Hughes visits Rowena and Alexander Jelliffe, directors of the settlement playhouse "Karamu House," home of the black theatre troupe the Gilpin Players. Rowena Jelliffe explains that she has obtained the rights to a play entitled *Mule Bone* by Zora Neale Hurston.

January 16, 1931: Hughes phones Hurston to protest her action. Hurston denies knowledge of play being sent to French or to Jelliffe. Hughes incredulous.

January 16, 1931: Hughes writes to Carl Van Vechten asking for his advice.

January 17, 1931: Louise Thompson arrives in Cleveland, in her capacity as official of the American Interracial Seminar.

January 18, 1931: Hurston visits Van Vechten, and "cried and carried on no end."

January 19, 1931: Hughes mails copy of play to U.S. copyright office, in name of Hurston and himself. Received January 22.

January 20, 1931: Hughes receives Hurston's letter denying joint authorship and complaining about Louise Thompson's compensation.

January 20, 1931: French's company wires Jelliffe refusing Hurston's permission to authorize production. Demands return of script.

January 20–21, 1931: Hurston sends three telegrams reversing her decision; authorizes the production and agrees to collaborate with Hughes.

January 21, 1931: Hughes receives Hurston letter of January 18, denying Hughes's collaboration and revealing resentment over Hughes's friendship with Louise Thompson.

January 21–26, 1931: Hurston agrees to come to Cleveland to collaborate with Hughes on rewrites; first performance scheduled for February 15.

February 1, 1931: Hughes's twenty-ninth birthday. Hurston arrives in Cleveland, meets with Hughes, resolves differences, misses scheduled meeting with Gilpin Players. That evening, the Gilpin Players meet and vote to cancel play, but reconsider. All seems set for a Cleveland opening and a Broadway run.

February 2, 1931: Hurston learns that Louise Thompson has visited Cleveland and seen Hughes. Hurston berates Mrs. Jelliffe.

February 3, 1931: Hurston visits Hughes at his home and rudely cancels production.

August 1931: Wallace Thurman (estranged husband of Louise Thompson) hired to revise *Mule Bone.* Hughes writes to Dramatists Guild declaring joint authorship.

1940: Hughes publishes account in *The Big Sea.*

1964: Hughes publishes act three in *Drama Critique.*

This, in barest outline, is an account of the bizarre events of an extremely ugly affair. As Hemenway and Rampersad make clear, Hurston justified her denial of Hughes's collaboration by claiming anger over Hughes's apparent proposal that Louise Thompson be given a share of all royalties, and that she be made the business manager of any Broadway production that might evolve. In Hurston's words:

> In the beginning, Langston, I was very eager to do the play with you. ANYthing you said would go over big with me. But scarcely had we gotten underway before you made three propositions that shook me to the foundation of myself. First: that three way split with Louise. Now Langston, nobody has in the history of the world given a typist an interest in a work for typing it. Nobody would think of it unless they were prejudiced in favor of the typist.

If this seems scant reason, sixty years later, for Hurston's protest over Thompson's financial role to assume such an extreme form, her behavior was no doubt also motivated, as Hemenway and Rampersad argue, by Hughes's deteriorating relationship with Mrs. Mason and Hurston's desire to continue hers, even if at Hughes's expense. Hurston kept Mrs. Mason abreast of these developments over the play, and even sent her copies of Hughes's letters to her, all the while denying his claims to Mason. What seems clear, however, is that Hurston's behavior was not justified by her anger over Hughes's friendship with Thompson, and that her claim of sole authorship should not have been made. As Hughes concluded, "our art was broken," as was both their friendship and the promise of a new and bold direction in black theatre.

IV

Certainly one tragic aspect of the failure of Hughes and Hurston to produce and publish *Mule Bone* was the interruption of the impact that it might have had on the shape and direction of Afro-American theatre. Among all of the black arts, greater expectations were held for none more than for black theatre. As early as 1918, W. E. B. Du Bois, writing in *The Crisis,* argued that "the value of [a sustained Afro-American theatre] for Negro art can scarcely be overestimated." In 1925, Du Bois would help to found Krigwa, a black theatre group in Harlem, dedicated to drama that is "by," "for," "about," and "near *us,* " a self-contained and self-sustaining Afro-American theatre. Du Bois was just one of many critics who felt that the drama was the most crucial form of all of the arts for the future of black artistic development, and that it was precisely in this area that blacks had most signally failed. As Alain Locke put it, "Despite the fact that Negro life is somehow felt to be particularly rich in dramatic values, both as folk experience and as a folk temperament, its actual yield, so far as worthwhile drama goes, has been very inconsiderable." And, in another essay published in 1927, Locke wrote:

In the appraisal of the possible contribution of the Negro to the American theatre, there are those who find the greatest promise in the rising drama of Negro life. Others see possibilities of a deeper, though subtler influence upon what is after all more vital, the technical aspects of the arts of the theatre. Until very recently the Negro influence upon American drama has been negligible, whereas even under the handicaps of second-hand exploitation and restriction to the popular amusement stage, the Negro actor has already considerably influenced our stage and its arts. One would do well to imagine

what might happen if the art of the Negro actor
should really become artistically lifted and liber-
ated. Transpose the possible resources of Negro
song and dance and pantomime to the serious stage,
envisage an American drama under the galvanizing
stimulus of a rich transfusion of essential folk-arts
and you may anticipate what I mean. ("The Negro
and the American Theatre")

There can be little doubt that Locke here voices the theory of
black drama that Hurston and Hughes sought to embody in
their unwritten black opera and in *Mule Bone.* (Hurston had,
by the way, once described the relationship among the three
as that of a triangle, with Hughes and her forming the base,
and Locke the apex.)

There are many reasons for the supposed primacy of the
theatre among the arts of the Harlem Renaissance. Many
scholars date the commencement of the Renaissance itself to
the phenomenal and unprecedented success of Eubie Blake's
and Noble Sissle's all-black Broadway musical, *Shuffle Along,*
which opened in 1921. (Blake and Sissle did the score, and
Aubrey Lyles and Flournoy Miller did the book.) As Bruce
Kellner informs us, "Often the week's first run business was
so heavy that the street on which it was playing had to be
designated for one-way traffic only." Josephine Baker, Flor-
ence Mills, and Paul Robeson were just a few of the performers who played in this musical.

Predictably, the success of *Shuffle Along* spawned a whole
host of imitators, including *Alabama Bound, Bandana Land,
Black Bottom Revue, Black Scandals, Blackbirds, Chocolate Blondes,
Chocolate Browns, Chocolate Dandies, Darktown Scandals, Darktown Strutters, Goin' White, Lucky Sambo, North Ain't South,
Raisin' Cane, Strut Miss Lizzie, Seven-Eleven, Dixie to Broadway,*
and *Runnin' Wild* (which introduced "The Charleston"), to
list just a few. Jazz, the dance, acting, and an extraordinarily

large white and sympathetic audience made the theatre an enormously promising venue for a black art that would transform the public image of the Negro. Its effect was both broad and immediate; there was not the sort of mediation necessary between artist and audience as is the case with a printed book. What's more, theatre as a combination of several arts—poetry, narrative, music, the dance, acting, the visual arts—allowed blacks to bring together the full range of their traditions, vernacular and formal, rather than just one. The great potential of the theatre was hard to resist.

Resistance, however, arose from tradition itself. The roots of black theatre in the twenties were buried in the soil of minstrelsy and vaudeville. Musicals such as *Shuffle Along* did indeed reach tens of thousands more Americans than would any book before *Native Son* (1940). But what image did they represent, and at what cost? Reviews of *Shuffle Along* often turned on phrases such as "extreme energy," "the sun of their good humor." Especially notable were the dancers' "jiggling," "prancing," "wiggling," and "cavorting." In other words, what this sort of black theatre did was to reinforce the stereotype of black people as happy-go-lucky, overly sensual bodies. And while it was (and remains) difficult to disrupt the integrity of jazz and Afro-American dance, even in association with quasi-minstrel forms, it is difficult to imagine how the *intelligence* of these artistic traditions could shine through the raucous humor of this kind of theatre. Broadway, in other words, stood as the counterpoint to the sort of written art that Hughes and Hurston were determined to create, even if they envied Broadway's potential and actual market. Accordingly, they decided to intervene, to do for the drama what Hughes had done for poetry and what Hurston would do (in *Jonah's Gourd Vine* [1934] and *Their Eyes Were Watching God* [1937]) for the novel, which was to shape a formal written art out of the vast and untapped black vernacular tradition.

Mule Bone was based on a Hurston short story, "The

Bone of Contention," which Hurston never published. For the Hurston scholar, it is particularly fascinating as a glimpse into Hurston's manner of revising or transforming the oral tradition (she had collected the story in her folklore research) and because of its representation of various characters (such as Eatonville, an all-black town where Hurston was born, Joe Clarke and his store, the yellow mule and his mock burial) who would recur in subsequent works, such as *Mule Bone* and *Their Eyes Were Watching God.*

The story's plot unfolds as follows: Dave Carter and Jim Weston are hunting turkeys one evening. Carter claims to have shot a turkey, while Weston is loading his gun. Weston claims that it is his shot that killed the turkey. They struggle. Jim Weston strikes Dave Carter on the head with "de hockbone" of a mule, Carter alleges, and steals his turkey.

The remainder of the plot depicts the trial, held at the Baptist Church and presided over by Mayor Joe Clarke. Weston is a Methodist while Clarke is a Baptist, and the townspeople are equally divided between the two denominations. They are also fiercely competitive, bringing a religious significance to the quarrel. In fact, Carter and Weston would be represented in court by their ministers, Rev. Simms (Methodist) and Elder Long (Baptist). "The respective congregations were lined up behind their leaders," the text tells us.

The resolution of the dilemma turns on traditional African-American biblical exegesis: can a mule-bone be a weapon? If it can, then it follows that its use could constitute a criminal act. Using Judges 15:16, Elder Long proves that since a donkey is the father of a mule, and since Samson slew one thousand Philistines with the jaw-bone of an ass, and since "de further back on a mule you goes, do mo' dangerous he gits," then "by de time you gits clear back tuh his hocks hes rank pizen." Jim Weston is banished from town.

The plot of *Mule Bone* is very similar. The play consists of three acts, and includes Jim Weston and Dave Carter (best friends), Joe Clarke, but now Daisy Taylor, over whom Weston and Clarke will, inevitably, quarrel. Weston will strike Carter with the hock-bone of "Brazzle's ole yaller mule," during an argument over Daisy on the front porch of Clarke's store. Weston is arrested, Carter is rushed off to be treated, leaving Daisy alone wondering who's going to walk her home.

Act Two consists of two scenes. The first reveals the subtext of the trial—the struggle between Joe Clarke and Elder Simms for mayor, and the class tension between the Baptists and the Methodists. Scene Two occurs mostly in the Macedonia Baptist Church, newly transformed into a courthouse, with Joe Clarke presiding. As in the short story, the Methodists and Baptists seat themselves on opposite sides, even singing competing hymns (Baptists, "Onward Christian Soldiers" and the Methodists, "All Hail the Power of Jesus's Name") when the mayor asks that the proceedings commence with a hymn. Act Two proceeds as does the short story, with Judges 18:18 coming to bear in exactly the same manner as had Judges 15:16. Jim Weston, found guilty, is banished from town for two years.

Act Three depicts the reconciliation of Jim and Dave, and Jim's return to Eatonville, following their joint rejection of Daisy, who as it turns out, wants her husband to "work for her white folks." What is most interesting about this scene is that the tension between Dave and Jim is resolved in a witty and sustained verbal dual, in which the two trade cleverly improvised hyperbolic claims of their love for Daisy, in an elaborate ritual of courtship. As Hemenway puts it:

> When Dave asks Jim how much time he would do for Daisy on the chain gang, Jim answers, "Twenty years and like it." Dave exults, "See dat, Daisy, Dat nigger ain't willin to do no time for you. I'd beg de judge to gimme life."

Again a significant stage direction interrupts the dialogue. By telling us that "both Jim and Dave laugh," Hurston and Hughes were trying to show the sense of verbal play and rhetorical improvisation characteristic of Eatonville generally, and Joe Clark's store-front porch specifically. . . . The contest is a ritual, designed to defuse the violence implicit in the conflict, to channel the aggression into mental rather than physical terms. The manner in which the courting contest ends suggests its ritualistic nature: Dave says to Daisy, "Don't you be skeered, baby. Papa kin take keer o you [To Jim: suiting the action to the word] Countin from de finger back to de thumb. . . . Start anything, I got you some." Jim is taken aback: "Aw, I don't want no more fight wid you, Dave." Dave replies, "Who said anything about fighting? We just provin who love Daisy de best."

This courtship ritual, like so much of the verbal "signifying" rituals in which the characters engage throughout the play, are both reflections of historical folk rituals practiced by African Americans as well as their extensions or elaborations. As Hemenway shows so carefully in his essay appended to this volume, often the characters' dialogues are taken directly from the black vernacular tradition. As often, however, Hughes and Hurston are *imitating* that tradition, improvising upon a historical foundation of ritualized oral discourse, which Hurston had been collecting as part of her graduate research in anthropology with Franz Boas. Hughes and Hurston, in other words, were drawing upon the black vernacular tradition both to "ground" their drama in that discourse but also to "extend" the vernacular itself.

Mule Bone, then, was not a mere vehicle for black folklore, rather, black folklore served as the basis, the foundation, for what they hoped would be a truly new art form: an art form that would stand in relation to traditional American drama in the way that Hughes's "blues poetry" stood to American poetry and Hurston's vernacular fictions stood to the American novel. *Mule Bone,* in other words, was meant to be the dramatic embodiment of James Weldon Johnson's demand that "the colored poet in the United States needs to do . . . something like what Synge did for the Irish; he needs to find a form that will express the racial spirit by symbols from within rather than by symbols from without, such as the mere mutilation of English spelling and pronunciation. He needs a form that is freer and larger than dialect, but which will still hold the racial flavor; a form expressing the imagery, the idioms, the peculiar turns of thought, and the distinctive humor and pathos, too, of the Negro, but which will also be capable of voicing the deepest and highest emotions and aspirations, and allow of the widest range of subjects and the widest scope of treatment." Dialect, Johnson continued, was doomed by its racist textual heritage:

> Negro dialect is at present a medium that is not capable of giving expression to the varied conditions of Negro life in America, and much less is it capable of giving the fullest interpretation of Negro character and psychology. This is no indictment against the dialect as dialect, but against the mould of convention in which Negro dialect in the United States has been set.

Mule Bone was also a refutation of Johnson's claim that "Negro dialect" "is an instrument with but two full stops, humor and pathos," because of the racist minstrel and vaudeville representations of black characters and their language. This is what they meant when they subtitled their play "A Comedy of

Negro Life" and when they claimed that *Mule Bone* was "the first real Negro folk comedy."

By using the vernacular tradition as the foundation for their drama—indeed, as the basis for a new *theory* of black drama—Hughes and Hurston succeeded quite impressively in creating a play that implicitly *critiqued* and explicitly *reversed* the racist stereotypes of the ignorant dialect-speaking darky that had populated the stages of the minstrel and vaudeville traditions. Indeed, we can only wonder at the effect that a successful Broadway production of *Mule Bone* might have had on the subsequent development of black theatre, given the play's sheer novelty and freshness of language.

With their turn to the vernacular, however, Hurston and Hughes also seem at times to reinscribe the explicit sexism of that tradition, through the discussions of physical abuse and wife-beatings as agents of control, which the male characters on Joe Clarke's store-front porch seem to take for granted as a "natural" part of sexual relations. These exchanges are quite disturbing for our generation of readers, demanding as they do a forceful critique by the reader. Daisy's representation in a triangle of desire as the *object* of her lovers' verbal dueling rather than as one who duels herself, a mode of dueling that demands great intelligence, is also a concern, even if this concern is tempered somewhat by the fact that it is she who controls their complex relationship all along, as demonstrated when she dismisses them both when they will not accede to her demands that they get jobs and provide support for her own efforts at self-sufficiency: "Both of you niggers can git yo' hat on yo' heads and git on down de road. Neither one of y'all don't have to have me. I got a good job and plenty men beggin' for yo' change." Despite this, however, the depiction of female characters and sexual relations in *Mule Bone* almost never escapes the limitation of the social realities that the vernacular tradition reflects.

Mule Bone was never completed. Hurston, in a frantic

attempt to demonstrate to Hughes's lawyer, Arthur Spingarn, that she had indeed been the play's sole author, sent him more handwritten revisions of large sections of the play, creating still another version. We have reprinted here, however, the last version on which Hughes and Hurston collaborated. Despite its limitations as a work-in-progress, it stands as a daring attempt to resurrect black poetic language from the burial grounds of racist stereotypes. Had it been performed, the power of its poetic language could very well have altered forever the evolution of African-American drama enabling the theatre to fulfill its great—and still unfulfilled—potential among the African-American arts.

Selected Bibliography

Baker, Houston A., Jr. *Modernism and the Harlem Renaissance.* Chicago: University of Chicago Press, 1987.

Du Bois, W. E. B. "Can the Negro Save the Drama?" *Theatre Magazine* XXXVIII (July 1923): 12, 68.

Du Bois, W. E. B. "The Krigwa Players Little Negro Theatre." *Amsterdam News* (October 5, 1927) and *Crisis* XXXII, No. 3 (July 1926): 134–36.

Du Bois, W. E. B. "The Negro and the American Stage." *Crisis* XXVIII, No. 2 (June 1924): 55–60.

Du Bois, W. E. B. "The Negro Theatre." *Crisis* XV (February 1918): 165.

Fabre, Geneviève. *Drumbeats, Masks, and Metaphors: Contemporary Afro-American Theatre.* Cambridge, Mass.: Harvard University Press, 1983.

Hemenway, Robert. *Zora Neale Hurston: A Literary Biography.* Urbana, Ill.: University of Illinios, 1977.

Huggins, Nathan Irvin. *Harlem Renaissance.* New York: Oxford University Press, 1971.

Johnson, James Weldon. "Preface." In *The Book of American Negro Poetry.* New York: Harcourt, Brace, Jovanovich, 1931.

Kellner, Bruce. *The Harlem Renaissance: A Historical Dictionary of the Era.* New York: Methuen, 1987.

Lewis, David Levering. *When Harlem Was in Vogue*. New York: Alfred A. Knopf, 1981.

Locke, Alain. "The Drama of Negro Life." *Theatre Arts Monthly* 10 (October 1926): 701–6.

Locke, Alain. "The Negro and the American Stage." *Theatre Arts Monthly* 10 (February 1926): 112–20.

Rampersad, Arnold. *The Life of Langston Hughes. Vol. 1: 1902–1941: I, Too, Sing America*. New York: Oxford University Press, 1986.

"THE BONE OF CONTENTION"

a short story by

ZORA NEALE HURSTON

I

Eatonville Florida is a colored town and has its colored interests. It has not now, nor ever has had anything to rank Brazzle's yellow mule. His Yaller Highness was always mentioned before the weather, the misery of the back or leg, or the hard times.

The mule was old, rawbony and mean. He was so rawbony that he creaked as he ambled about the village street with his meanness shining out through every chink and cranny in his rattling anatomy. He worked little, ate heartily, fought every inch of the way before the plow and even disputed with Brazzle when he approached to feed him. Sale, exchange or barter was out of the question, for everybody in the county knew him.

But one day he died. Everybody was glad, including Brazzle. His death was one of those pleasant surprises that people hope for, but never expect to happen.

The city had no refuse plant so H.Y.H. went the way of

all other domestic beasts who died among us. Brazzle borrowed Watson's two grey plugs and dragged the remains out to the edge of the cypress swamp, three miles beyond the city limits and abandoned them to the natural scavengers. The town attended the dragging out to a man. The fallen gladiator was borne from the arena on his sharp back, his feet stiffly raised as if [in] a parting gesture of defiance. We left him on the edge of the cypress swamp and returned to the village satisfied that the only piece of unadulterated meanness that the Lord had ever made was gone from among us forever.

Three years passed and his bones were clean and white. They were scattered along the swamp edge. The children still found them sufficiently interesting to tramp out to gaze upon them on Sunday afternoons. The elders neglected his bones, but the mule remained with them in song and story as a simile, as a metaphor, to point a moral or adorn a tale. But as the mean old trouble-making cuss, they considered him gone for good.

II

It was early night in the village. Joe Clarke's store porch was full of chewing men. Some chewed tobacco, some chewed cane, some chewed straws, for the villager is a ruminant in his leisure. They sat thus every evening ostensibly waiting for the mail from Number 38, the south-bound express. It was seldom that any of them got any but it gave them a good excuse to gather. They all talked a great deal, and every man jack of them talked about himself. Heroes all, they were, of one thing or another.

Ike Pearson had killed a six-foot rattler in a mighty battle that grew mightier every time Ike told about it; Walter Thomas had chinned the bar twenty times without stopping; Elijah Moseley had licked a "cracker"; Brazzle had captured a live catamount; Hiram Lester had killed a bear; Sykes Jones

had won the soda-cracker eating contest; AND JOE CLARKE
HAD STARTED THE TOWN!

Reverend Simms, the Methodist preacher, a resident of
less than a year, had done nothing to boast of, but it was
generally known that he aspired to the seat of Joe Clarke. He
wanted to be the mayor. He had observed to some of his
members that it wasnt no sense in one man staying in office all
the time.

"Looka heah," Clarke cut across whoever it was that
[was] talking at the time, "When Ah started dis town, Ah
walked right up to de white folks an' laid down TWO
HUN'DED DOLLAHS WID DIS RIGHT HAND YOU
SEE BEFO' YOU AN' GOT MAH PAPERS AN' PUT DIS
TOWN ON DE MAP! It takes uh powerful lot uh sense an'
grit tuh start uh town, yessirree!"

"Whut map did you put it on, Joe?" Lindsay disrespect-
fully asked. "Ah aint seed it on no map."

Seeing Clarke gored to his liver, Rev. Simms let out a
gloating snicker and tossed a cane knot to Tippy, the Lewis'
dejected dog frame hovering about the group hoping for
something more tempting to a dog's palate than cane chews
and peanut shells might drop. He tossed the knot and waited
for Clarke to answer. His Honor ignored the thrust as being
too low for him to stoop to and talked on. Was he not mayor,
postmaster, storekeeper and Pooh Bah general? Insults must
come to him from at least the county seat.

"Nother thing," Clarke continued, giving Simms a
meaning look, "There's a heap goin' on 'round heah under
the cover dat Ahm gointer put a stop to. Jim Weston done
proaged through mah hen house enough. Last Sat'day Ah
missed three uh mah bes' layin' hens, an' Ah been tol' he
buried feathers in his backyard the very next day. Cose Ah
caint prove nothin', but de minute he crooks his little finger,
he goes 'way from mah town. He aint de onliest one Ah got
mah eye on neither."

Simms accepted the challenge thrown at him.

"Fact is, the town aint run lak it might be. We oughta stop dat foolishness of runnin' folks outa town. We oughta jail'em. They's got jails in all de other towns, an' we oughta bring ours up to date."

"Ah'll be henfired! Simms, you tries to know mo' 'bout runnin' de town than me! Dont you reckon a man thats got sense enough to start uh town, knows how tuh run it. Dont you reckon if de place had uh needed uh jailhouse Ah would have got one built 'long befo' you come heah?"

"We do so need a jail," Lindsay contended. "Jus' cause you stahted the town, dat dont make yo' mouf no prayer book nor neither yo' lips no Bible. They dont flap lak none tuh *me.*"

Lindsay was a little shriveled up man with grey hair and bow-legs. He was the smallest man in the village, who nevertheless did the most talk of fighting. That was because the others felt he was too small for them to hit. He was harmless, but known to be the nastiest threatener in the county.

Clarke merely snorted contemptuously at his sally and remarked dryly that the road was right there for all those who were not satisfied with the way he was running the town.

"Meaning to insult me?" Lindsay asked belligerently.

"Ah dont keer HOW yuh take it. Jus' take yo' rawbony cow an' gwan tuh de woods, fuh all I keer," Clarke answered.

Lindsay leaped from the porch and struck his fighting pose. "Jus' hit de ground an' Ah'll strow yuh all over Orange County! Aw, come on! Come on! Youse a big seegar, but Ah kin smoke yuh!"

Clarke looked at the little man, old, and less that half his size and laughed. Walter Thomas and 'Lige Moseley rushed to Lindsay and pretended to restrain him.

"That's right," Lindsay panted, "you better hold me offen him. Cause if I lay de weight uh dis right hand on him, he wont forget it long as he live."

"Aw, shet up, Lin'say, an' set down. If you could fight as

good as you kin threaten, you'd be world's champeen 'stead
uh Jack Dempsey. Some uh dese days when youse hollerin'
tuh be let loose, somebody's gointer take you at yo' word,
then it will be jus' too bad about yuh," Lester admonished.

"Who?—"

The war was about to begin all over on another front
when Dave Carter, the local Nimrod, walked, almost ran up
the steps of the porch. He was bareheaded, excited and even
in the poor light that seeped to the porch from the oil lamps
within, it was seen that he was bruised and otherwise unusu-
ally mussed up.

"Mist' Clarke, Ah wants tuh see yuh, Me said. "Come on
inside."

"Sholy, Dave, sholy." The mayor responded and followed the young man into the store and the corner reserved
for City Administration. The crowd from the porch followed
to a man.

Dave wiped a bruise spot on his head. "Mist' Clarke, Ah
wants uh warrant took out fuh Jim Weston. Ahm gointer law
him outa dis town. He caint lam me over mah head wid no
mule bone and steal mah turkey and go braggin' about it!"

Under the encouraging quiz of the mayor, Dave told his
story. He was a hunter and fisherman, as everybody knew. He
had discovered a drove of wild turkeys roosting in the trees
along the edge of the cypress swamp near the spot where
Brazzle's old mule had been left. He had watched them for
weeks, had seen the huge gobbler that headed the flock and
resolved to get him.

"Yes," agreed Clarke, "you said something to me about
it yesterday when you bought some shells."

"Yes, and thats how Jim knowed Ah was goin' turkey
huntin'. He was settin' on de store porch and heard me talkin'
to you. Today when Ah started out, jes 'bout sundown—dats
de bes' time tuh get turkeys, when they goes tuh roost—he ups
and says he's goin' long. Ah didnt keer 'bout dat, but when

them birds goes tuh roost, he aint even loaded, so Ah had shot
dat gobbler befo' he took aim. When he see dat great big
gobbler fallin' he fires off his gun and tries tuh grab him. But
Ah helt on. We got tuh pushin' and shovin' and tusslin' 'till
we got to fightin'. Jim's a bully, but Ah wuz beatin' his socks
offa him till he retched down and picked up de hock-bone of
Brazzle's ol' mule and lammed me ovah mah head wid it and
knocked me out. When Ah come to, he had done took mah
turkey and gone. Ah wants uh warrant, Mist' Clarke. Ahm
gointer law him outa dis town."

"An' you sho gointer get, Dave. He oughter be run out.
Comes from bad stock. Every last one of his brothers been run
out as fast as they grow up. Daddy hung for murder."

Clarke busied himself with the papers. The crowd looking on and commenting.

"See whut you Meth'dis' niggahs will do?" asked Brazzle, a true Baptist. "Goin' round lammin' folks ovah the head
an' stealin' they turkeys."

"Cose everybody knows dem Westons is a set uh bullies,
but you Baptists aint such a much," Elijah Moseley retorted.

"Yas, but Ah know yuh know," put in Lindsay. "No
Baptis' aint never done nothin' bad as dat. Joe Clarke is right.
Jail is too good fuh 'em. The last one uh these heah half-
washed christians oughta be run 'way from heah."

"When it comes tuh dat, theres jus' as many no count
Baptists as anybody else. Jus' aint caught 'em," Thomas said,
joining the fray.

"Yas," Lindsay retorted, "but we done kotched yo'
Meth'dis' niggah. Kotched him knockin' people ovah de head
wid mule bones an' stealin' they turkeys, an' wese gointer run
him slap outa town sure as gun's iron. The dirty onion!"

"We dont know whether you will or no, Joe Lindsay.
You Baptists aint runnin' this town exactly."

"Trial set for three oclock tomorrow at de Baptis'
church, that being the largest meetin' place in town," Clarke

announced with a satisfied smile and persuaded the men to go back to the porch to argue.

Clarke, himself, was a Methodist, but in this case, his interests lay with the other side. If he could get Jim to taste the air of another town, chicken mortality of the sudden and unexplained variety, would drop considerably, he was certain. He was equally certain that the ambitious Simms would champion Jim's cause and losing the fight, lose prestige. Besides, Jim was a troublesome character. A constant disturber of the village peace.

III

It was evident to the simplest person in the village long before three oclock that this was to be a religious and political fight. The assault and the gobbler were unimportant. Dave was a Baptist, Jim a Methodist, only two churches in the town and the respective congregations had lined up solidly.

At three the house was full. The defendant had been led in and seated in the amen corner to the left of the pulpit. Rev. Simms had taken his place beside the prisoner in the role of defense counsel. The plaintiff, with Elder Long, shepherd of the Baptist flock in the capacity of prosecution, was seated at the right. The respective congregations were lined up behind their leaders.

Mutual glances of despisement and gloating are exchanged across the aisle. Not a few verbal sorties were made during this waiting period as if they were getting up steam for the real struggle.

Wize Anderson (Meth) Look at ole Dave tryin' to make out Jim hurt his head! Yuh couldnt hurt a Baptist head wid a hammer—they're that hard.

Brother Poke (Bapt.) Well, anyhow we dont lie an' steal an' git run outa town lak de softhead Meth'dis niggahs.

Some Baptist wag looked over at Jim and crowed like a

rooster, the others took it up immediately and the place was full of hen-cackling and barnyard sounds. The implication was obvious. Jim stood up and said, "If I had dat mule bone heah, Ahd teach a few mo' uh you mud-turtles something."

Enter His Honor at this moment. Lum Boger pompously conducted him to his place, the pulpit, which was doing duty as the bench for the occasion. The assembly unconsciously moderated its tone. But from the outside could still be heard the voices of the children engaged in fisticuffy trials of the case.

The mayor began rapping for order at once. "Cote is set. Cote is set! Looka heah, DIS COTE IS DONE SET! Ah wants you folks tuh dry up."

The courtroom grew perfectly still. The mayor prepared to read the charge to the prisoner, when Brother Stringer (Meth.) entered, hot and perspiring with coat over his arm. He found a seat near the middle of the house against the wall. To reach it, he must climb over the knees of a bench length of people. Before seating himself, he hung his coat upon an empty lamp bracket above his head.

Sister Lewis of the Baptist persuasion, arose at once, her hands akimbo, her eyes flashing.

"Brothah Stringah, you take yo' lousy coat down off dese sacred walls! Aint you Methdis got no gumption in the house uh washup?"

Stringer did not answer her, but he cast over a glance that said as plain as day 'Just try and make me do it!

Della Lewis snorted, but Stringer took his seat complacently. He took his seat, but rose up again as if he had sat on a hot needle point. The reason for this was that Brother Hambo on the Baptist side, a nasty scrapper, rose and rolled his eyes to the fighting angle, looking at Stringer. Stringer caught the look, and hurriedly pawed that coat down off that wall.

Sister Taylor (M) took up the gauntlet dropped like a hot

potato by Stringer. "Some folks" she said with a meaning look, "is a whole lot mo' puhtic'lar bout a louse in they church than they is in they house." A very personal look at Sister Lewis.

"Well" said that lady, "mah house mought not be exactly clean. But nobody caint say *dat*"—indicating an infinitesimal amount on the end of her finger—"about my chaRACter! They didnt hafta git de sheriff to make Ike marry ME!"

Mrs. Taylor leaped to her feet and struggled to cross the aisle to her traducer but was restrained by three or four men. "Yas, they did git de sheriff tuh make Sam marry me!" She shouted as she panted and struggled, "And Gawd knows you sho oughter git him again and make *some* of these men marry yo' Ada."

Mrs. Lewis now had to be restrained. She gave voice and hard, bone-breaking words flew back and forth across the aisle. Each was aided and abetted by her side of the house. His Honor was all the time beating the pulpit with his gavel and shouting for order. At last he threatened to descend in person upon the belligerents.

"Heah! You moufy wimmen! Shet up. Aint Ah done said cote was set? Lum Boger, do yo' duty. Make them wimmen dry up or put 'em outa heah."

Marshall Boger who wore his star for the occasion was full of the importance of his office for nineteen is a prideful age; he hurried over to Mrs. Taylor. She rose to meet him. "You better gwan 'way from me, Lum Boger. Ah jes' wish you would lay de weight of yo' han' on me! Ahd kick yo' cloes up round yo' neck lak a horse collar. You impident limb you."

Lum retreated before the awful prospect of wearing his suit about his neck like a horse-collar. He crossed the aisle to the fiery Della and frowned upon her. She was already standing and ready to commence hostilities. One look was enough. He said nothing, but her threats followed him down the aisle as he retreated to the vestibule to shoo the noisy children away. The women subsided and the Mayor began.

"We come heah on very important business," he said. "Stan' up dere, Jim Weston. You is charged wid 'ssaultin' Dave Carter here wid a mule bone, and robbin' him uh his wild turkey. Is you guilty or not guilty?"

Jim arose, looked insolently around the room and answered the charge: "Yas, Ah hit him and took de turkey cause it wuz mine. Ah hit him and Ahll hit him agin, but it wasnt no crime this time."

His Honor's jaw dropped. There was surprise on the faces of all the Baptist section, surprise and perplexity. Gloating and laughter from the Methodists. Simms pulled Jim's coattail.

"Set down Jim," he cooed, "youse one of mah lambs. Set down. Yo' shepherd wil show them that walks in de darkness wid sinners and republicans de light."

Jim sat down and the pastor got to his feet.

"Looka heah, Jim, this aint for no foolishness. Do you realize dat if youse found guilty, youse gonna be run outa town?"

"Yeah" Jim answered without rising. "But Ah aint gonna be found no guilty. You caint find me." There was a pleasurable stir on his side of the house. The Baptists were still in the coma which Jim's first statement had brought on.

"Ah say too, he aint guilty," began Rev. Simms with great unction in his tones. "Ah done been to de cot-house at Orlando an' set under de voice of dem lawyers an' heard 'em law from mornin' tell night. They says you got tuh have a weepon befo' you kin commit uh 'ssault. Ah done read dis heah Bible fum lid tuh lid (he made a gesture to indicate the thoroughness of his search) and it aint in no Bible dat no mule bone is a weepon, an' it aint in no white folks law neither. Therefo' Brother Mayor, Ah ast you tuh let Jim go. You gotta turn 'im loose, cause nobody kin run 'im outa town when he aint done no crime."

A deep purple gloom settled down upon the Mayor and his followers. Over against this the wild joy of the Methodists. Simms already felt the reins of power in his hands. Over the protest of the Mayor he raised a song and he and his followers sang it with great gusto.

> "Oh Mary dont you weep, dont you mourn
> Oh Mary, dont you weep dont you mourn
> Pharaoh's army got drownded,
> O-O-oh Mary, dont you weep"

The troubled expression on the face of the Baptist leader, Elder Long, suddenly lifted. He arose while yet the triumphant defense is singing its hallelujah. Mayor Clarke quieted the tumult with difficulty. Simms saw him rise but far from being worried, he sank back upon the seat, his eyes half closed, hands folded fatly across his fat stomach. He smirked. Let them rave! He had built his arguments on solid rock, and the gates of Baptist logic could not prevail against it!

When at last Long got the attention of the assembly, he commanded Dave to stand.

"Ah jus want you all tuh take a look at his head. Anybody kin see dat big knot dat Jim put on dere." Jim, the Rev. Simms and all his communicants laughed loudly at this, but Long went on calmly. "Ah been tuh de cote-house tuh Orlando an' heard de white folks law as much as any body heah. And dey dont ast whether de thing dat a person gits hurt wid is uh weepon or not. All dey wants tuh fin' out is, 'did it hurt?' Now you all kin see dat mule bone did hurt Dave's head. So it must be a weepon cause it hurt 'im."

Rev. Simms had his eyes wide open now. He jumped to his feet.

"Never mind bout dem white folks laws at O'landa, Brother Long. Dis is a colored town. Nohow we oughter run by de laws uh de Bible. Dem white folks laws dont go befo' whuts in dis sacred book."

"Jes' hold yo' hot potater, Brother Simms, Ahm comin' tuh dat part right now. Jes lemme take yo' Bible a minute."

"Naw indeed. You oughter brought one of yo' own if you got one. Furthemo' Brother Mayor, we got work tuh do. Wese workin' people. Dont keep us in heah too long. Dis case is through wid."

"Oh, naw it aint" the Mayor disagreed, "you done talked yo' side, now you got tuh let Brother Long talk his. So fur as de work is concerned, it kin wait. One thing at a time. Come on up heah in yo' pulpit an' read yo' own Bible, Brother Long. Dont mind me being up heah."

Long ascended the pulpit and began to turn the leaves of the large Bible. The entire assembly slid forward to the edges of the seat.

"Ah done proved by de white folks law dat Jim oughter be run outa town an' now Ahm gointer show by de Bible—"

Simms was on his feet again. "But Brother Mayor—"

"Set down Simms" was all the answer he got. "Youse *entirely* outa order."

"It says heah in Judges 15:16 dat Samson slewed a thousand Philistines wid de jaw-bone of a ass" Long drawled.

"Yas, but this wasnt no ass, this was a mule" Simms objected.

"And now dat bring us to de main claw uh dis subjick. It sho want no ass, but everybody knows dat a donkey is de father of every mule what ever wuz born. Even little chillen knows dat. Everybody knows dat dat little as a donkey is, dat if he is dangerous, his great big mule son is mo' so. Everybody knows dat de further back on a mule you goes, de mo' dangerous he gits. Now if de jawbone is as dangerous as it says heah, in de Bible, by de time you gits clear back tuh his hocks hes rank pizen."

"AMEN!! Specially Brazzle's ol' mule," put in Hambo.

"An' dat makes it double 'ssault an' batt'ry," Long continued. "Therefo' Brother Mayor, Ah ast dat Jim be run outa town fuh 'ssaultin Dave wid a deadly weepon an' stealin' his turkey while de boy wuz unconscious."

It was now the turn of the Baptists to go wild. The faint protests of Simms were drowned in the general uproar.

"I'll be henfired if he aint right!" The Mayor exclaimed when he could make himself heard. "This case is just as plain as day."

Simms tried once more. "But Brother Mayor—"

"Aw be quiet, Simms. You done talked yo'self all outa joint already." His Honor cut him short. "Jim Weston, you git right outa *mah* town befo sundown an' dont lemme ketch you back heah under two yeahs, neither. You folks dats so rearin' tuh fight, gwan outside an' fight all you wants tuh. But dont use no guns, no razors nor no mule-bones. Cote's dismissed."

A general murmur of approval swept over the house. Clarke went on, unofficially, as it were. "By ziggity, dat ol' mule been dead three years an' still kickin'! An' he done kicked more'n one person outa whack today." And he gave Simms one of his most personal looks.

THE END

MULE BONE
A COMEDY OF NEGRO LIFE

by

LANGSTON HUGHES

and

ZORA NEALE HURSTON

A Note on the Text

Several drafts of *Mule Bone* exist, housed at Howard and at Yale. The most complete draft, however, and the only one containing two scenes in Act Two, is that dated "Cleveland, 1931." It is this draft that we have published here.

Since the manuscript for *Mule Bone* was never copyedited during the authors' lifetimes, there are some apparent inconsistencies in characters' names and relationships to one another. For instance, Daisy Taylor is the daughter of Mrs. Blunt, and is seemingly unrelated to Mrs. Taylor. We have noted any name changes in the text.

CHARACTERS

Principal Characters

JIM WESTON: Guitarist, Methodist, slightly arrogant, aggressive, somewhat self-important, ready with his tongue.

DAVE CARTER: Dancer, Baptist, soft, happy-go-lucky character, slightly dumb and unable to talk rapidly and wittily.

DAISY TAYLOR: Methodist, domestic servant, plump, dark and sexy, self-conscious of clothes and appeal, fickle.

JOE CLARKE: The Mayor, storekeeper and postmaster, arrogant, ignorant and powerful in a self-assertive way, large, fat man, Methodist.

ELDER SIMMS: Methodist minister, newcomer in town, ambitious, small and fly, but not very intelligent.

ELDER CHILDERS: Big, loose-jointed, slow spoken but not dumb. Long resident in the town, calm and sure of himself.

KATIE CARTER: Dave's aunt, little old wisened dried-up lady.

MRS. MATTIE CLARKE: The Mayor's wife, fat and flabby mulatto, high-pitched voice.

THE MRS. REV. SIMMS: Large and aggressive.

THE MRS. REV. CHILDERS: Just a wife who thinks of details.

LUM BOGER: Young town marshall about twenty, tall, gangly, with big flat feet, liked to show off in public.

TEETS MILLER: Village vamp who is jealous of DAISY.

LIGE MOSELY: A village wag.

WALTER THOMAS: Another village wag.

ADA LEWIS: A promiscuous lover.

DELLA LEWIS: Baptist, poor housekeeper, mother of ADA.

BOOTSIE PITTS: A local vamp.

MRS. DILCIE ANDERSON: Village housewife, Methodist.

WILLIE NIXON: Methodist, short runt.

Minor Characters

HAMBO

GOODWIN

BRAZZLE

CODY

JONES

SAM MOSELY

TAYLOR

MRS. TAYLOR

MRS. JAKE ROBERTS

(VOICE OF MRS. MOSELY)

SENATOR BAILEY (BOY)

LITTLE MATILDA

OLD MAN

FRANK WARRICK

OLD WOMAN

SISTER THOMAS

SISTER JONES
MARY ELLA
SISTER PITTS
SISTER LUCAS
MRS. HAMBO
MRS. NIXON
MRS. BLUNT
(CHILDREN)
(LOUNGERS)

ACT ONE

SETTING: *The raised porch of* JOE CLARKE'S *Store and the street in front. Porch stretches almost completely across the stage, with a plank bench at either end. At the center of the porch three steps leading from street. Rear of porch, center, door to the store. On either side are single windows on which signs, at left,* "POST OFFICE", *and at right,* "GENERAL STORE" *are painted. Soap boxes, axe handles, small kegs, etc., on porch on which townspeople sit and lounge during action. Above the roof of the porch the "false front", or imitation second story of the shop is seen with large sign painted across it* "JOE CLARKE'S GENERAL STORE". *Large kerosine street lamp on post at right in front of porch.*

Saturday afternoon and the villagers are gathered around the store. Several men sitting on boxes at edge of porch chewing sugar cane, spitting tobacco juice, arguing, some whittling, others eating peanuts. During the act the women all dressed up in starched dresses parade in and out of store. People buying groceries, kids playing in the street, etc. General noise of conversation, laughter and children shouting. But when the curtain rises there is a momentary lull for cane-chewing. At left of porch four men are playing cards on a soap box, and seated on the edge of the porch at extreme right two children are engaged in a checker game, with the board on the floor between them.

When the curtain goes up the following characters are discovered on the porch: MAYOR JOE CLARKE, *the storekeeper;* DEACON HAMBO; DEACON GOODWIN; *Old Man* MATT BRAZZLE: WILL CODY; SYKES JONES: LUM BOGER, *the young town marshall:* LIGE MOSELY *and* WALTER THOMAS, *two village wags;* TOM NIXON *and* SAM MOSELY, *and several others, seated on boxes, kegs, benches and floor of the porch.* TONY TAYLOR *is sitting on steps of porch with empty basket.* MRS. TAYLOR *comes out with her arms full of groceries, empties them into basket and goes back in store. All the men are chewing sugar cane earnestly with varying facial expressions. The noise of the breaking and sucking of cane can be clearly heard in the silence. Occasionally the laughter and shouting of children is heard nearby off stage.*

HAMBO: (*To* BRAZZLE) Say, Matt, gimme a jint or two of dat green cane—dis ribbon cane is hard.

LIGE: Yeah, and you ain't got de chears in yo' parlor you useter have.

HAMBO: Dat's all right, Lige, but I betcha right now wid dese few teeth I got I kin eat up more cane'n you kin grow.

LIGE: I know you kin and that's de reason I ain't going to tempt you. But youse gettin' old in lots of ways—look at dat bald-head—just as clean as my hand. (*Exposes his palm.*)

HAMBO: Don't keer if it tis—I don't want nothin'—not even hair—between me and God. (*General laughter*—LIGE *joins in as well. Cane chewing keeps up. Silence for a moment.*)

(*Off stage a high shrill voice can be heard calling:*)

VOICE: Sister Mosely, Oh, Sister Mosely! (*A pause*) Miz Mosely! (*Very irritated*) Oh, Sister Mattie! You hear me out here—you just won't answer!

VOICE OF MRS. MOSELY: Whoo-ee . . . somebody calling me?

VOICE OF MRS. ROBERTS: (*Angrily*) Never mind now—you couldn't come when I called you. I don't want yo' lil ole weasley turnip greens. (*Silence*)

MATT BRAZZLE: Sister Roberts is en town agin! If she was mine, I'll be hen-fired if I wouldn't break her down in de lines (loins)—good as dat man is to her!

HAMBO: I wish she was mine jes' one day—de first time she open her mouf to beg *anybody,* I'd lam her wid lightning.

JOE CLARKE: I God, Jake Roberts buys mo' rations out dis store than any man in dis town. I don't see to my Maker whut she do wid it all. . . . Here she come. . . .

(Enter MRS. JAKE ROBERTS, *a heavy light brown woman with a basket on her arm. A boy about ten walks beside her carrying a small child about a year old straddle of his back. Her skirts are sweeping the ground. She walks up to the step, puts one foot upon the steps and looks forlornly at all the men, then fixes her look on* JOE CLARKE.*)*

MRS. ROBERTS: Evenin', Brother Mayor.

CLARKE: Howdy do, Mrs. Roberts. How's yo' husband?

MRS. ROBERTS: *(Beginning her professional whine)* He ain't much and I ain't much and my chillun is poly. We ain't got 'nough to eat! Lawd, Mr. Clarke, gimme a lil piece of side meat to cook us a pot of greens.

CLARKE: Aw gwan, Sister Roberts. You got plenty bacon home. Last week Jake bought . . .

MRS. ROBERTS: *(Frantically)* Lawd, Mist' Clarke, how long you think dat lil piece of meat last me an' my chillun? Lawd, me and my chillun is *hongry!* God knows, Jake don't fee-eed me! *(*MR. CLARKE *sits unmoved.* MRS. ROBERTS *advances upon him)* Mist' Clarke!

CLARKE: I God, woman, don't keep on after me! Every time I look, youse round here beggin' for everything you see.

LIGE: And whut she don't see she whoops for it just de same.

MRS. ROBERTS: *(In dramatic begging pose)* Mist' Clarke! Ain't you goin' do nuthin' for me? And you see me and my poor chillun is starvin'. . . .

CLARKE: *(Exasperated, rises)* I God, woman, a man can't git no peace wid somebody like you in town. *(He goes angrily into the store followed by* MRS. ROBERTS. *The boy sits down on the edge of the porch sucking the baby's thumb.)*

VOICE OF MRS. ROBERTS: A piece 'bout dis wide. . . .

VOICE OF CLARKE: I God, naw! Yo' husband done bought you plenty meat, nohow.

VOICE OF MRS. ROBERTS: *(In great anguish)* Ow! Mist' Clarke! Don't you cut dat lil tee-ninchy piece of meat for me and my chillun! *(Sound of running feet inside the store.)* I ain't a going to tetch it!

VOICE OF CLARKE: Well, don't touch it then. That's all you'll git outa me.

VOICE OF MRS. ROBERTS: *(Calmer)* Well, hand it chear den. Lawd, me and my chillun is *so* hongry. . . . Jake don't fee-eed me. *(She re-enters by door of store with the slab of meat in her hand and an outraged look on her face. She gazes all about her for sympathy.)* Lawd, me and my poor chillun is *so* hungry . . . and some folks has *every*thing and they's so *stingy* and gripin'. . . . Lawd knows, Jake don't fee-eed me! *(She exits right on this line followed by the boy with the baby on his back.)*

(All the men gaze behind her, then at each other and shake their heads.)

HAMBO: Poor Jake . . . I'm really sorry for dat man. If she was mine I'd beat her till her ears hung down like a Georgy mule.

WALTER THOMAS: I'd beat her till she smell like onions.

LIGE: I'd romp on her till she slack like lime.

NIXON: I'd stomp her till she rope like okra.

VOICE OF MRS. ROBERTS: *(Off stage right)* Lawd, Miz Lewis, you goin' give me dat lil han'ful of greens for me and my chillun. Why dat ain't a eyefull. I ought not to take 'em . . . but me and my chillun is *so* hongry . . . Some folks is so stingy and gripin'! Lawd knows, Jake don't *feed* me!

(The noise of cane-chewing is heard again. Enter JOE LINDSAY *left with a gun over his shoulder and the large leg bone of a mule in the other hand. He approaches the step wearily.)*

HAMBO: Well, did you git any partridges, Joe?

JOE: *(Resting his gun and seating himself)* Nope, but I made de feathers fly.

HAMBO: I don't see no birds.

JOE: Oh, the feathers flew off on de birds.

LIGE: I don't see nothin' but dat bone. Look lak you done kilt a cow and et 'im raw out in de woods.

JOE: Don't y'all know dat hock-bone?

WALTER: How you reckon we gointer know every hock-bone in Orange County sight unseen?

JOE: *(Standing the bone up on the floor of the porch)* Dis is a hock-bone of Brazzle's ole yaller mule.

(General pleased interest. Everybody wants to touch it.)

BRAZZLE: *(Coming forward)* Well, sir! *(Takes bone in both hands and looks up and down the length of it)* If 'tain't my ole mule! This sho was one hell of a mule, too. He'd fight every inch in front of de plow . . . he'd turn over de mowing machine . . . run away wid de wagon . . . and you better not look like you wanter *ride* 'im!

LINDSAY: *(Laughing)* Yeah, I 'member seein' you comin' down de road just so . . . *(He limps wid one hand on his buttocks)* one day.

BRAZZLE: Dis mule was so evil he used to try to bite and kick when I'd go in de stable to feed 'im.

WALTER: He was too mean to git fat. He was so skinny you could do a week's washing on his ribs for a washboard and hang 'em up on his hip-bones to dry.

LIGE: I 'member one day, Brazzle, you sent yo' boy to Winter Park after some groceries wid a basket. So here he went down de road ridin' dis mule wid dis basket on his arm. . . . Whut you reckon dat ole contrary mule done when he got to dat crooked place in de road going round Park Lake? He turnt right round and went through de handle of dat basket . . . wid de boy still up on his back. *(General laughter)*

BRAZZLE: Yeah, he up and died one Sat'day just for spite . . . but he was too contrary to lay down on his side like a mule orter and die decent. Naw, he made out to lay down on his narrer contracted back and die wid his feets sticking straight up in de air just so. *(He gets down on his back and illustrates.)* We drug him out to de swamp wid 'im dat way, didn't we, Hambo?

JOE CLARKE: I God, Brazzle, we all seen it. Didn't we all go to de draggin' out? More folks went to yo' mule's draggin' out than went to last school closing . . . Bet there ain't been a thing right in mule-hell for four years.

HAMBO: Been dat long since he been dead?

CLARKE: I God, yes. He died de week after I started to cuttin' dat new ground. *(The bone is passing from hand to hand. At last a boy about twelve takes it. He has just walked up and is proudly handling the bone when a woman's voice is heard off stage right.)*

VOICE: Senator! Senator!! Oh, you Senator?

BOY: *(Turning, displeased, mutters)* Aw, shux. *(Loudly)* Ma'm?

VOICE: If you don't come here you better!

SENATOR: Yes ma'am. *(He drops bone on ground down stage and trots off frowning.)* Soon as we men git to doing something dese wimmen. . . . *(Exits, right.)*

(Enter TEETS and BOOTSIE left, clean and primped in voile dresses just alike. They speak diffidently and enter store. The men admire them casually.)

LIGE: Them girls done turned out to be right good-looking.

WALTER: Teets ain't as pretty now as she was a few years back. She used to be fat as a butter ball wid legs just like two whiskey-kegs. She's too skinny since she got her growth.

CODY: Ain't none of 'em pretty as dat Miss Daisy. God! She's pretty as a speckled pup.

LIGE: But she was sho nuff ugly when she was little . . . little ole hard black knot. She sho has changed since she been away up North. If she ain't pretty now, there ain't a hound dog in Georgy.

(Re-enter SENATOR BAILEY *and stops on the steps. He addresses* JOE CLARKE.*)*

SENATOR: Mist' Clarke. . . .

HAMBO: *(To* SENATOR*)* Ain't you got no manners? We all didn't sleep wid you last night.

SENATOR: *(Embarrassed)* Good evening, everybody.

ALL THE MEN: Good evening, son, boy, Senator, etc.

SENATOR: Mist' Clarke, mama said is Daisy been here dis evenin'?

JOE CLARKE: Ain't laid my eyes on her. Ain't she working over in Maitland?

SENATOR: Yessuh . . . but she's off today and mama sent her down here to get de groceries.

JOE CLARKE: Well, tell yo' ma I ain't seen her.

SENATOR: Well, she say to tell you when she come, to tell her ma say she better git hime and dat quick.

JOE CLARKE: I will. *(Exit* BOY *right.)*

LIGE: Bet she's off somewhere wid Dave or Jim.

WALTER: I don't bet it . . . I know it. She's got them two in de go-long.

(Re-enter TEETS *and* BOOTSIE *from store.* TEETS *has a letter and* BOOTSIE *two or three small parcels. The men look up with interest as they come out on the porch.)*

WALTER: *(Winking)* Whut's dat you got, Teets . . . letter from Dave?

TEETS: *(Flouncing)* Naw indeed! It's a letter from my B-I-T-sweetie! *(Rolls her eyes and hips.)*

WALTER: *(Winking)* Well, ain't Dave yo' B-I-T-sweetie? I thought y'all was 'bout to git married. Everywhere I looked dis summer 'twas you and Dave, Bootsie and Jim. I thought all of y'all would've done jumped over de broomstick by now.

TEETS: *(Flourishing letter)* Don't tell it to me . . . tell it to the ever-loving Mr. Albert Johnson way over in Apopka.

BOOTSIE: *(Rolling her eyes)* Oh, tell 'em 'bout the ever-loving Mr. Jimmy Cox from Altamont. Oh, I can't stand to see my baby lose.

HAMBO: It's lucky y'all girls done got some more fellers, cause look like Daisy done treed both Jim and Dave at once, or they done treed her one.

TEETS: Let her have 'em . . . nobody don't keer. They don't handle de "In God we trust" lak my Johnson. He's head bellman at de hotel.

BOOTSIE: Mr. Cox get money's grandma and old grandpa change. *(The girls exit huffily.)*

LINDSAY: *(To* HAMBO, *pseudo-seriously)* You oughtn't tease dem gals lak dat.

HAMBO: Oh, I laks to see gals all mad. But dem boys *is* crazy sho nuff. Before Daisy come back here they both had a good-looking gal a piece. Now they 'bout to fall out and fight over half a gal a piece. Neither one won't give over and let de other one have her.

LIGE: And she ain't thinking too much 'bout no one man. *(Looks off left.)* Here she come now. God! She got a mean walk on her!

WALTER: Yeah, man. She handles a lot of traffic! Oh, mama, throw it in de river . . . papa'll come git it!

LINDSAY: Aw, shut up, you married men!

LIGE: Man don't go blind cause he gits married, do he? *(Enter* DAISY *hurriedly. Stops at step a moment. She is dressed in sheer organdie, white shoes and stockings.)*

DAISY: Good evening, everybody. *(Walks up on the porch.)*

ALL THE MEN: *(Very pleasantly)* Good evening, Miss Daisy.

DAISY: *(To* CLARK*)* Mama sent me after some meal and flour and some bacon and sausage oil.

CLARKE: Senator been here long time ago hunting you.

DAISY: *(Frightened)* Did he? Oo . . . Mist' Clarke, hurry up and fix it for me. *(She starts on in the store.)*

LINDSAY: *(Giving her his seat)* You better wait here, Daisy. *(*WALTER *kicks* LIGE *to call his attention to* LINDSAY*'s attitude)* It's powerful hot in dat store. Lemme run fetch 'em out to you.

LIGE: *(to* LINDSAY*) Run!* Joe Lindsay, you ain't been able to run since de big bell rung. Look at dat gray beard.

LINDSAY: Thank God, I ain't gray all over. I'm just as good a man right now as any of you young 'uns. *(He hurries on into the store.)*

WALTER: Daisy, where's yo' two body guards? It don't look natural to see you thout nary one of 'em.

DAISY: *(Archly)* I ain't got no body guards. I don't know what you talkin' about.

LIGE: Aw, don' try to come dat over us, Daisy. You know who we talkin' 'bout all right . . . but if you want me to come out flat footed . . . where's Jim and Dave?

DAISY: Ain't they playin' somewhere for de white folks?

LIGE: *(To* WALTER*)* Will you listen at dis gal, Walter? *(To* DAISY*)* When I ain't been long seen you and Dave going down to de Lake.

DAISY: *(Frightened)* Don't y'all run tell mama where I been.

WALTER: Well, you tell us which one you laks de best and we'll wipe our mouf *(Gesture)* and say nothin'. Dem boys been de best of friends all they life, till both of 'em took after you . . . then good-bye, Katy bar de door!

DAISY: *(Affected innocence)* Ain't they still playin' and dancin' together?

LIGE: Yeah, but that's 'bout all they do 'gree on these days. That's de way it is wid men, young and old. . . . I don't keer how long they been friends and how thick they been . . . a woman kin come between 'em. David and Jonather never would have been friends so long if Jonather had of been any great hand wid de wimmen. You ain't never seen no two roosters that likes one another.

DAISY: I ain't tried to break 'em up.

WALTER: Course you ain't. You don't have to. All two boys need to do is go git stuck on de same girl and they done broke up . . . *right now!* Wimmen is something can't be divided equal.

(Re-enter JOE LINDSAY *and* CLARKE *with the groceries.* DAISY *jumps up and grabs the packages.)*

LIGE: *(To* DAISY*)* Want some of us . . . me . . . to go long and tote yo' things for you?

DAISY: *(Nervously)* Naw, mama is riding her high horse today. Long as I been gone it wouldn't do for me to come walking up wid nobody. *(She exits hurriedly right.)*

(All the men watch her out of sight in silence.)

CLARKE: *(Sighing)* I God, know whut Daisy puts me in de mind of?

HAMBO: No, what? *(They all lean together.)*

CLARKE: I God, a great big mango . . . a sweet smell, you know, with a strong flavor, but not something you could mash up like a strawberry. Something with a body to it.

(General laughter, but not obscene.)

HAMBO: *(Admiringly)* Joe Clarke! I didn't know you had it in you! *(MRS. CLARKE enters from store door and they all straighten up guiltily)*

CLARKE: *(Angrily to his wife)* Now whut do you want? I God, the minute I set down, here you come. . . .

MRS. CLARKE: Somebody want a stamp, Jody. You know you don't 'low me to bove wid de post office. *(HE rises sullenly and goes inside the store.)*

BRAZZLE: Say, Hambo, I didn't see you at our Sunday School picnic.

HAMBO: *(Slicing some plug-cut tobacco)* Nope, wan't there dis time.

WALTER: Looka here, Hambo. Y'all Baptist carry dis close-communion business too far. If a person ain't half drownded in de lake and half et up by alligators, y'all think he ain't baptized, so you can't take communion wid him. Now I reckon you can't even drink lemonade and eat chicken perlow wid us.

HAMBO: My Lord, boy, youse just *full* of words. Now, in de first place, if this year's picnic was lak de one y'all had last year . . . you ain't had no lemonade for us Baptists to turn down. You had a big ole barrel of rain water wid about a pound of sugar in it and one lemon cut up over de top of it.

LIGE: Man, you sho kin mold 'em!

WALTER: Well, I went to de Baptist picnic wid my mouf all set to eat chicken, when lo and behold y'all had chitlings! Do Jesus!

LINDSAY: Hold on there a minute. There was plenty chicken at dat picnic, which I do know is right.

WALTER: Only chicken I seen was a half a chicken yo' pastor musta tried to swaller whole cause he was choked stiff as a board when I come long . . . wid de whole deacon's board beating him in de back, trying to knock it out his throat.

LIGE: Say, dat puts me in de mind of a Baptist brother that was crazy 'bout de preachers and de preacher was crazy 'bout feeding his face. So his son got tired of trying to beat dese stump-knockers to de grub on the table, so one day he throwed out some slams 'bout dese preachers. Dat made his old man mad, so he tole his son to git out. He boy ast him, "Where must I go, papa?" He says, "Go on to hell I reckon. . . . I don't keer where you go."

So de boy left and was gone seven years. He come back one cold, windy night and rapped on de door. "Who dat?" de old man ast him. "It's me, Jack." De old man opened de door, so glad to see his son agin, and tole Jack to come in. He did and looked all round de place. Seven or eight preachers was sitting round de fire eatin' and drinkin'.

"Where you been all dis time, Jack?" de old man ast him.

"I been to hell," Jack tole him.

"Tell us how it is down there, Jack."

"Well," he says, "It's just like it is here . . . you cain't git to de fire for de preachers."

HAMBO: Boy, you kin lie just like de cross-ties from Jacksonville to Key West. De presidin' elder must come round on his circuit teaching y'all how to tell 'em, cause you couldn't lie dat good just natural.

WALTER: Can't nobody beat Baptist folks lying . . . and I ain't never found out how come you think youse so important.

LINDSAY: Ain't we got de finest and de biggest church? Macedonia Baptist will hold more folks than any two buildings in town.

LIGE: Thass right, y'all got a heap more church than you got members to go in it.

HAMBO: Thass all right . . . y'all ain't got neither de church nor de members. Everything that's had in this town got to be held in our church. (Re-enter JOE CLARKE.)

CLARKE: What you-all talkin'?

HAMBO: Come on out, Tush Hawg, lemme beat you some checkers. I'm tired of fending and proving wid dese boys ain't got no hair on they chest yet.

CLARKE: I God, you mean you gointer get beat. You can't handle me. . . . I'm a tush hawg.

HAMBO: Well, I'm going to draw dem tushes right now. *(To two small boys using checker board on edge of porch.)* Here you chilluns, let de Mayor and me have that board. Go on out an' play an' give us grown folks a little peace. *(The children go down stage and call out:)*

SMALL BOY: Hey, Senator. Hey, Marthy. Come on let's play chick-me, chick-me, cranie-crow.

CHILD'S VOICE: *(Off stage)* All right! Come on, Jessie! *(Enter several children, led by* SENATOR, *and a game begins in front of the store as* JOE CLARKE *and* HAMBO *play checkers.)*

JOE CLARKE: I God! Hambo, you can't play no checkers.

HAMBO: *(As they seat themselves at the checker board)* Aw, man, if you wasn't de Mayor I'd beat you all de time.

(The children get louder and louder, drowning out the men's voices.)

SMALL GIRL: I'm gointer be de hen.

BOY: And I'm gointer be de hawk. Lemme git maself a stick to mark wid.

(The boy who is the hawk squats center stage with a short twig in his hand. The largest girl lines up the other children behind her.)

GIRL: *(Mother Hen) (Looking back over her flock)* Y'all ketch holt of one 'nother's clothes so de hawk can't git yuz. *(They do.)* You all straight now?

CHILDREN: Yeah. *(The march around the hawk commences.)*

HEN AND CHICKS: Chick mah chick mah craney crow
Went to de well to wash ma toe
When I come back ma chick was gone
What time, ole witch?

HAWK: *(Making a tally on the ground)* One!

HEN AND CHICKS: *(Repeat song and march.)*

HAWK: *(Scoring again)* Two! *(Can be repeated any number of times.)*

HAWK: Four. *(He rises and imitates a hawk flying and trying to catch a chicken. Calling in a high voice:)* Chickee.

HEN: *(Flapping wings to protect her young)* My chickens sleep.

HAWK: Chickee. *(During all this the hawk is feinting and darting in his efforts to catch a chicken, and the chickens are dancing defensively, the hen trying to protect them.)*

HEN: My chicken's sleep.

HAWK: I shall have a chick.

HEN: You shan't have a chick.

HAWK: I'm goin' home. *(Flies off)*

HEN: Dere's de road.

HAWK: My pot's a boilin'.

HEN: Let it boil.

HAWK: My guts a growlin'.

HEN: Let 'em growl.

HAWK: I must have a chick.

HEN: You shan't have n'airn.

HAWK: My mama's sick.

HEN: Let her die.

HAWK: Chickie!

HEN: My chicken's sleep. *(HAWK darts quickly around the hen and grabs a chicken and leads him off and places the captive on his knees at the store porch. After a brief bit of dancing he catches another, then a third, etc.)*

HAMBO: *(At the checker board, his voice rising above the noise of the playing children, slapping his sides jubilantly)* Ha! Ha! I got you now. Go ahead on and move, Joe Clarke . . . jus' go ahead on and move.

LOUNGERS: *(Standing around two checker players)* Ol' Deacon's got you now.

ANOTHER VOICE: Don't see how he can beat the Mayor like that.

ANOTHER VOICE: Got him in the Louisville loop. *(These remarks are drowned by the laughter of the playing children directly in front of the porch.* MAYOR JOE CLARKE *disturbed in his concentration on the checkers and peeved at being beaten suddenly turns toward the children, throwing up his hands.)*

CLARKE: Get on 'way from here, you limbs of Satan, making all that racket so a man can't hear his ears. Go on, go on! (THE MAYOR *looks about excitedly for the town marshall. Seeing him playing cards on the other side of porch, he bellows:)* Lum Boger, whyn't you git these kids away from here! What kind of a marshall is you? All this passle of young'uns around here under grown people's feet, creatin' disorder in front of my store. (LUM BOGER *puts his cards down lazily, comes down stage and scatters the children away. One saucy little girl refuses to move.)*

LUM BOGER: Why'nt you go on away from here, Matilda? Didn't you hear me tell you-all to move?

LITTLE MATILDA: *(Defiantly)* I ain't goin' nowhere. You ain't none of my mama. *(Jerking herself free from him as* LUM *touches her.)* My mama in the store and she told me to wait out here. So take that, ol' Lum.

LUM BOGER: You impudent little huzzy, you! You must smell yourself . . . youse so fresh.

MATILDA: The wind musta changed and you smell your own top lip.

LUM BOGER: Don't make me have to grab you and take you down a buttonhole lower.

MATILDA: *(Switching her little head)* Go ahead on and grab me. You sho can't kill me, and if you kill me, you sho can't eat me. *(She marches into the store.)*

SENATOR: *(Derisively from behind stump)* Ol' dumb Lum! Hey! Hey! *(LITTLE BOY at edge of stage thumbs his nose at the marshall.)* *(LUM lumbers after the small boy. Both exit.)*

HAMBO: *(To CLARKE who has been thinking all this while what move to make)* You ain't got but one move . . . go ahead on and make it. What's de matter, Mayor?

CLARKE: *(Moving his checker)* Aw, here.

HAMBO: *(Triumphant)* Now! Look at him, boys. I'm gonna laugh in notes. *(Laughing to the scale and jumping a checker each time)* Do, sol, fa, me, lo . . . one! *(Jumping another checker)* La, sol, fa, me, do . . . two! *(Another jump.)* Do, sol, re, me, lo . . . three! *(Jumping a third.)* Lo, sol, fa, me, re . . . four! *(The crowd begins to roar with laughter. LUM BOGER returns, looking on. Children come drifting back again playing chick-me-chick-me-cranie crow.)*

VOICE: Oh, ha! Done got the ol' tush hog.

ANOTHER VOICE: Thought you couldn't be beat, Brother Mayor?

CLARKE: *(Peeved, gets up and goes into the store mumbling)* Oh, I coulda beat you if I didn't have this store on my mind. Saturday afternoon and I got work to do. Lum, ain't I told you to keep them kids from playin' right in front of this store? *(LUM makes a pass at the nearest half-grown boy. The kids dart around him teasingly.)*

ANOTHER VOICE: Eh, heh . . . Hambo done run him in his store . . . done run the ol' coon in his hole.

ANOTHER VOICE: That ain't good politics, Hambo, beatin' the Mayor.

ANOTHER VOICE: Well, Hambo, you done got to be so hard at checkers, come on let's see what you can do with de cards. Lum Boger there got his hands full nursin' the chilluns.

ANOTHER VOICE: *(At the table)* We ain't playin' for money, nohow, Deacon. We just playin' a little Florida Flip.

HAMBO: Ya all can't play no Florida Flip. When I was a sinner there wasn't a man in this state could beat me playin' that game. But I'm a deacon in Macedonia Baptist now and I don't bother with the cards no more.

VOICE AT CARD TABLE: All right, then, come on here Tony *(To man with basket on steps.)* let me catch your jack.

TAYLOR: *(Looking toward door)* I don't reckon I got time. I guess my wife gonna get through buying out that store some time or other and want to go home.

OLD MAN: *(On opposite side of porch from card game)* I bet my wife would know better than expect me to sit around and wait for her with a basket. Whyn't you tell her to tote it on home herself?

TAYLOR: *(Sighing and shaking his head)* Eh, Lawd!

VOICE AT CARD TABLE: Look like we can't get nobody to come into this game. Seem like everybody's scared a us. Come on back here, Lum, and take your hand. *(*LUM *makes a final futile gesture at the children.)*

LUM: Ain't I tole you little haitians to stay away from here?

*(*CHILDREN *scatter teasingly only to return to their play in front of the store later on.* LUM *comes up on the porch and re-joins the card*

game. Just as he gets seated, MRS. CLARKE *comes to the door of the store and calls him.)*

MRS. CLARKE: *(Drawlingly)* Columbus!

LUM: *(Wearily)* Ma'am?

MRS. CLARKE: De Mayor say for you to go round in de back yard and tie up old lady Jackson's mule what's trampin' sup all de tomatoes in my garden.

LUM: All right. *(Leaving card game.)* Wait till I come back, folkses.

LIGE: Oh, hum! *(Yawning and putting down the deck of cards)* Lum's sho a busy marshall. Say, ain't Dave and Jim been round here yet? I feel kinder like hearin' a little music 'bout now.

BOY: Naw, they ain't been here today. You-all know they ain't so thick nohow as they was since Daisy Bailey come back and they started runnin' after her.

WOMAN: You mean since she started runnin' after them, the young hussy.

MRS. CLARKE: *(In doorway)* She don't mean 'em no good.

WALTER: That's a shame, ain't it now? *(Enter* LUM *from around back of store. He jumps on the porch and takes his place at the card box.)*

LUM: *(To the waiting players)* All right, boys! Turn it on and let the bad luck happen.

LIGE: My deal. *(He begins shuffling the cards with an elaborate fan-shape movement.)*

VOICE AT TABLE: Look out there, Lige, you shuffling mighty lot. Don't carry the cub to us.

LIGE: Aw, we ain't gonna beat you . . . we gonna beat you. *(He slams down the cards for* LUM BOGER *to cut.)* Wanta cut 'em?

LUM: No, ain't no need of cutting a rabbit out when you can twist him out. Deal 'em. *(*LIGE *deals out the cards.)*

CLARKE'S VOICE: *(Inside the store)* You, Mattie! *(*MRS. CLARKE, *who has been standing in the door, quickly turns and goes inside.)*

LIGE: Y-e-e-e! Spades! *(The game is started.)*

LUM: Didn't snatch that jack, did you?

LIGE: Aw, no, ain't snatched no jack. Play.

WALTER: *(*LUM'S *partner)* Well, here it is, partner. What you want me to play for you?

LUM: Play jus' like I'm in New York, partner. But we gotta try to catch that jack.

LIGE: *(Threateningly)* Stick out your hand and draw back a nub. *(*WALTER THOMAS *plays.)*

WALTER: I'm playin' a diamond for you, partner.

LUM: I done tole you you ain't got no partner.

LIGE: Heh, Heh! Partner, we got 'em. Pull off wid your king. Dey got to play 'em. *(When that trick is turned, triumphantly:)* Didn't I tell you, partner? *(Stands on his feet and slams down with his ace violently)* Now, come up under this ace. Aw, hah, look at ol' low, partner. I knew I was gonna catch 'em. *(When* LUM *plays)* Ho, ho, there goes the queen . . . Now, the jack's a gentlemen. . . . Now, I'm playin' my knots. *(Everybody plays and the hand is ended.)* Partner, high, low, jack and the game and four.

WALTER: Give me them cards. I believe you-all done give me the cub that time. Look at me . . . this is Booker T Washington dealing these cards. *(Shuffles cards grandly and gives them to* LIGE *to cut.)* Wanta cut 'em?

LIGE: Yeah, cut 'em and shoot 'em. I'd cut behind my ma. *(He cuts the cards.)*

WALTER: *(Turning to player at left,* FRANK, LIGE's *partner)* What you saying, Frank?

FRANK: I'm beggin'. *(*LIGE *is trying to peep at cards.)*

WALTER: *(Turning to* LIGE*)* Stop peepin' at them cards, Lige. *(To* FRANK*)* Did you say you was beggin' or standin'?

FRANK: I'm beggin'.

WALTER: Get up off your knees. Go ahead and tell 'em I sent you.

FRANK: Well, that makes us four.

WALTER: I don't care if you is. *(Pulls a quarter out of his pocket and lays it down on the box.)* Twenty-five cents says I know the best one. Let's go. *(Everybody puts down a quarter.)*

FRANK: What you want me to play for you partner?

LIGE: Play me a club. *(The play goes around to dealer, WAL-TER, who gets up and takes the card off the top of the deck and slams it down on the table.)*

WALTER: Get up ol' deuce of deamonds and gallop off with your load. *(To LUM)* Partner, how many times you seen the deck?

LUM: Two times.

WALTER: Well, then I'm gonna pull off, partner. Watch this ol' queen. *(Everyone plays)* Ha! Ha! Wash day and no soap. *(Takes the jack of diamonds and sticks him up on his forehead. Stands up on his feet.)* Partner, I'm dumping to you . . . play your king. *(When it comes to his play LUM, too, stands up. The others get up and they, too, excitedly slam their cards down.)* Now, come on in this kitchen and let me splice that cabbage! *(He slams down the ace of diamonds. Pats the jack on his forehead, sings:)* Hey, hey, back up, jenny, get your load. *(Talking)* Dump to that jack, boys, dump to it. High, low, jack and the game and four. One to go. We're four wid you, boys.

LIGE: Yeah, but you-all playin' catch-up.

FRANK: Gimme them cards . . . lemme deal some.

LIGE: Frank, now you really got responsibility on you. They's got one game on us.

FRANK: Aw, man, I'm gonna deal 'em up a mess. This deal's in the White House. *(He shuffles and puts the cards down for* WALTER *to cut.)* Cut 'em.

WALTER: Nope, I never cut green timber. *(*FRANK *deals and turns the card up.)*

FRANK: Hearts, boys. *(He turns up an ace.)*

LUM: Aw, you snatched that ace, nigger.

WALTER: Yeah, they done carried the cub to us, partner.

LIGE: Oh, he didn't do no such a thing. That ace was turned fair. We jus' too hard for you . . . we eats our dinner out a the blacksmith shop.

WALTER: Aw, you all cheatin'. You know it wasn't fair.

FRANK: Aw, shut up, you all jus' whoopin' and hollerin' for nothin'. Tryin' to bully the game. *(*FRANK *and* LIGE *rise and shake hands grandly.)*

LIGE: Mr. Hoover, you sho is a noble president. We done stuck these niggers full of cobs. They done got scared to play us.

LUM: Scared to play you? Get back down to this table, let me spread my mess.

LOUNGER: Yonder comes Elder Simms. You all better squat that rabbit. They'll be having you all up in the church for playin' cards.

*(*FRANK *grabs up the cards and puts them in his pocket quickly. Everybody picks up the money and looks unconcerned as the preacher*

enters. Enter ELDER SIMMS *with his two prim-looking little children by the hand.)*

ELDER SIMMS: How do, children. Right warm for this time in November, ain't it?

VOICE: Yes sir, Reverend, sho is. How's Sister Simms?

SIMMS: She's feelin' kinda po'ly today. *(Goes on in store with his children)*

VOICE: *(Whispering loudly)* Don't see how that great big ole powerful woman could be sick. Look like she could go bear huntin' with her fist.

ANOTHER VOICE: She look jus' as good as you-all's Baptist pastor's wife. Pshaw, you ain't seen no big woman, nohow, man. I seen one once so big she went to whip her little boy and he run up under her belly and hid six months 'fore she could find him.

ANOTHER VOICE: Well, I knowed a woman so little that she had to get up on a soap box to look over a grain of sand.

*(*REV. SIMMS *comes out of store, each child behind him sucking a stick of candy.)*

SIMMS: *(To his children)* Run on home to your mother and don't get dirty on the way. *(The two children start primly off down the street but just out of sight one of them utters a loud cry.)*

SIMMS'S CHILD: *(Off stage)* Papa, papa. Nunkie's trying to lick my candy.

SIMMS: I told you to go on and leave them other children alone.

VOICE ON PORCH: *(Kidding)* Lum, whyn't you tend to your business.

*(*TOWN MARSHALL *rises and shoos the children off again.)*

LUM: You all varmints leave them nice chillun alone.

LIGE: *(Continuing the lying on porch)* Well, you all done seen so much, but I bet you ain't never seen a snake as big as the one I saw when I was a boy up in middle Georgia. He was so big couldn't hardly move his self. He laid in one spot so long he growed moss on him and everybody thought he was a log, till one day I set down on him and went to sleep, and when I woke up that snake done crawled to Florida. *(Loud laughter.)*

FRANK: *(Seriously)* Layin' all jokes aside though now, you all remember that rattlesnake I killed last year was almost as big as that Georgia snake.

VOICE: How big, you say it was, Frank?

FRANK: Maybe not quite as big as that, but jus' about four-teen feet.

VOICE: *(Derisively)* Gimme that lyin' snake. That snake wasn't but four foot long when you killed him last year and you done growed him ten feet in a year.

ANOTHER VOICE: Well, I don't know about that. Some of the snakes around here is powerful long. I went out in my front yard yesterday right after the rain and killed a great big ol' cottonmouth.

SIMMS: This sho is a snake town. I certainly can't raise no chickens for 'em. They kill my little biddies jus' as fast as they hatch out. And yes . . . if I hadn't cut them weeds out of the street in front of my parsonage, me or some of my folks woulda been snake-bit right at our front door. *(To whole crowd)* Whyn't you all cut down these weeds and clean up these streets?

HAMBO: Well, the Mayor ain't said nothin' 'bout it.

SIMMS: When the folks misbehaves in this town I think they oughta lock 'em up in a jail and make 'em work their fine out on the streets, then these weeds would be cut down.

VOICE: How we gonna do that when we ain't got no jail?

SIMMS: Well, you sho needs a jail . . . you-all needs a whole lot of improvements round this town. I ain't never pastored no town so way-back as this one here.

CLARKE: *(Who has lately emerged from the store, fanning himself, overhears this last remark and bristles up)* What's that you say 'bout this town?

SIMMS: I say we needs some improvements here in this town . . . that's what.

CLARKE: *(In a powerful voice)* And what improvements you figgers we needs?

SIMMS: A whole heap. Now, for one thing we really does need a jail, Mayor. We oughta stop runnin' these people out of town that misbehaves, and lock 'em up. Others towns has jails, everytown I ever pastored had a jail. Don't see how come we can't have one.

CLARKE: *(Towering angrily above the preacher)* Now, wait a minute, Simms. Don't you reckon the man who knows how to start a town knows how to run it? I paid two hundred dollars out of this right hand for this land and walked out here and started this town befo' you was born. I ain't like some of you new niggers, come here when grapes' ripe. I was here to cut new ground, and I been Mayor ever since.

SIMMS: Well, there ain't no sense in no one man stayin' Mayor all the time.

CLARKE: Well, it's my town and I can be mayor jus' as long as I want to. It was me that put this town on the map.

SIMMS: What map you put it on, Joe Clarke? I ain't seen it on no map.

CLARKE: *(Indignant)* I God! Listen here, Elder Simms. If you don't like the way I run this town, just' take your flat feets right on out and git yonder crost the woods. You ain't been here long enough to say nothin' nohow.

HAMBO: *(From a nail keg)* Yeah, you Methodist niggers always telling people how to run things.

TAYLOR: *(Practically unheard by the others)* We do so know how to run things, don't we? Ain't Brother Mayor a Methodist, and ain't the schoolteacher a . . . ? *(His remarks are drowned out by the others.)*

SIMMS: No, we don't like the way you're runnin' things. Now looka here, *(Pointing at the Marshall)* You got that lazy

Lum Boger here for marshall and he ain't old enough to be dry behind his ears yet . . . and all these able-bodied mens in this town! You won't 'low nobody else to run a store 'ceptin' you. And looka yonder *(happening to notice the street light)* only street lamp in town, you got in front of your place. *(Indignantly)* We pay the taxes and you got the lamp.

VILLAGER: Don't you-all fuss now. How come you two always yam-yamming at each other?

CLARKE: How come this fly-by-night Methodist preacher over here . . . ain't been here three months . . . tries to stand up on my store porch and tries to tell me how to run my town? *(MATTIE CLARKE, the Mayor's wife, comes timidly to the door, wiping her hands on her apron.)* Ain't no man gonna tell me how to run my town. I God, I 'lected myself in and I'm gonna run it. *(Turns and sees wife standing in door. Commandingly.)* I God, Mattie, git on back in there and wait on that store!

MATTIE: *(Timidly)* Jody, somebody else wantin' stamps.

CLARKE: I God, woman, what good is you? Gwan, git in. Look like between women and preachers a man can't have no peace. *(Exit CLARKE.)*

SIMMS: *(Continuing his argument)* Now, when I pastored in Jacksonville you oughta see what kinda jails they got there . . .

LOUNGER: White folks needs jails. We colored folks don't need no jail.

ANOTHER VILLAGER: Yes, we do, too. Elder Simms is right . . .

(The argument becomes a hubbub of voices.)

TAYLOR: *(Putting down his basket)* Now, I tell you a jail . . .

MRS. TAYLOR: *(Emerging from the store door, arms full of groceries, looking at her husband)* Yeah, and if you don't shut up and git these rations home I'm gonna be worse on you than a jail and six judges. Pickup that basket let's go. *(TONY meekly picks up the basket and he and his wife exit as the sound of an approaching guitar is heard off stage.)*

(Two carelessly dressed, happy-go-lucky fellows enter together. One is fingering a guitar without playing any particular tune, and the other has his hat cocked over his eyes in a burlesque, dude-like manner. There are casual greetings.)

WALTER: Hey, there, bums, how's tricks?

LIGE: What yo' sayin', boys?

HAMBO: Good evenin', sons.

LIGE: How did you-all make out this evening', boys?

JIM: Oh, them white folks at the party shelled out right well. Kept Dave busy pickin' it up. How much did we make today, Dave?

DAVE: *(Striking his pocket)* I don't know, boy, but feels right heavy here. Kept me pickin' up money just like this . . . *(As JIM picks a few dance chords, DAVE gives a dance imitation of how he picked up the coins from the ground as the white folks threw them.)* We count it after while. Woulda divided up with you already if you hadn't left me when you seen Daisy comin' by. Let's sit down on the porch and rest now.

LIGE: She sho is lookin' stylish and pretty since she come back with her white folks from up North. Wearin' the swellest clothes. And that coal-black hair of hers jus' won't quit.

MATTIE CLARKE: *(In doorway)* I don't see what the mens always hanging after Daisy Taylor for.

CLARKE: *(Turning around on the porch)* I God, you back here again. Who's tendin' that store? *(*MATTIE *disappears inside.)*

DAVE: Well, she always did look like new money to me when she was here before.

JIM: Well, that's all you ever did get was a look.

DAVE: That's all you know! I bet I get more than that now.

JIM: You might git it but I'm the man to use it. I'm a bottom fish.

DAVE: Aw, man. You musta been walking round here fast asleep when Daisy was in this county last. You ain't seen de go I had with her.

JIM: No, I ain't seen it. Bet you didn't have no letter from her while she been away.

DAVE: Bet you didn't neither.

JIM: Well, it's just cause she can't write. If she knew how to scratch with a pencil I'd had a ton of 'em.

DAVE: Shaw, man! I'd had a post office full of 'em.

OLD WOMAN: You-all ought to be shame, carrying on over a brazen heifer like Daisy Taylor. Jus' cause she's been up North and come back, I reckon you cutting de fool sho 'nough now. She ain't studying none of you-all nohow. All she wants is what you got in your pocket.

JIM: I likes her but she won't git nothin' outa me. She never did. I wouldn't give a poor consumpted cripple crab a crutch to cross the River Jurdon.

DAVE: I know I ain't gonna give no woman nothin'. I wouldn't give a dog a doughnut if he treed a terrapin.

LIGE: Youse a cottontail dispute . . . both of you. You'd give her anything you got. You'd give her Georgia with a fence 'round it.

OLD MAN: Yeah, and she'd take it, too.

LINDSAY: Don't distriminate the woman like that. That ain't nothing but hogism. Ain't nothin' the matter with Daisy, she's all right. *(Enter* TEETS *and* BOOTSIE *tittering coyly and switching themselves.)*

BOOTSIE: Is you seen my mama?

OLD WOMAN: You know you ain't lookin' for no mama. Jus' come back down here to show your shape and fan around awhile. *(*BOOTSIE *and* TEETS *going into the store.)*

BOOTSIE & TEETS: No, we ain't. We'se come to get our mail.

OLD WOMAN: *(After girls enter store)* Why don't you all keep up some attention to these nice girls here, Bootsie and Teets. They wants to marry.

DAVE: Aw, who thinkin' 'bout marryin' now? They better stay home and eat their own pa's rations. I gotta buy myself some shoes.

JIM: The woman I'm gonna marry ain't born yet and her maw is dead. *(GIRLS come out giggling and exit.)* *(JIM begins to strum his guitar lightly at first as the talk goes on.)*

CLARKE: *(To DAVE and JIM)* Two of the finest gals that ever lived and friendly jus' like you-all is. You two boys better take 'em back and stop them shiftless ways.

HAMBO: Yeah, hurry up and do somethin'! I wants to taste a piece yo' weddin' cake.

JIM: *(Embarrassed but trying to be jocular)* Whut you trying to rush me up so fast? . . . Look at Will Cody here *(Pointing to little man on porch)* he been promising to bring his already wife down for two months . . . and nair one of us ain't seen her yet.

DAVE: Yeah, how you speck me to haul in a brand new wife when he can't lead a wagon-broke wife eighteen miles? Me, I'm going git one soon's Cody show me his'n. *(General sly laughter at CODY's expense.)*

WALTER: *(Snaps his fingers and pretends to remember something)* Thass right, Cody. I been intending to tell you . . . I know where you kin buy a ready-built house for you and yo' wife. *(Calls into the store.)* Hey, Clarke, come on out here and tell Cody 'bout dat Bradley house. *(To CODY.)* I know you wants to git a place of yo' own so you kin settle down.

HAMBO: He done moved so much since he been here till every time he walk out in his back yeard his chickens lay down and cross they legs.

LINDSAY: Cody, I thought you tole us you was going up to Sanford to bring dat 'oman down here last Sat'day.

LIGE: That ain't de way he tole me 'bout it. Look, fellers, *(Getting up and putting one hand on his hips and one finger of the other hand against his chin coquettishly)* Where you reckon I'll be next Sat'day night? . . . Sittin' up side of Miz Cody. *(Great burst of laughter.)*

SYKES JONES: *(Laughing)* Know what de folks tole me in Sanford? Dat was another man's wife. *(Guffaws.)*

CODY: *(Feebly)* Aw, you don't know whut you talkin' bout.

JONES: Naw, I don't know, but de folks in Sanford does. *(Laughing)* Day tell me when dat lady's husband come home Sat'day night, ole Cody jumped out de window. De man grabbed his old repeater and run out in de yard to head him off. When Cody seen him come round de corner de house *(Gesture)* he flopped his wings and flew up on de fence. De man thowed dat shotgun dead on him. *(Laughs)* Den, man! Cody flopped his wings lak a buzzard *(Gesture)* and sailed on off. De man dropped to his knees lak dis *(Gesture of kneeling on one knee and taking aim)* Die! die! die! *(Supposedly sound of shots as the gun is moved in a circle following the course of Cody's supposed flight)* Cody just flew right on off and lit on a hill two miles off. Then, man! *(Gesture of swift flight)* In ten minutes he was back here in Eatonville and in he bed.

WALTER: I passed there and seen his house shakin', but I didn't know how come.

HAMBO: Aw, leave de boy alone. . . . If you don't look out some of y'all going to have to break his record.

LIGE: I'm prepared to break it now. *(General laughter.)*

JIM: Well, anyhow, I don't want to marry and leave Dave . . . yet awhile. *(Picking a chord.)*

DAVE: And I ain't gonna leave Jim. We been palling around together ever since we hollered titty mama, ain't we, boy?

JIM: Sho is. *(Music of the guitar increases in volume.* DAVE *shuffles a few steps and the two begin to sing.)*

JIM: Rabbit on the log.
       I ain't got no dog.
       How am I gonna git him?
       God knows.

DAVE: Rabbit on the log.
        Ain't got no dog.
        Shoot him with my rifle
        Bam! Bam!

(Some of the villagers join in song and others get up and march around the porch in time with the music. BOOTSIE *and* TEETS *re-enter,* TEETS *sticking her letter down the neck of her blouse.* JOE LINDSAY *grabs* TEETS *and* WALTER THOMAS *grabs* BOOTSIE. *There is dancing, treating and general jollification. Little children dance the parse-me-la. The music fills the air just as the sun begins to go down. Enter* DAISY TAYLOR *coming down the road toward the store.)*

CLARKE: *(Bawls out from the store porch)* I God, there's Daisy again.

(Most of the dancing stops, the music slows down and then stops completely. DAVE *and* JIM *greet* DAISY *casually as she approaches the porch.)*

JIM: Well, Daisy, we knows you, too.

DAVE: Gal, youse jus' as pretty as a speckled pup.

DAISY: *(Giggling)* I see you two boys always playin' and singin' together. That music sounded right good floating down the road.

JIM: Yeah, child, we'se been playin' for the white folks all week. We'se playin' for the colored now.

DAVE: *(Showing off, twirling his dancing feet)* Yeah, we're standin' on our abstract and livin' on our income.

OLD MAN: Um-ump, but they ain't never workin'. Just round here playing as usual.

JIM: Some folks think you ain't workin' lessen you smellin' a mule. *(He sits back down on box and picks at his guitar.)* Think you gotta be beatin' a man to his barn every mornin'.

VOICE: Glad to be round home with we-all again, ain't you Daisy?

DAISY: Is I glad? I jus' got off special early this evenin' to come over here and see everybody. I was kinda 'fraid sundown would catch me 'fore I got round that lake. Don't know how I'm gonna walk back to my workin' place in the dark by muself.

DAVE: Don't no girl as good-lookin' as you is have to go home by herself tonight.

JIM: No, cause I'm here.

DAVE: *(To* DAISY*)* Don't you trust yourself round that like wid all them 'gators and moccasins with that nigger there, Daisy *(Pointing at* JIM*)* He's jus' full of rabbit blood. What you need is a real man . . . with good feet. *(Cutting a dance step.)*

DAISY: I ain't thinking 'bout goin' home yet. I'm goin' in the store.

JIM: What you want in the store?

DAISY: I want some gum.

DAVE: *(Starting toward door)* Girl, you don't have to go in there to git no gum. I'll go in there and buy you a carload of gum. What kind you want?

DAISY: Bubble gum. *(*DAVE *goes in the store with his hand in his pocket. The sun is setting and the twilight deepens.)*

JIM: *(Pulling package out of his pocket and laughing)* Here your gum, baby. What it takes to please the ladies, I totes it. I don't have to go get it, like Dave. What you gimme for it?

DAISY: A bushel and a peck, and a hug around the neck. *(She embraces* JIM *playfully. He hands her the gum, patting his shoulder as he sits on box.)* Oh, thank you. Youse a ready man.

JIM: Yeah, there's a lot of good parts to me. You can have West Tampa if you want it.

DAISY: You always was a nice quiet boy, Jim.

DAVE: *(Emerging from the store with a package of gum)* Here's your gum, Daisy.

JIM: Oh, youse late. She's done got gum now. Chaw that yourself.

DAVE: *(Slightly peeved and surprised)* Hunh, you mighty fast here now with Daisy but you wasn't that fast gettin' out of that white man's chicken house last week.

JIM: Who you talkin' 'bout?

DAVE: Hoo-oo? *(Facetiously)* You ain't no owl. Your feet don't fit no limb.

JIM: Aw, nigger, hush.

DAVE: Aw, hush, yourself. *(He walks away for a minute as* DAISY *turns to meet some newcomers.* DAVE *throws his package of gum down on the ground. It breaks and several children scramble for the pieces. An old man, very drunk, carrying an empty jug enters on left and staggers tipsily across stage.) (*MAYOR JOE CLARKE *emerges from the store and looks about for his marshall.)*

CLARKE: *(Bellowing)* Lum Boger!

LUM BOGER: *(Eating a stalk of cane)* Yessir!

CLARKE: I God, Lum, take your lazy self off that keg and go light that town lamp. All summer long you eatin' up my melon, and all winter long you chawin' up my cane. What you think this town is payin' you for? Laying round here doin' nothin'? Can't you see it's gettin' dark?

(LUM BOGER rises lazily and takes the soap box down stage, stands on it to light the lamp, discovers no oil in it and goes in store. In a few moments he comes out of store, fills the lamp and lights it.)

DAISY: *(Coming back toward JIM)* Ain't you all gonna play and sing a little somethin' for me? I ain't heard your all's music much for so long.

JIM: Play anything you want, Daisy. Don't make no difference what 'tis I can pick it. Where's that old coon, Dave? *(Looking around for his partner.)*

LIGE: *(Calling DAVE, who is leaning against post at opposite end of porch)* Come here, an' get warmed up for Daisy.

DAVE: Aw, ma throat's tired.

JIM: Leave the baby be.

DAISY: Come on, sing a little, Dave.

DAVE: *(Going back toward JIM)* Well, seeing who's asking . . . all right. What song you like, Daisy?

DAISY: Um-m. Lemme think.

VOICE ON PORCH: "Got on the train, didn't have no fare".

DAISY: *(Gaily)* Yes, that one. That's a good one.

JIM: *(Begins to tune up. DAVE touches DAISY's hand.)*

VOICE: *(In fun)* Hunh, you all wouldn't play at the hall last week when we asked you.

VOICE OF SPITEFUL OLD WOMAN: Daisy wasn't here then.

ANOTHER VOICE: *(Teasingly)* All you got to do to some men is to shake a skirt tail in their face and they goes off their head.

DAVE: *(To* JIM *who is still tuning up)* Come if you're comin' boy, let's go if you gwine. *(The full melody of the guitar comes out in a lively, old-fashioned tune.)*

VOICE: All right now, boys, do it for Daisy jus' as good as you do for dem white folks over in Maitland.

DAVE & JIM: *(Beginning to sing)*
          Got on the train,
          Didn't have no fare,
          But I rode some,
          I rode some.
          Got on the train,
          Didn't have no fare,
          But I rode some,
          But I rode some.
          Got on the train,
          Didn't have no fare,
          Conductor asked me what I'm doin' there,
          But I rode some!

          Grabbed me by the neck
          And led me to the door.
          But I rode some,
          But I rode some.
          Grabbed me by the neck
          And led me to the door.
          But I rode some,

But I rode some.
Grabbed me by the neck,
And led me to the door.
Rapped me cross the head with a forty-four,
But I rode some!

First thing I saw in jail
Was a pot of peas.
But I rode some,
But I rode some.
First thing I saw in jail
Was a pot of peas.
But I rode some,
But I rode some.
The peas was good,
The meat was fat,
Fell in love with the chain gang jus' for that,
But I rode some.

(DAVE *acts out the song in dancing pantomime and when it ends there are shouts and general exclamations of approval from the crowd.*)

VOICES: I don't blame them white folks for goin' crazy 'bout that . . .

OLD MAN: Oh, when I was a young boy I used to swing the gals round on that piece.

DAISY: *(To* JIM*)* Seem like your playin' gits better and better.

DAVE: *(Quickly)* And how 'bout my singin'? *(Everybody laughs.)*

VOICES IN THE CROWD: Ha! Ha! Ol' Dave's gittin' jealous when she speaks o' Jim.

JIM: *(To* DAVE, *in fun)* Ain't nothin' to it but my playin'. You ain't got no singin' voice. If that's singin', God's a gopher.

DAVE: *(Half-seriously)* My singin' is a whole lot better'n your playin'. You jus' go along and fram. The reason why the white folks gives us money is cause I'm singin'.

JIM: Yeah?

DAVE: And you can't dance.

VOICE IN THE CROWD: You oughta dance. Big as your feet is, Dave.

DAISY: *(Diplomatically)* Both of you all is wonderful and I would like to see Dave dance a little.

DAVE: There now, I told you. What did I tell you. *(To* JIM*)* Stop woofing and pick a little tune there so that I can show Daisy somethin'.

JIM: Pick a tune? I bet if you fool with me I'll pick your bones jus' like a buzzard did the rabbit. You can't sing and now you wants to dance.

DAVE: Yeah, and I'll lam your head. Come on and play, good-for-nothing.

JIM: All right, then. You say you can dance . . . show these people what you can do. But don't bring that little stuff I been seein' you doin' all these years. (JIM *plays and* DAVE *dances,*

various members of the crowd keep time with their hands and feet,
DAISY *looks on enjoying herself immensely.)*

DAISY: *(As* DAVE *cuts a very fancy step)* I ain't seen nothin'
like this up North. Dave you sho hot.

(As DAVE *cuts a more complicated step the crowd applauds, but just
as the show begins to get good, suddenly* JIM *stops playing.)*

DAVE: *(Surprised)* What's the matter, buddy?

JIM: *(Envious of the attention* DAVE *has been getting from*
DAISY, *disgustedly)* Oh, nigger, I'm tired of seein' you cut the
fool. 'Sides that, I been playin' all afternoon for the white
folks.

DAISY: But I though you was playin' for me now, Jim.

JIM: Yeah, I'd play all night long for you, but I'm gettin' sick
of Dave round here showin' off. Let him git somethin' and
play for himself if he can. *(An* OLD MAN *with a lighted lantern
enters.)*

DAISY: *(Coyly)* Well, honey, play some more for me then,
and don't mind Dave. I reckon he done danced enough. Play
me "Shake That Thing".

OLD MAN WITH LANTERN: Sho, you ain't stopped, is you,
boy? Music sound mighty good floatin' down that dark road.

OLD WOMAN: Yeah, Jim, go on play a little more. Don't get
to acting so niggerish this evening.

DAVE: Aw, let the ol' darky alone. Nobody don't want to
hear him play, nohow. I know I don't.

JIM: Well, I'm gonna play. *(And he begins to pick "Shake That Thing".* TEETS *and* BOOTSIE *begin to dance with* LIGE MOSELY *and* FRANK WARRICK. *As the tune gets good,* DAVE *cannot resist the music either.)*

DAVE: Old nigger's evil but he sho can play. *(He begins to do a few steps by himself, then twirls around in front of* DAISY *and approaches her.* DAISY, *overcome by the music, begins to step rhythmically toward* DAVE *and together they dance unobserved by* JIM, *absorbed in picking his guitar.)*

DAISY: Look here, baby, at this new step I learned up North.

DAVE: You can show me anything, sugar lump.

DAISY: Hold me tight now. *(But just as they begin the new movement* JIM *notices* DAISY *and* DAVE. *He stops playing again and lays his guitar down.)*

VOICES IN THE CROWD: *(Disgustedly)* Aw, come on, Jim . . . You must be jealous . . .

JIM: No, I ain't jealous. I jus' get tired of seein' that ol' nigger clownin' all the time.

DAVE: *(Laughing and pointing to* JIM *on porch)* Look at that mad baby. Take that lip up off the ground. Got your mouth stuck out jus' because some one is enjoying themselves. *(He comes up and pushes* JIM *playfully.)*

JIM: You better go head and let me alone. *(To* DAISY*)* Come here, Daisy!

LIGE: That's just what I say. Niggers can't have no fun without someone getting mad . . . specially over a woman.

JIM: I ain't mad . . . Daisy, 'scuse me, honey, but that fool, Dave . . .

DAVE: I ain't mad neither . . . Jim always tryin' to throw off on me. But you can't joke him.

DAISY: *(Soothingly)* Aw, now, now!

JIM: You ain't jokin'. You means that, nigger. And if you tryin' to get hot, first thing, you can pull off my blue shirt you put on this morning.

DAVE: Youse a got that wrong. I ain't got on no shirt of yours.

JIM: Yes, you is got on my shirt, too. Don't tell me you ain't got on my shirt.

DAVE: Well, even if I is, you can just lift your big plantations out of my shoes. You can just foot it home barefooted.

JIM: You try to take any shoes offa me!

LIGE: *(Pacifying them)* Aw, there ain't no use of all that. What you all want to start this quarreling for over a little jokin'.

JIM: Nobody's quarreling . . . I'm just playin' a little for Daisy and Dave's out there clownin' with her.

CLARKE: *(In doorway)* I ain't gonna have no fussin' round my store, no way. Shut up, you all.

JIM: Well, Mayor Clarke, I ain't mad with him. We'se been friends all our lives. He's slept in my bed and wore my clothes and et my grub. . . .

DAVE: I et your grub? And many time as you done laid down with your belly full of my grandma's collard greens. You done et my meat and bread a whole lot more times than I et your stewed fish-heads.

JIM: I'd rather eat stewed fish-heads than steal out of other folkses houses so much till you went to sleep on the roost and fell down one night and broke up the settin' hen. *(Loud laughter from the crowd)*

DAVE: Youse a liar if you say I stole anybody's chickens. I didn't have to. But you . . . 'fore you started goin' around with me, playin' that little box of yours, you was so hungry you had the white mouth. If it wasn't for these white folks throwin' *me* money for *my* dancin', you would be thin as a whisper right now.

JIM: *(Laughing sarcastically)* Your dancin'! You been leapin' around here like a tailless monkey in a wash pot for a long time and nobody was payin' no 'tention to you, till I come along playing.

LINDSAY: Boys, boys, that ain't no way for friends to carry on.

DAISY: Well, if you all gonna keep up this quarrelin' and carryin' on I'm goin' home. 'Bout time for me to be gittin' back to my white folks anyhow. It's dark now. I'm goin', even if I have to go by myself. I shouldn't a stopped by here nohow.

JIM: *(Stopping his quarrel)* You ain't gonna go home by yourself. I'm goin' with you.

DAVE: *(Singing softly)*
It may be so,

I don't know.
But it sounds to me
Like a lie.

WALTER: Dave ain't got as much rabbit blood as folks thought.

DAVE: Tell 'em 'bout me. *(Turns to* DAISY*)* Won't you choose a treat on me, Miss Daisy, 'fore we go?

DAISY: *(Coyly)* Yessir, thank you. I wants a drink of soda water.

*(*DAVE *pulls his hat down over his eyes, whirls around and offers his arm to* DAISY. *They strut into the store,* DAVE *gazing contemptuously at* JIM *as he passes. Crowd roars with laughter, much to the embarrassment of* JIM.*)*

LIGE: Ol' fast Dave jus' runnin' the hog right over you, Jim.

WALTER: Thought you was such a hot man.

LUM BOGER: Want me to go in there and put Daisy under arrest and bring her to you?

JIM: *(Sitting down on the edge of porch with one foot on the step and lights a cigarette pretending not to be bothered.)* Aw, I'll get her when I want her. Let him treat her, but see who struts around that lake and down the railroad with her by and by.

*(*DAVE *and* DAISY *emerge from the store, each holding a bottle of red soda pop and laughing together. As they start down the steps* DAVE *accidentally steps on* JIM*'s outstretched foot.* JIM *jumps up and pushes* DAVE *back, causing him to spill the red soda all over his white shirt front.)*

JIM: Stay off my foot, you big ox.

DAVE: Well, you don't have to wet me all up, do you, and me in company? Why don't you put your damn foot in your pocket?

DAISY: (*Wiping* DAVE's *shirt front with her handkerchief*) Aw, ain't that too bad.

JIM: (*To* DAVE) Well, who's shirt did I wet? It's mine, any-how, ain't it?

DAVE: (*Belligerently*) Well, if it's your shirt, then you come take it off me. I'm tired of your lip.

JIM: Well, I will.

DAVE: Well, put your fist where you lip is. (*Pushing* DAISY *aside.*)

DAISY: (*Frightened*) I want to go home. Now, don't you-all boys fight.

(JIM *attempts to come up the steps.* DAVE *pushes him back and he stumbles and falls in the dust. General excitement as the crowd senses a fight.*)

LITTLE BOY: (*On the edge of crowd*) Fight, fight, you're no kin. Kill one another, won't be no sin. Fight, fight, you're no kin.

(JIM *jumps up and rushes for* DAVE *as the latter starts down the steps.* DAVE *meets him with his fist squarely in the face and causes him to step backward, confused.*)

DAISY: *(Still on porch, half crying)* Aw, my Lawd! I want to go home.

(General hubbub, women's cries of "Don't let 'em fight." "Why don't somebody stop 'em?" "What kind of men is you all, sit there and let them boys fight like that." Men's voices urging the fight: "Aw, let 'em fight." "Go for him, Dave." "Slug him, Jim." JIM makes another rush toward the steps. He staggers DAVE, DAVE knocks JIM sprawling once more. This time JIM grabs the mule bone as he rises, rushes DAVE, strikes DAVE over the head with it and knocks him out. DAVE falls prone on his back. There is great excitement.)

OLD WOMAN: *(Screams)* Lawdy, is he kilt? *(Several men rush to the fallen man.)*

VOICE: Run down to the pump and get a dipper o' water.

CLARKE: *(To his wife in door)* Mattie, come out of that store with a bottle of witch hazely oil quick as you can. Jim Weston, I'm gonna arrest you for this. You Lum Boger. Where is that marshall? Lum Boger! *(LUM BOGER detaches himself from the crowd.)* Arrest Jim.

LUM: *(Grabs JIM's arm, relieves him of the mule bone and looks helplessly at the Mayor.)* Now I got him arrested, what's I going to do with him?

CLARKE: Lock him up back yonder in my barn till Monday when we'll have the trial in de Baptist Church.

LINDSAY: Yeah, just like all the rest of them Methodists . . . always tryin' to take undercurrents on people.

WALTER: Ain't no worse then some of you Baptists, nohow.

You all don't run this town. We got jus' as much to say as you have.

CLARKE: *(Angrily to both men)* Shut up! Done had enough arguing in front of my place. *(To* LUM BOGER*)* Take that boy on and lock him up in my barn. And save that mule bone for evidence.

*(*LUM BOGER *leads* JIM *off toward the back of the store. A crowd follows him. Other men and women are busy applying restoratives to* DAVE. DAISY *stands alone, unnoticed in the center of the stage.)*

DAISY: *(Worriedly)* Now, who's gonna take me home?

CURTAIN

ACT TWO

Scene I

SETTING: *Village street scene; huge oak tree upstage center; a house or two on back drop. When curtain goes up,* SISTER LUCY TAYLOR *is seen standing under the tree. She is painfully spelling it out. (Enter* SISTER THOMAS, *a younger woman [In her thirties] at left.)*

SISTER THOMAS: Evenin', Sis Taylor.

SISTER TAYLOR: Evenin'. *(Returns to the notice)*

SISTER THOMAS: What you doin'? Readin' dat notice Joe Clarke put up 'bout de meeting? *(Approaches tree)*

SISTER TAYLOR: Is dat whut it says? I ain't much on readin' since I had my teeth pulled out. You know if you pull out dem eye teeth you ruins yo' eye sight. *(Turns back to notice)* Whut it say?

SISTER THOMAS: *(Reading notice)* "The trial of Jim Weston for assault and battery on Dave Carter wid a dangerous wee- pon will be held at Macedonia Baptist Church on Monday, November 10, at three o'clock. All are welcome. By order of J. Clarke, Mayor of Eatonville, Florida." *(Turning to* SISTER TAYLOR*)* Hit's makin' on to three now.

SISTER TAYLOR: You mean it's right *now.* *(Locks up at sun to tell time)* Lemme go git ready to be at de trial 'cause I'm sho goin' to be there an' I ain't goin' to bite my tongue neither.

SISTER THOMAS: I done went an' crapped a mess of collard greens for supper. I better go put 'em on 'cause Lawd knows when we goin' to git outa there an' my husband is one of them dat's gointer eat don't keer what happen. I bet if judgment day was to happen tomorrow he'd speak I orter fix him a bucket to carry long. *(She moves to exit, right)*

SISTER TAYLOR: All men favors they guts, chile. But what you think of all dis mess they got goin' on round here?

SISTER THOMAS: I just think it's a sin en' a shame befo' de livin' justice de way dese Baptis' niggers is runnin' round here carryin' on.

SISTER TAYLOR: Oh, they been puttin' out the brags ever since Sat'day night 'bout shut they gointer do to Jim. They thinks they runs this town. They tell me Rev. Childers preached a sermon on it yistiddy.

SISTER THOMAS: Lawd help us! He can't preach em' let lone gittin' up dere tryin' to throw slams at us. Now all Elder Simms done wus to explain to us our rights . . . what you think 'bout Joe Clarke runnin' round here takin' up for these ole Baptist niggers?

SISTER TAYLOR: De puzzle-gut rascal . . . we oughter have him up in conference an' put him out de Methdis' faith. He don't b'long in there—wanter tun dat boy outa town for nothin'.

SISTER THOMAS: But we all know how come he so hot to law Jim outa town—hit's to dig de foundation out from under Elder Simms.

SISTER TAYLOR: Whut he wanta do dat for?

SISTER THOMAS: 'Cause he wants to be a God-know-it-all an' a God-do-it-all an' Simms is de onliest one in this town whut will buck up to him. *(Enter* SISTER JONES, *walking leisurely)*

SISTER JONES: Hello, Boyt, hello, Lucy.

SISTER TAYLOR: Goin' to de meetin'?

SISTER JONES: Done got my clothes on de line an' I'm bound to be dere.

SISTER THOMAS: Gointer testify for Jim?

SISTER JONES: Naw, I reckon—don't make such difference to me which way de drop fall. . . . 'Tain't neither one of 'em much good.

SISTER TAYLOR: I know it. I know it, Ida. But dat ain't de point. De crow we wants to pick is: Is we gointer set still an' let dese Baptist tell us when to plant an' when to pluck up?

SISTER JONES: Dat *is* something to think about when you come to think 'bout it. *(Starts to move on)* Guess I better go ahead—see y'all later an tell you straighter.

(Enter ELDER SIMMS, *right, walking fast, Bible under his arm, almost collides with* SISTER JONES *as she exits.)*

SIMMS: Oh, 'scuse me, Sister Jones. *(She nods and smiles and exits.)* How you do, Sister Taylor, Sister Thomas.

BOTH: Good evenin', Elder.

SIMMS: Sho is a hot day.

SISTER TAYLOR: Yeah, de bear is walkin' de earth lak a natural man.

SISTER THOMAS: Reverend, look like you headed de wrong way. It's almost time for de trial an' youse all de dependence we got.

SIMMS: I know it. I'm tryin' to find de marshall so we kin go after Jim. I wants a chance to talk wid him a minute before court sets.

SISTER TAYLOR: Y'think he'll come clear?

SIMMS: *(Proudly)* I *know* it! *(Shakes the Bible)* I'm goin' to law 'em from Genesis to Revelation.

SISTER THOMAS: Give it to 'em, Elder. Wear 'em out!

SIMMS: We'se liable to have a new Mayor when all dis dust settle. Well, I better scuffle on down de road. *(Exits, left.)*

SISTER THOMAS: Lord, lemme gwan home an' put dese greens on. *(Looks off stage left)* Here come Mayor Clarke now, wid his belly settin' out in front of him like a cow catcher! His name oughter be Mayor Belly.

SISTER TAYLOR: *(Arms skimbo)* Jus' look at him! Tryin' to look like a jigadier Breneral. *(Enter* CLARKE *hot and perspiring. They look at him coldly.)*

CLARKE: I God, de bear got me! *(Silence for a moment)* How y'all feelin', ladies?

SISTER TAYLOR: Brother Mayor, I ain't one of these folks dat bite my tongue an' bust my gall—what's inside got to come out! I can't see to my rest why you cloakin' in wid dese Baptist buzzards 'ginst yo' own church.

MAYOR CLARKE: I ain't cloakin' in wid *none.* I'm de Mayor of dis whole town. I stands for de right an' ginst de wrong—I don't keer who it kill or cure.

SISTER THOMAS: You think it's right to be runnin' dat boy off for nothin'?

CLARKE: I God! You call knockin' a man in de head wid a mule bone nothin'? 'Nother thing, I done missed nine of my best-layin' hens. I ain't sayin' Jim got 'em, but different people has tole me he burries a powerful lot of feathers in his back yard. I God, I'm a ruint man! *(He starts towards the right exit, but* LUM BOGER *enters right.)* I God, Lum, I bean lookin' for you all day. It's almost three o'clock. *(Hands him a key from his ring)* Take dis key an' go fetch Jim Weston on to de church.

LUM: Have you got yo' gavel from de lodge-room?

CLARKE: I God, that's right, Lum. I'll go get it from de lodge room whilst you go git de bone an' de prisoner. Hurry up! You walk like dead lice droppin' off you. *(He exits right while* LUM *crosses stage towards left.)*

SISTER TAYLOR: Lum, Elder Simms been huntin' you—he's gone on down 'bout de barn. *(She gestures)*

LUM BOGER: I reckon I'll overtake him. *(Exit left.)*

SISTER THOMAS: I better go put dose greens on. My husband will kill me if he don't find no supper ready. Here come Mrs. Blunt. She oughter feel like a penny's worth of have-mercy wid all dis stink behind her daughter.

SISTER TAYLOR: Chile, some Folks don't keer. They don't raise they chillon, they drags 'em up. God knows if dat Daisy wus mine, I'd throw her down an' put a hundred lashes on her back wid a plow-line. Here she come in de store Sat'day night *(Acts coy and coquettish, burlesques* DAISY's *walk)* a wringing and a twisting!

*(*REV. CHILDERS *enters left with* DAVE *and* DEACON LINDSAY *and* SISTER LEWIS. *Very hostile glances from* SISTERS THOMAS *and* TAYLOR *towards the others.)*

CHILDERS: Good evenin', folks.

(Sisters THOMAS *and* TAYLOR *just grunt.* MRS. THOMAS *moves a step or two towards exit. Flirts her skirts and exits.)*

MARY ELLA: Y'all ole Meth'dis' ain't got no window panes in yo' church down yonder in de swamp.

ANOTHER GIRL: *(Takes center of stand, hands akimbo and shakes her hips)* I don't keer whut y'all say, I'm a Meth'dis' bred an' uh Meth'dis' born an' when I'm dead there'll be uh Meth'- dis' gone.

MARY ELLA: *(Snaps fingers under other girl's nose and starts singing. Several join her.)*
>Oh Baptis', Baptis' is my name
>My name's written on high
>I got my lick in de Baptis' church
>Gointer eat up de Meth'dis' pie.

(The Methodist children jeer and make faces. The Baptist camp make faces back; for a full minute there is silence while each camp tries to outdo the other in face making. The Baptist makes the last face.)

METHODIST BOY: Oo e on, less us don't notice 'em. Less gwan down to de church an' hear de trial.

MARY ELLA: Y'all ain't de onliest ones kin go. We goin', too.

WILLIE: Aw, haw! Copy cats! *(Makes face)* Dat's right. Follow on behind us lak uh puppy dog tail. *(They start walking toward right exit, switching their clothes behind.)*

(Baptist children stage a rush and struggle to get in front of the Methodists. They finally succeed in flinging some of the Methodist children to the ground and come behind them and walk towards right exit haughtily switching their clothes.)

WILLIE: (*Whispers to his crowd*) Less go round by Mosely's lot an' beat 'em there!

OTHERS: All right!

WILLIE: (*Yellin' to Baptists*) We wouldn't walk behind no ole Baptists!

(*The Methodists turn and walk off towards left exit, switching their clothes as the Baptists are doing.*)

SLOW CURTAIN

ACT TWO

Scene II

SETTING: *Interior of Macedonia Baptist Church, a rectangular room. Windows on each side, two Amen Corners. Pulpit with a plush cover with heavy fringe, door in front of church, two oil brackets with reflectors on each side wall, with lamps missing on all but one. One big oil lamp in center.*

ACTION: *At the rise, church is about full. A buzz and hum fills the church. Voices of children angry and jeering heard from the street. The church bell begins to toll for death. Everybody looks shocked.*

SISTER LEWIS: Lawd! Is Dave done died from dat lick?

SISTER THOMAS: (*to her husband*) Walter, go see. (*He gets up and starts down the aisle to front door. Enter* DEACON HAMBO *by front door.*)

WALTER: Who dead?

HAMBO: *(Laughing)* Nobody. Jus' tollin' de bell for dat Meth'dis' gopher dat's gointer be long, long gone after dis trial. *(Laughter from Baptist side. Enter* TONY TAYLOR *and his wife.* TONY *is about to go to front of church but* MRS. TAYLOR *jerks him down into a seat on the aisle on the Methodist side.)*

WALTER: Y'all sho thinks you runs dis town, dontcher? But Elder Simms'll show you somethin' t'day. If he don't God's up gopher.

HAMBO: He can't show us nothin' cause he don't know nothin' hisself.

WALTER: He got mo' book-learnin' than Rev. Childers* got.

HAMBO: Childers mought be unletter-learnt, but he kin drive over Simms like a road plow.

METHODIST CHORUS: Aw naw! Dat's a lie!

(Enter REV. SIMMS *by front door with open* Bible *in hand. A murmur of applause rises on the Methodist side. Grunts on the Baptist side. Immediately behind him, comes* LUM BOGER *leading* JIM WESTON. *They parade up to the right Amen Corner and seat themselves on the same bench.* JIM *between the Marshall and preacher. A great rooster-crowing and hen-cackling arises on the Baptist side.* JIM WESTON *jumps angrily to his feet.)*

JIM: Wisht tuh God I had dat mule bone agin! Ah'd make some uh you mud turtles cackle out de other side yo' mouf. *(Loud laughter of derision from the Baptists.* LUM *looks scared.)*

---

*At this point in the original manuscript, for unknown reasons, the name *Childers* changed to *Singletary*. We have kept *Childers* for consistency.

SIMMS: Sit down, son; sit down. Be c'am.

(Enter by front door REV. CHILDERS *and* DAVE. DAVE's *head is bandaged, but he walks firmly and seems not ill at all. They sit in the left Amen Corner. Jeering grunts from the Methodist side.)*

SISTER THOMAS: Look at ol' Dave tryin' to make out he's hurt.

METHODIST VOICE: And Childers lookin' like ten cents worth of have-mercy.

BAPTIST VOICE: Yes, but you ought to heard that hell fire sermon he preached yesterday on fightin'.

METHODIST VOICE: Yeah, tryin de case fo' de trial come up.

BAPTIST VOICE: Well, sho is a sin to split a man's head, aint it?

LIGE: Everybody know uh Baptis' head is harder'n uh rock. Look like they'd be skeered tuh go in swimmin; do, they heads would drown 'em. *(General laughter on Methodist side.)*

SISTER TAYLOR: Some folks is a whole lot more keerful 'bout a louse in de church than dey is in dey house. *(Looks pointedly at Sister Lewis)*

SISTER LEWIS: *(bristling)* Whut you gazin' at me for? Wid your popeyes lookin' like skirt ginny-nuts?

SISTER TAYLOR: I hate to tell you whut yo' mouf looks like. I thinks you an' soap an' water musta had some words.

Evertime you lifts yo' arm you smell like a nest of yellow hammers.

SISTER LEWIS: Well, I ain't seen no bath tubs in your house.

SISTER TAYLOR: Mought not have no tub, but tain't no lice on me though.

SISTER LEWIS: Aw, you got just as many bed-bugs and chinces as anybody else. I seen de bed-bugs marchin' out of yo' house in de mornin', keepin' step just like soldiers drillin'.

SISTER TAYLOR: You got that wrong, I—

(Enter BROTHER NIXON *with his junper jacket on his arm and climbs over the knees of a bench full of people and finds a seat against the wall directly beneath an empty lamp bracket. He looks around for some place to dispose of his coat. Sees the lamp-bracket and hangs the coat there. Hitches up his pants and sits down.*)

SISTER LEWIS: Wait a minute *(rising and glaring at* NIXON*)* Shank Nixon, you take yo' lousy coat down off these sacred walls. Ain't you Meth'dis' niggers got no gumption in de house of wash-up!

(NIXON *mocks her by standing akimbo and shaking himself like a woman. General laughter. He prepares to resume his seat, but looks over and sees* DEACON HAMBO *on his feet, and glaring angrily at him. He quickly reaches up and takes the coat down and folds it across his knee.*)

SISTER TAYLOR: *(Looks very pointedly at* SISTER LEWIS, *then takes a dip of snuff and looks sneering at* LEWIS *again.)* If I kept de dirty house you keeps ma mouth would be a closed book. *(Loud laughter from the Meth'dis' side.)*

SISTER LEWIS: *(furious, rises arms akimbo.)* Well, my house might not be exactly clean, but there's no fly-specks on my chara*c*ter! They didn't have to git de sheriff to make Willie marry *me* like they did to make Tony marry *you.*

SISTER TAYLOR: *(jumping up and starting across the aisle. She is pulled back out of the aisle by friends.)* Yeah, they got de sheriff to make Tony marry me, but he married me and made me a good husband too. I sits in my rocking cheer on my porch every Sat'day evenin' an' say: "Here come Tony and them"

SISTER LEWIS: *(scornfully)* Them what?

SISTER TAYLOR: Them dollars, that's what! Now you sho orter go git de sheriff and a shot gun and make some of dese men marry yo' daughter, Ada.

SISTER LEWIS: *(Jumpin' up an' startin' across the aisle. She is restrained, but struggles hard.)* Lemme go, Jim Merchant! Turn me go! I'm goin' to stomp her till she can't sit down.

SISTER TAYLOR: *(also struggling)* Let her come on! If I get my hands on her I'll turn her every way but loose.

SISTER LEWIS: Just come on out dis church, Lucy Taylor. I'll beat you on everything but yo' tongue, and I'll give dat a lick if you stick it out. *(to the men holding her)* Turn me go! I'm goin' to fix her so her own Mammy won't know her.

SISTER TAYLOR: *(trying to free herself.)* Why don't y'all turn dat ole twist mouth 'oman loose? All I wants to do is hit her one lick. I betcha I'll take her 'way from here faster than de word of God.

SISTER LEWIS: *(to men holding Mrs. Taylor)* I don't see how come y'all won't let old Lucy Taylor a loose. Make out she so bad, now. She may be red hot but I kin cool her. I'll ride her just like Jesus rode a jackass.

(As they subside into their seats again, but glare at each other, MAYOR CLARKE comes thru the pulpit door. He is annoyed at the clamor going on. He tries to quell the noise with a frown.)

SISTER TAYLOR: Dat ain't nothin' but talk. You looks lak de Devil before day, but you ain't so bad; not half as bad as you smell.

MAYOR CLARKE: Order, please, court is set.

SISTER LEWIS: You looks like de devil's doll baby, but all I want you to do is put it where I kin git it an' I'll sho use it.

MAYOR CLARKE: *(booming)* Here! Here! *(feeling everywhere for the gavel)* Lum Boger! Where's dat gavel I done told you to put here?

LUM BOGER: *(from beside prisoner)* You said *you* was gonna bring it yo'self.

MAYOR CLARKE: *(going up in the air)* I God, Lum, you gointer stand there like a bump on a log and see I ain't got nothin' to open court wid? Go 'head an' fetch me dat gavel. Make haste quick before dese wimmen folks tote off dis church house. *(LUM exits by front door.)*

SISTER TAYLOR: *(to LEWIS)* Aw, shut up, you big ole he-looking rascal you! Nobody don't know whether youse a man or a woman.

CLARKE: You wimmen, shut up! Hush! Just hush! *(He wipes his face with a huge handkerchief.)*

SISTER LEWIS: *(To* SISTER TAYLOR*)* Air Lawd! Dat ain't your trouble. They all knows whut you is eg-zackly.

LINDSAY: Aw? why don't you wimmen cut dat out in de church house? Jus' jawin' an chewin' de rag!

SISTER TAYLOR: Joe Lindsay, if you'd go home an' feed dat rawbony horse of yourn, you wouldn't have so much time to stick yo' bill in business that ain't yourn.

SISTER LEWIS: Joe Lindsay, don't you know no better than to strain wid folks ain't got sense enough to tote guts to a bear? If they ain't born wid no sense, you can't learn 'em none.

LINDSAY: You sho done tole whut God love now. *(glaring across the aisle)* Ain't got enough gumption to bell a buzzard. *(Enter* LUM *by front door with gavel in one hand and mule bone in the other. He walks importantly up the aisles and hands* CLARKE *the gavel and lays the bone atop the pulpit.)*

WALTER: Huh! Marshall had done forgot de bone.

METHODIST SISTER: It's a wonder he ain't forgot hisself.

CLARKE: *(rapping sharply with gavel)* Here! you moufy wimmen shut up. *(to* LUM*)* Lum you go on back there and shut dem wimmen up or put 'em outa here. They shan't contempt this court. *(He wipes his eye glasses.)*

(LUM *starts walking importantly down the aisle towards* SISTER TAYLOR. *She almost rises to meet him.)*

SISTER TAYLOR: Lum Boger, you fresh little snot you! Don't you dast to come here trying to put me out; many diapers as I done pinned on you! *(fiercely)* Git away from me before I knock every nap off of yo' head, one by one. (LUM BOGER *hurries away from her apologetically. He turns towards* MRS. LEWIS.*)*

MRS. LEWIS: *(calmly)* Deed God knows you better not lay de weight of yo' hand on me, Lum. Gwan way from here before I kick yo' clothes up round yo' neck like a horse collar. *(All the men laugh.* LUM *looks worried and finally goes back and takes his seat beside the prisoner.)*

CLARKE: *(glaring ferociously)* This court is set an' I'm bound to have some order or else. *(The talking ceases. Absolute quiet.)*

CLARKE: Now less git down to business. We got folks in dis town dat's just like a snake in de grass.

SISTER PITTS: Brother Mayor! We ain't got no business goin' into no trial for nothin' else 'thout a word of prayer to be sure de right spirit is wid us.

VOICE ON METHODIST SIDE: Thass right, Elder Simms. Give us a word of prayer. *(He rises hurriedly.)*

VOICE ON BAPTIST SIDE: This is a Baptist church an' de paster is sittin' right here. How come he can't pray in his own church?

TAYLOR: Y'all done started all dis mess, how you goin' to git de right spirit here? Go 'head Rev. Simms.

LEWIS: He cain't pray over me. Dis church says: One Lord, one faith, one Baptism, and a man that ain't never been baptised at all ain't got no business prayin' over nobody.

CLARKE: *(rapping with gavel)* Less sing. Somebody raise a tune.

VOICE ON BAPTIST SIDE: *(begins)* "Onward Christian Soldiers" *(and the others join in)*

VOICE ON METHODIST SIDE: *(Begins)* "All hail the power of Jesus name", *(and the Methodists join in. Both shout as loud as they can to the end of the verse. Clarke lifts his hands rapidly as if to bless a table.)*

CLARKE: *(Praying, quickly)* Lowd be with us and bless these few remarks we are about to receive amen. Now this court is open for business. All of us know we come here on serious business. This town is bout to be tore up by backbiting and malice and mouthy women. *(Glaring at the Sisters)* Now everybody that's a witness in this case, stand up. I wants the witness to take the front seat. *(Nearly everybody in the room rises. Clarke tries to count them.)*

HAMBO: *(Frowns across the aisle at* MRS. LUCAS, *who is standing.)* Whut you doing standing up for a witness? I know you wuzn't there.

SISTER LUCAS: I got just as much right to testify as you is. I don't keer if I wasn't there. Any man that treats they wife bad as you can't tell nobody else they eye is black. You clean round yo' own door before you go sweeping round other folks.

SISTER LINDSAY: *(to* NIXON*)* Whut you doing up there testifyin? When you done let yo' hawg root up all my p'tater patch?

NIXON: Aw, shut up woman. You ain't had no taters for no pig to root up.

SISTER LINDSAY: Who ain't had no taters? *(to* LIGE*)* Look here, Lige, didn't I git a whole crokus sack full of tater slips from yo' brother, Sam?

LIGE: *(Reluctantly)* Yeah.

SISTER LINDSAY: Course I had sweet p'taters! And if you stand up there and tell me I aint had no p'taters, I'll be all over you just like gravy over rice.

NIXON: AW, shut up. We ain't come here to talk about yo' tater vines. We come—

SISTER LINDSAY: *(to her husband)* Joe! Whut kind of a husband is you? Sit here and let Nixon 'buse me out lak dat.

WALTER THOMAS: How is Joe goin' give anybody a straightenin', when he needs straightenin' hisself?

SISTER HAMBO: Aw, you ain't got no right to talk, Walter. Not low down as you is. If somebody stump their toe in dis town you bolt over to Maitland an' puke yo' guts out to de white folks, and God knows I 'bominates a white folks nigger.

WALTER THOMAS: Aw, you jus' mad 'cause I wouldn't let your old starved-out cow eat up my cow-peas.

CLARKE: *(Pounding)* Hush and lemme count.

SISTER HAMBO: *(triumphantly)* UNhumh! I knowed you was the one knocked my cow's horn off! And you lied like a doodle-bug goin' backwards in his hole an' made out you didn't do it.

WALTER THOMAS: I didn't do no such a thing, woman.

SISTER HAMBO: I say you did, and I belong to Macedonia Baptist Church an' I can't lie.

DEACON HAMBO: Walter Thomas, talk dat biggity talk to me, not to my wife. Maybe you kin whip her, but if you can't whip me, too, don't bring de mess up.

CLARKE: *(rapping)* Y'all men folks shut up before I put you both under arrest. Come to order everybody.

LINDSAY: I just want a say this before we go any further. Nobody bet' not slur my wife in here. Do, I'll strow 'em over de country.

MRS. NIXON: Aw, youse de nastiest threatener in three states, but I ain't seen you do nothin'. De seat of yo' pants is too close to de ground for you to be crowin' so loud. You's so short you smell right earthy.

CLARKE: Shut up! We didn't come here to wash an' iron niggers! We come here for a trial. *(raps)*

MRS. NIXON: *(to CLARKE)* I ain't goin' to shut up nothin' of de kind.

CLARKE: Sister Nixon, shut up!

MRS. NIXON: You can't shut me up, not the way you live. When you quit beatin' Mrs. Mattie an' dominizing her all de time, then you kin tell other folks what to do. You ain't none of my boss, not de way you sells rancid bacon for fresh.

CLARKE: *(to* MARSHALL*)* Lum Boger, git me a pencil. *(to* MRS. NIXON*)* Big a bill as you owe ma store, you ain't gonna get nothin' else till you pay.

MRS. NIXON: Huh! I can trade in Maitland—an' see if I pays you now.

NIXON: AW, honey, hush a while, please, and less git started. You don't pay de bills no how. *(The men laugh.)*

JIM: Lawd! Lawd! We done set de whole town fightin'.

DAVE: Boy', we sho is!

CHILDERS: Son, don't talk wid yo' 'sailent. He's a wicked man.

DAVE: How come I can't talk wid him? Known him all ma life.

CHILDERS: Shss. He done tried to kill you.

DAVE: Was our fight, warn't it?

JIM: You niggers just tryin to get us messed up on some kind o' mess. Dave knows I ain't meant to hurt him.

SIMMS: *(to* JIM*)* Derserved to be hurt.

DAVE: No, he didn't. We's just friendly-fightin'-like.

CHILDERS: He sho tried to kill you!

(CLARKE raps. A momentary quiet falls on the place. MAYOR glowers all over the place.)

CLARKE: Here! Quiet till you's called on. *(Turns to LUM)* Lum, git a piece of paper an take de names of all de witnesses *who was there* while de fight was goin' on.

LUM: *(Pulling a small tablet and pencil out of his coat pocket)* I brought it with me.

CLARKE: Now everybody who was at de fight hold up yo' hands so Lum kin know who you are. *(Several hands go up. SISTER ANDERSON puts up her hand.)*

CLARKE: You wuzn't there, Sister Anderson, not at that time.

SISTER ANDERSON: I hadn't been gone more'n ten minutes.

CLARKE: But you didn't see it.

SISTER ANDERSON: It don't make no difference. My husband heered every word was spoke an' told me, jes' lak it happen. Don't tell me I can't testify.

DEACON HAMBO: Nobody can't testify but them what seen it.

SISTER ANDERSON: Dat's all right, but I know whut they was fightin' 'bout. It was Daisy Taylor*

---

*At this point in the original manuscript, for unknown reasons, Daisy *Taylor* is referred to as Daisy *Blunt*. We have kept *Taylor* for consistency. Likewise, *Dilcie* Anderson is referred to as *Becky*, and we have kept *Dilcie*.

MRS. BLUNT: Jus' you take my chile's name right out yo' mouf, Dilcie* Anderson. She was on her way back to her white folks when all this happen.

SISTER ANDERSON: Well, God knows if dat Daisy was mine, I'd throw her down an' put a hundred lashes on her back wid a plow-line. Here she come in de store Sat'day night *(Acts coy and coquettish, burlesques Daisy's walk).* A wringing and a twisting!

MRS. BLUNT: You better hush while you able! You niggers got my Daisy's name all mixed up in dis mess, an' she at work, can't defend herself.

MRS. TAYLOR: You musn't mind, Sister Blunt. People jus' *will* talk. They's talkin' in New York an' they's talkin' in Georgy an' they's talkin' in Italy.

SISTER PITTS: Chile, if you listen at folkses talk, they'll have you in de graveyard or in Chattahoochee—one. You can't pay no 'tention to talk.

MRS. BLUNT: Well, I know one thing. De man or woman, chick or child, grizzly or gray, that tells me to my face anythin' wrong 'bout *my* chile, I'm goin' to take *my* fist *(Rolling up right sleeve and gesturing with right fist)* and knock they teeth down they throat. *(She looks ferocious)* 'Case y'all know I raised my Daisy right round my feet till I let her go up North last year wid them white folks. I'd ruther her to be in de white folks' kitchen than walkin' de streets like some of dese gals round here. If I do say so, I done raised a lady. She can't help it if all dese mens get stuck on her.

MRS. TAYLOR: You'se tellin' de truth, Sister Blunt. That's whut I always say: Don't confidence dese niggers. Do, they'll sho put you in de street.

MRS. THOMAS: Naw indeed, never syndicate wid niggers. Do, they will distriminate you.

MRS. BLUNT: Just as sho as you snore. An' they better leave Daisy's name outa dis, too, an' Daisy better not leave them white folks' house today to come traipsin' over here scornin' her name all up wid dis nigger mess. Do, I'll kill her. No daughter of mine ain't goin' be mixed up in nothin' like this.

MRS. THOMAS: That's right, Sister Blunt. I glory in yo' spunk.

MAYOR CLARKE: Sit down, Sister Blunt an' shet up. Ain't gonna mention Daisy a-tall. Ain't gonna drag no woman's name in dis trial long as I's presidin'.

METHODIST SISTER: Dis ain't no trial. Dis is a mess!

REV. SIMMS: You sho said a mouthful, Sister. Dis sho is a mess. Can't help from bein' uh mess. (Glares at MAYOR) Holdin' a trial in de Baptist Church! Some folks ain't got sense enough to do 'em till four o'clock, an' its way after half past three right now.

MAYOR CLARKE: Shet up, dere, Simms! Set down! Who ast yo' pot to boil, nohow? A church trial is de bes' trial they is, anyhow, cause you better have a good experience here an' a strong determination. (Raps vigorously) Now lemme tel y'all somethin'. When de Mayor sets court, don't keer when I sets it nor where I sets it, you got to git quiet and stay quiet till I ast you tuh talk. Set down! All o' yuh! I God, you sound lak a tree full uh blackbirds! Dis ain't no barbecue, nor neither no camp meetin'. We 'sembled here tuh law uh boy on a serious charge. (A great buzz rises from the congregation. MAYOR raps hard for order and glares all about him.) Heah! Heah! All o' us kin sing at de same time, but can't but one o' us talk at a time. I'm doin' de talkin' now, so de res' o' you dry up till I git through. I God, you sound lak uh passel uh dog fights! We ain't here for no form and no fashion and no outside show to de worl'. We'se here to law!

(For a moment, there is silence, then a small boy, peeping in window on the Methodist side says:)

BOY: *(Thru window, right)* Aw, haw! Y'all ole Baptis' ain't got no bookcase in yo' church.

SMALL GIRL: *(In window on opposite side, left, with other children)* Y'all ole Meth'dis' ain't got no window panes in yo' church down yonder in de swamp.

CLARKE: *(Booming)* You chillun shut up and get out o' them winders. You, Lum! *(LUM stops taking names to go shoo the children. The old people aid him, and the children on left run off singing:)*

CHILDREN: Oh, Baptis', Baptis' is my name,
              My name's written on high.
              I got my lick in de Baptis' Church,
              Gointer eat up de Meth'dis' pie.

CLARKE: *(Rapping)* You done got all de witnesses straight an' got they names down?

LUM: Yassuh, I got it all straightened out.

CLARKE: Well, read de names out and let de witnesses take de front seats. Who is they?

LUM: *(Reading)* Mrs. Lucy Taylor, Sister Katie Pitts, Sister Doll Nixon, Deacon Hambo, Brother Lige Mosely, Brother Joe Lindsay. . . .

LINDSAY: Brother, my eye!

LUM: *(Continuing the reading of the list)* Mr. Sykes Jones, Sister Laura Carter, Mr. Pat Jenkins. And they was lots mo' there but they say they ain't gonna witness. *(Those whose names were read begin to rise and start forward.)*

JIM: They better not neither.

SIMMS: Shsss! De devil can't hurt you, son. An' them what speaks against you is devils.

CLARKE: Won't witness, heh? Huh-um! Well, I see they's some witnessin' whut warn't there. Lucy Taylor, you know you left mah store fo' dat fight come off!

SISTER TAYLOR: *(In attitude of defiance)* Well, I'm gonna witness! An' I ain't gonna bit mah tongue neither. You knows you cheated me outa half a pound o' salt pork Sat'day night. I weighed dat piece when I got home, and 'twarn't no bigger'n mah fist here.

SISTER PITTS: Huh! Dat's a common thing, chile.

CLARKE: *(Calmly)* Is dat all?

SISTER TAYLOR: No, that ain't all. You waters yo' cider, an' yo' sells bag meal.

CLARKE: An' yo' been buyin' outa mah store fo' God knows how long. Yo' owes me Thirty-eight Dollars and Ten Cents, an' can't nobody whuts in mah debt testify in this court. Set down!

SISTER TAYLOR: You'se a lie! You'se a . . . *(But the noise of the gavel drowns her out. In the meantime, the other witnesses are all seated at the front.)*

CLARKE: Now, we'll go on with this trial. We's tryin' Jim Weston fo' 'saultin' Dave Carter wid a dangerous weepon. Did he or did he not done it, that's what we got to fin' out? You, Lum! You was there. You'se de Marshall. You saw it. Now, what went on?

LUM: *(Startled, drawls)* Well . . .

DAVE: You better, "Well . . ." *(Mocking* LUM*)*

LUM: Daisy come. . . .

SISTER BLUNT: Uhm-uh! Not Daisy.

LUM: I mean *(turning to* CLARKE *in distress)* Well, you say I should take Jim and lock him up, an' that's whut I done, jus' like you tol' me.

CLARKE: You sho did, but I God, I ast you whut you seed befo' I told you to take Jim and lock him up? *(*DAVE, JIM *and* SISTER TAYLOR *eye* LUM *dangerously)*

LUM: *(Shifting nervously)* Well, I ain't seen much.

CLARKE: *(Rapping impatiently)* Whut did you see?

LUM: Well, ole lady Pitts' mule was tied in yo' back yard a-tearin' up Mis' Mattie's tomato vines, an' Mis' Mattie say,

'Lum, you go 'roun' an' tend to dat mule', an' I went, an' that mule sho drawed back to kick me.

CLARKE: *(To* SISTER PITTS*)* I God, yo' mule drawed a hoof on de marshall?

SISTER PITTS: Dat's a lie! Mah mule don't kick.

CLARKE: G'wan, Lum!

LUM: An' I was busy wid dat mule.

LIGE: Looks like de marshall warn't at de scene o' action.

SISTER LEWIS: Dat's de kin' o' men de Mayor hires to do de duties o' dis town.

CLARKE: Set down, Lum. Ain't worth de dust it took to make you. *(To* HAMBO*)* Hambo, you was settin' an' loafin' right on mah front porch all day Sat'day, and night, too. Get up an' tell whut you saw.

HAMBO: *(Rising)* Now, in de first place, Joe Clarke, I warn't loafin'. I'se a deacon in de church an' you knows I don't waste mah time wid dem low niggers whut hangs aroun' yo' store.

LIGE: Do you hear that?

HAMBO: An' furthermo', I don't know if I wuz there or not, now dat you so sure I wuz.

SISTER HAMBO: Make him prove it! Make him prove it!

CLARKE: I God, Hambo, you know you wuz there!

CHILDERS: *(Quickly)* He were there, yo' honery, but he warn't loafin'. *(To* HAMBO*)* You mah main witness, Brother Hambo. Now tell jus' how dis vileness was done. You sees our lamb all hurted here. *(Pointing to* DAVE'*s head.* JIM *laughs.)*

DAVE: Hush, fool! You'se in court.

JIM: Boy, yo' head sho is soft.

HAMBO: *(To* JIM*)* An' you'll soon be gone. *(To the* MAYOR*)* Clarke, it were like dis. These two boys here started fightin' over Dais . . . *(sees* SISTER BLUNT *half rise in her seat)* over somethin' or nother o' no importance . . . *(*BAPTISTS *all murmur in agreement)* an' dat there triflin' rascal, for no cause whatinsoever, hit this boy in de head with a mule bone.

CLARKE: Um-hmmm! Dat's right.

SISTER THOMAS: Hear him, Lord! How he kin lie!

SISTER NIXON: An' then re-lie!

HAMBO: *(To* CLARKE*)* You 'lows dese 'ruptions in de court?

CLARKE: *(To* WOMEN, *rapping)* Hush! I say, hush! Hambo, is you through?

HAMBO: *(Sitting down pompously)* I is.

CLARKE: *(To* OLD WOMAN*)* Sister Pitts, le's hear whut you got to say!

SISTER PITTS: Brother Mayor, I wan't there, but I been knowin' this boy Dave since he was knee-high to a duck an' that boy wouldn't hurt nobody, but that varmint yonder *(Pointing to* JIM*)* is de crookedist limb of Satan that de Lawd ever made. He is a scoundrel, a rat, a low-down dog, a . . .

SIMMS: *(Jumping up)* I objects! I objects! Nobody's got de right to call my charge no names like dat. *(As* CLARKE *is silent and* SISTER PITTS *goes on, "rascal, heathen, etc.")* I objects! *(Dances in front of* MAYOR*'s face)* I objects!

CLARKE: I God, Simms, if you don't set down an' stop spittin' in mah face I'll lam you over de head wid dis mallet.

SIMMS: *(Weakly)* I objects.

CLARKE: Dat'll do! Dat'll do! Dry up, suh! *(Turning to* DAVE*)* Stand up, Dave. Since youse de one got hurted, you tell me jus' whut went on out dere. *(*DAVE *rises slowly)*

MRS. TAYLOR: Dat's right, Dave. Git up dere an' lie lak de cross ties from New York to Texas. You greasy rascal, you! You better go wash yo'self befo' you go testifyin' on people.

DAVE: *(Calmly)* I'm jus' as clean as you. *(*JIM *laughs)*

CHILDERS: *(Jumping to his feet)* Wait a minute! 'Tain't none o' y'all got no call to be thowin' off on dis boy. He come here to git justice, not to be slurred an' low-rated. He ain't 'ssaulted nobody. He ain't stole no chickens. He's a clean boy. He set at mah feet in Sunday School since he was so high *(Measures knee height)* and he come through religion under de sound of mah voice an' I baptized him an' I know he's clean.

MRS. TAYLOR: It'll take more'n uh baptizin' to clean dat nigger.

DAVE: I goes in swimmin' nearly every day. I'm jus' as clean as anybody else.

MRS. TAYLOR: (MAYOR *begins rapping for order.* SHE *shouts out)* Swimming! Dat ain't gointer clean de crust offa you. You ain't had a good bath since de devil was a hatchet.

CLARKE: I'm goin' to have order heah or else! G'wan, Dave!

DAVE: It's jus' lak you seen it Sat'day night. You-all was there.

CLARKE: Yeah, but dat wuz at de store. Dis is in court an' it's got to be tole.

SIMMS: Just uh minute, Brother Clarke, before we any further go, I wants to ast de witness uh question dat oughter be answered before he open his mouf.

CLARKE: Whut *kind* of a question is dat?

SIMMS: Dave, tell de truth. Ain't yo' heart full of envy an' malice 'gainst dis chile? (*Gestures towards* JIM. DAVE *shakes his head and starts to deny the charge, but* SIMMS *hurries on)* Wait a minute, now! Wait till I git thru. Didn't y'all used to run aroun' everywhere playin' an' singin' an' everythin' till you got so full of envy an' malice an' devilment till y'all broke up? Now, Brother Mayor, make him tell de truth.

DAVE: Yeah, I useter be crazy 'bout Jim, and we was buddies till he tried to back bite me wid my girl.

JIM: Yo' girl! Never *was* yo' girl, nohow! I reckon I ain't none of yo' buddy. I ain't got no buddy, they kilt my buddy tryin' to raise me. But I did useter lak you till you tried to root me out wid Dais. . . .

SISTER BLUNT: Jes' dare!

MAYOR: Aw, table dat business, an' le's open up new business. We ain't here to fin' out whose girl it is an' we ain't gonna mention no woman's name. We wants to know 'bout dis fight, an' who hit de first lick, an' how come. Go 'head on, Dave, an' talk.

CHILDERS: Yes, Dave, talk, son.

DAVE: Well, we was all dancin' an' a singin' in front o' yo' store, an' seem like Jim kinder got mad 'bout somethin' or nother an' so I went in de store an' left de ole nigger. Well, near as I can remember, when I come out seems like I kinder step on his ole big foot whut had no business where it wuz nohow. An' then he up and knocks mah soda all ovah mah clean shirt.

JIM: Who's shirt?

DAVE: De shirt I had on. An' then I hits him. An' fo' I knowed it, he done picked up that bone an' lammed me ovah de head wid it.

CHILDERS: He hit you, didn't he?

DAVE: Yes, sir.

CHILDERS: He assaulted you, didn't he?

DAVE: I reckon he did.

CLARKE: Uh-humm!

(DAVE *resumes his seat and* JIM *drops his head for a moment then snatches it up arrogantly and glares at the* BAPTISTS. *The whole place is very silent for a moment. Then* MAYOR CLARKE *clears his throat, raps with his gavel and looks sternly at* JIM.)

Jim Weston, stand up, suh! (JIM *rises sullenly*) You'se charged wid 'ssaultin' Dave Carter wid uh dangerous weepon. You heard de charge. Guilty or not guilty?

JIM: (*Arrogantly*) Yeah, I hit him an' I'll hit him agin if he crowd me. But I ain't guilty of no crime. (HE *hitches up his pants and sits down arrogantly.*)

CLARKE: (*Surprised*) Whut's dat you say, Jim? (*Raps sharply*) Git up from there, sir! Whut's dat you say?

JIM: (*Rising*) I say, yeah, I lammed ole Dave wid de mule bone, but I ain't guilty uh nothin'. (*There is a stark silence for a few seconds. Then* CLARKE *raps nervously.*)

CLARKE: How come you ain't guilty?

SIMMS: (*To* JIM) Set down, Jim, and lemme show dese people dat walks in de darkness wid sinners an' republicans de light.

(JIM *sets down amid jubilant smiles of* METHODISTS. SIMMS *chuckles out loud and wipes his face with his handkerchief. He gets to his feet still laughing.*)

CHILDERS: You jus' as well tuh hush up befo' you start then, Simms. You can't show nobody uh light when you ain't got none tuh show.

HAMBO: Ain't dat de gospel?

NIXON: Aw, let de man talk! Y'all soun' lak uh tree full uh blackbirds. Go 'head on, Elder Simms.

WALTER THOMAS: Yeah, you can't teach 'em nothin', but talk on. We know whut you talkin' 'bout.

CLARKE: *(Rapping once or twice)* I God, tell it . . . whutever 'tis you got tuh tell!

SISTER NIXON: Law 'em from Genesis to Revelations, Elder.

SISTER LEWIS: Aw yeah, hurry up an' tell it. I know it ain't goin' tuh be nothin' after you git it tole, but hurry up an' say it so you kin rest easy.

THOMAS: Aw, shet up an' give de man uh chance.

SISTER LEWIS: My shetters ain't workin' good. Sposin' you come whet me up, Walter. Den you'll know it's done right.

LIGE: Aw, whyn't y'all ack lak folks an' leave de man talk!

CLARKE: *(Rapping repeatedly)* Order in dis court, I God, jus' like you wuz in Orlando! *(Silence falls)* Now, Simms, talk yo' chat.

SIMMS: *(Glances down into his open Bible, then looks all around the room with great deliberation. It is evident he enjoys being the center of attraction. He smiles smugly as he turns his face towards the pulpit. He speaks slowly and accents his words so that none will be lost on his audience.)* De Bible says, be sho you're right, then go ahead. *(He looks all around to collect the admiration he feels he has earned.)* Now, we all done gathered an' 'sembled here tuh law dis young lad of uh boy on uh mighty serious charge. Uh whole passel of us is rarin' tuh drive him way from home lak you done drove off his daddy an' his brothers.

HAMBO: We never drove off his pappy. De white folks took an' hung him for killin' dat man in Kissimmee for nothin'.

SIMMS: Dat ain't de point, Brother Hambo.

HAMBO: It's jes' as good uh pint as any. If you gointer talk, tell de truth. An' if you can't tell de truth, set down an' leave Reverend Childers talk.

SIMMS: Brother Mayor, how come you let dese people run they mouf lak uh passel uh cowbells? Ain't I got de floor? I ain't no breath-an'-britches. I was *people* in middle Georgy befo' I ever come to Floridy. Whut kin' of chairman is you, nohow?

CLARKE: *(Angrily)* Heah! Heah! Don't you come tryin' show yo'self round me! I God, I don't keer whut you wuz in Georgy. I kin eat fried chicken when you cain't git rainwater tuh drink. Hurry up an' say what you got in yo' craw an' set down. We needs yo' space more'n we needs yo' comp'ny.

NIXON: Don't let him skeer yo', Elder Simms. You got plenty shoulders tuh back yo' fallin'.

HAMBO: Well, each an' every shoulder kin hit de groun' an' I'll git wid 'em.

THOMAS: Hambo, everybody in Orange county knows you love tuh fight. But dis is uh law hearin', not no wrassle.

HAMBO: Oh, you Meth'dis' niggers wants tuh fight, bad enough, but youse skeered. Youse jus' as hot as Tucker when de mule kicked his mammy. But you know you got plenty coolers.

SISTER TAYLOR: Aw, ain't nobody skeered uh you half-pint Baptists. God knows ah'm ready an' willin'. *(She glares at* MRS. LEWIS. SISTER LEWIS *jumps to her feet, but is pulled back into her seat.* MAYOR CLARKE *raps for order and the room gets quiet.)*

CLARKE: Aw right, now, Simms. I God, git through!

SIMMS: *(Pompously)* Now y'all done up an' took dis po' boy an' had him locked up in uh barn ever since Sat'day night an' done got him 'ccused uh 'ssault an' I don't know whut all, an' you ain't got no business wid yo' hands on him a-tall. He ain't done no crime, an' if y'all knowed anythin' 'bout law, I wouldn't have tuh tell you so.

CLARKE: I God, he *is* done uh crime an' he's gointer ketch it, too.

SIMMS: But not by law, Brother Mayor. You tryin' tuh lay uh hearin' on dis boy an' you can't do it 'cause he ain't broke no law. I don't keer whut he done so long as he don't break no law you can't touch him.

CHILDERS: He committed assault, didn't he? Dat sho is breakin' de law!

SIMMS: Naw, he ain't committed no 'ssault. He jus' lammed Dave over de head, dat's all. *(Triumphantly)* Yuh see y'all don't know whut you talkin' 'bout. Now I done set in de court house an' heard de white folks law from mornin' till night. *(He flips his Bible shut.)* I done read dis book from lid tuh lid an' I knows de law. You got tuh have uh weepon tuh commit uh 'ssault. An' 'tain't in no white folks law an' 'tain't in dis Bible dat no mule bone is no weepon.

CLARKE: *(After a moment of dead silence)* I God, whut's dat you say?

SIMMS: *(Sitting down and crossing his legs and folding his hands upon his Bible.)* You heard me. I say you ain't got no case 'ginst dis boy an' you got tuh turn him loose.

CHILDERS: *(Jumping up)* Brother Chairman!

CLARKE: *(Raps once and nods recognition)* You got de floor.

CHILDERS: I ain't book-learnt an' I ain't rubbed de hair offen my head agin no college wall, but I know when uh 'ssault's been committed. I says Jim Weston did 'ssault Dave. *(He points at Dave's head.)*

SIMMS: *(Arrogantly)* Prove it!

CHILDERS: Stands silent and puzzled.

(The METHODIST *side breaks into a triumphant shout of* "Oh, Mary don't you weep, don't you moan, Pharaoh's Army got Drownded". CHILDERS *sinks into his seat. When they have shouted out three choruses,* SIMMS *rises to speak.)*

SIMMS: I move dat we sing doxology an' bring dis meetin' to uh close. We'se all workin' people, Brother Mayor. Dismiss us so we kin g'wan back to our work. De sun is two hours high yet. *(Looks towards the* METHODIST *side.)* I second de motion.

CHILDERS: *(Arising slowly)* Hol' on there uh minute wid dat motion. Dis ain't no lodge meetin'. Dis is uh court an' bofe sides got uh right tuh talk. *(Motions towards* SIMMS*'s Bible)* Youse uh letter-learnt man, but I kin read dat Bible some, too. Lemme take it uh minute.

SIMMS: I ain't uh gointer do it. Any preacher dat amounts to uh hill uh beans would have his own Bible.

CLARKE: I God, Childers, you right here in yo' own church. Come on up here an' read out yo' pulpit Bible. I God, don't mind me bein' up here. Come on up. *(A great buzzing breaks out all over the church for order.* CHILDERS *mounts the pulpit.* SIMMS *begins to turn the leaves of his Bible.)*

SIMMS: Brother Mayor, you oughter let us outa here. You ain't got no case 'ginst dis boy. Don't waste our time for nothin'. Leave us go home.

CLARKE: Aw, dry up, Simms, you done talked yo' talk. I God, leave Childers talk his. *(To* CHILDERS*)* Step on out when you ready, Reverend.

CHILDERS: *(Reading)* It says here in Judges 18:18 dat Samson slewed three thousand Philistines wid de jaw-bone of an ass.

SIMMS: *(On his feet)* Yeah, but dis wasn't no ass. Dis was uh mule, Brother Mayor. Dismiss dis meetin' an le's all go home.

CHILDERS: Yeah, but he was half-ass. A ass is uh mule's daddy, and he's bigger'n uh ass, too. *(Emphatic gestures)* Everybody knows dat, even de lil chillun.

SIMMS: *(Standing)* Yeah, but we didn't come here to talk about no asses, neither no half-asses, nor no mule daddies. *(Laughter from* METHODISTS*)* We come to law uh boy for 'ssault an' larceny.

CHILDERS: *(Very patiently)* We'se comin' to dat pint now. Dat's de second claw uh de sentence we'se expoundin'. I say Jim Weston did have uh weepon in his hand when he 'ssaulted Dave. 'Cause y'all knows if de daddy is dangerous, den de son is dangerous too. An y'all knows dat de further back you gits on uh mule de more dangerous he gits an' if de jaw-bone slewed three thousand people, by de time you gits back tuh his hocks, it's pizen enough tuh kill ten thousand. 'Tain't no knives nor no razors ever kilt no three thousand people. Now, folkses, I ast y'all whut kin be mo' dangerous dan uh mule bone? *(To* CLARKE*)* Brother Mayor, Jim didn't jes' lam Dave an' walk off . . . *(very emphatic)* he 'ssaulted him with de deadliest weepon there is in de worl' an' left him layin' unconscious. Brother Mayor, he's uh criminal an' oughter be run outa dis peaceful town! *(Great chorus of approval from Baptists.* CLARKE *begins to rap for order.)*

SIMMS: *(Standing)* Brother Mayor, I objects. I done studied jury and I know whut I'm talkin' 'bout.

CLARKE: Aw, dry up, Simms. You'se entirely out of order. You may be slick, but you kin stand another greasing. Reverend Childers is right. I God, I knows de law when I hear it. Stand up dere, Jim! *(*JIM *rises very slowly.* SIMMS *rises also.* DAVE *looks worried.)*

CLARKE: Set down, Simms! I God, I know where to find you when I want you. *(SIMMS sits.)* Jim, I find you guilty as charged an' I wants you to git outa my town an' stay gone for two years. *(To LUM)* Brother Marshall, you see dat he gits outa town befo' dark. An' you folks dat's so anxious to fight, fit on off dis church grounds befo' you starts. An' don't use no knives an' no guns an' no mule bones. Court's dismissed.

CURTAIN

ACT THREE

SETTING: *A high stretch of railroad track thru a luxurious Florida forest. It is near sundown.*

ACTION: *When the curtain rises there is no one on the stage, but there is a tremendous noise and hubbub off-stage right. There are yells of derision and shouts of anger. Part of the mob is trying to keep JIM in town, and part is driving him off. After a full minute of this, JIM enters with his guitar hanging around his neck and his coat over his shoulder. The sun is dropping low and red thru the forest. He is looking back angrily and shouting at the mob. A missile is thrown after him. JIM drops his coat and guitar and grabs up a piece of brick, and makes threatening gestures of throwing it.*

JIM: *(Running back the way he came and hurling the brick with all his might)* I'll kill some o' you old box-ankled niggers. *(Grabs up another piece of brick.)* I'm out o' your old town. Now just let some of you old half-pint Baptists let yo' wooden God and Cornstalk Jesus fool you into hittin' me. *(Threatens to throw again. There are some frightened screams and the mob is heard running back.)* I'm glad I'm out o' yo' ole town anyhow. I ain't never comin' back no mo', neither. You ole ugly-rump niggers done ruint de town anyhow.

(There is complete silence off stage. JIM *walks a few steps with his coat and guitar, then sits down on the railroad embankment facing the audience. He pulls off one shoe and pours the sand out. He holds the shoe in his hand a moment and looks wistfully back down the railroad track.)*

JIM: Lawd, folks sho is deceitful. *(He puts on the shoe and looks back down the track again.)* I never woulda thought people woulda acted like that. *(Laces up the shoe)* Specially Dave Carter, much as me and him done progue'd 'round together goin' in swimmin' an' playin' ball an' serenadin' de girls an' de white folks. *(He sits there gloomily silent for awhile, then looks behind him and picks up his guitar and begins to pick a tune. The music is very sad, but he trails off into, "YOU MAY LEAVE AN' GO TO HALIMUHFACKS, BUT MY SLOW DRAG WILL BRING YOU BACK." When he finishes he looks at the sun and picks up his coat.)*

JIM: Reckon I better git on down de road and git somewhere. Lawd knows where. *(Stops suddenly in his tracks and turns back toward the village. Takes a step or two.)* All dat mess and stink for nothin'. Dave know good an' well I didn't meant to hurt him much. *(He takes off his cap and scratches his head thoroughly. Then turns again and starts on down the road left. Enter* DAISY, *left, walking fast and panting, her head down. They meet.)*

DAISY: Oh, hello, Jim. *(A little surprised and startled)*

JIM: *(Not expecting her)* Hello, Daisy. *(Embarrassed silence.)*

DAISY: I was just coming over town to see how you come out.

JIM: You don't have to go way over there to find dat out . . . you and Dave done got me run outa town for nothin'.

DAISY: *(Putting her hand on his arm)* Dey didn't run you outa town, did dey?

JIM: *(Shaking her hand off)* Whut you reckon I'm countin' Mr. Railroad's ties for . . . just to find out how many ties between here and Orlando?

DAISY: *(Hand on his arm again)* Dey *cain't* run you off like dat!

JIM: Take yo' hands off me, Daisy! How come they cain't run me off wid you and Dave an' . . . *every*body 'ginst me?

DAISY: I ain't opened my mouf 'gainst you, Jim. I ain't said one word . . . I wasn't even at de old trial. My madame wouldn't let me git off. I wuz just comin' to see 'bout you now.

JIM: Aw, go 'head on. You figgered I was gone too long to talk about. You was haulin' it over to town to see Dave . . . dat's whut you was doin' . . . after gittin' *me* all messed up.

DAISY: *(Making as if to cry)* I wasn't studyin' 'bout no Dave.

JIM: *(Hopefully)* Aw, don't tell me. *(Sings)* Ashes to ashes, dust to dust, show me a woman that a man can trust. *(*DAISY *is crying now.)*

JIM: What you crying for? You know you love Dave. I'm yo' monkey-man. He always could do more wid you that I could.

DAISY: Naw, you ain't no monkey-man neither. I don't want you to leave town. I didn't want y'all to be fightin' over me, nohow.

JIM: Aw, rock on down de road wid dat stuff. A two-timin' cloaker like you don't keer whut come off. Me and Dave been good friends ever since we was born till you had to go flouncing yourself around.

DAISY: What did I do? All I did was to come over town to see you and git a mouf-ful of gum. Next thing I know y'all is fighting and carrying on.

JIM: *(Stands silent for a while)* Did you come over there Sat'-day night to see me sho nuff, sugar babe?

DAISY: Everybody could see dat but you.

JIM: Just like I told you, Daisy, before you *ever* left from round here and went up North. I could kiss you every day . . . just as regular as pig-tracks.

DAISY: And I tole you I could stand it too—just as regular as you could.

JIM: *(Catching her by the arm and pulling her down with him onto the rail)* Set down, here, Daisy. Less talk some chat. You want me sho nuff? Hones' to God?

DAISY: *(Coyly)* 'Member whut I told you out on de lake last summer?

JIM: Sho nuff, Daisy? (DAISY *nods smilingly*)

JIM: *(Sadly)* But I got to go 'way. Whut we gointer do 'bout dat?

DAISY: Where you goin', Jim?

JIM: *(Looking sadly down the track)* God knows.

(Off stage from the same direction from which JIM *entered comes the sound of whistling and tramping of feet on the ties.)*

JIM: *(Brightening)* Dat's Dave! *(Frowning)* Wonder whut he doin' walkin' dis track? *(Looks accusingly at* DAISY*)* I bet he's goin' to yo' work-place.

DAISY: Whut for?

JIM: He ain't goin' to see de madame—must be goin' to see you. *(He starts to rise petulantly as* DAVE *comes upon the scene.* DAISY *rises also.)*

DAVE: *(Looks accusingly from one to the other)* Whut y'all jumpin' up for? I . . .

JIM: Whut you gut to do wid us business? Tain't none of yo' business if we stand up, set down or fly like a skeeter hawk.

DAVE: Who said I keered? Dis railroad belongs to de *man*—I kin walk it good as you, cain't I?

JIM: *(Laughing exultantly)* Oh, yeah, Mr. Do-Dirty! You figgered you had done run me on off so you could git Daisy all by yo'self. You was headin' right for her work-place.

DAVE: I wasn't no such a thing.

JIM: You was. Didn't I hear you coming down de track all whistling and everything?

DAVE: Youse a big ole Georgy-something-ain't-so! I done got my belly full of Daisy Sat'day night. She can't snore in my ear no more.

DAISY: *(Indignantly)* Whut you come here low-ratin' me for, Dave Carter? I ain't done nothin' to you but treat you white. Who come rubbed yo' ole head for you yestiddy if it wasn't me?

DAVE: Yeah, you rubbed my head all right, and I lakted dat. But everybody say you done toted a pan to Joe Clarke's barn for Jim before I seen you.

DAISY: Think I was going to let Jim lay there 'thout nothing fitten for a dog to eat?

DAVE: That's all right, Daisy. If you want to pay Jim for knockin' me in de head, all right. But I'm a man in a class . . . in a class to myself and nobody knows my name.

JIM: *(Snatching Daisy around to face him)* Was you over to Dave's house yestiddy rubbing his ole head and cloaking wid him to run me outa town . . . and me looked up in dat barn wid de cows and mules?

DAISY: *(Sobbing)* All both of y'all hollerin' at me an' fussin' me just cause I tries to be nice . . . and neither one of y'all don't keer nothin' bout me.
(BOTH BOYS glare at each other over DAISY's head and both try to hug her at the same time. She violently wrenches herself away from both and makes as if to move on.)

DAISY: Leave me go! Take yo' rusty pams offen me. I'm going on back to my work-place. I just got off to see bout y'all and look how y'all treat me.

JIM: Wait a minute, Daisy. I love you like God loves Gabriel . . . and dat's His best angel.

DAVE: Daisy, I love you harder than de thunder can bump a sump . . . if I don't . . . God's a gopher.

DAISY: *(Brightening)* Dat's de first time you ever said so.

DAVE & JIM: Who?

JIM: Whut you hollering "Who" for? Yo' fat don't fit no limb.

DAVE: Speak when you spoken to . . . come when you called, next fall you'll be my coon houn' dog.

JIM: Table dat discussion. *(Turning to* DAISY*)* You ain't never give me no chance to talk wid you right.

DAVE: You made *me* feel like you was trying to put de Ned book on me all de time. Do you love me sho nuff, Daisy?

DAISY: *(Blooming again into coquetry)* Aw, y'all better stop dat. You know you don't mean it.

DAVE: Who don't mean it? Lemme tell you something, mama, if you was mine I wouldn't have you counting no ties wid *yo'* pretty lil toes. Know whut I'd do?

DAISY: *(Coyly)* Naw, whut would you do?

DAVE: I'd buy you a whole passenger train . . . and hire some mens to run it for you.

DAISY: *(Happily)* Oo-ooh, Dave.

JIM: *(To* DAVE*)* De wind may blow, de doorway slam
                    Dat shut you shootin' ain't worth a dam.
         (To DAISY*)* I'd buy you a great big ole ship . . . and
         then, baby, I'd buy you a ocean to sail yo' ship on.

DAISY: *(Happily)* Oo-ooh, Jim.

DAVE: *(To* JIM*)*   A long tain, a short caboose
                    Dat lie whut you shootin', ain't no use.
         (To DAISY*)* Miss Daisy, know what I'd do for you?

DAISY: Naw, whut?

DAVE: I'd come down de river riding a mud cat and loading
         a minnow.

DAISY: Lawd, Dave, you sho is propaganda.

JIM: *(Peevishly)* Naw he ain't . . . he's just lying . . . he's a
         noble liar. Know whut I'd do if you was mine?

DAISY: Naw, Jim.

JIM: I'd make a panther wash yl' dishes and a 'gater chop yo'
         wood for you.

DAVE: Daisy, how come you let Jim lie lak dat? He's as big
         as a liar as he is a man. But sho nuff now, laying all sides to
         jokes, Jim there don't even know how to answer you. If you
         don't b'lieve it . . . ast him something.

DAISY: *(To* JIM*)* You like me much, Jim?

JIM: *(Enthusiastically)* Yeah, Daisy I sho do.

DAVE: *(Triumphant)* See dat! I tole you he didn't know how to answer nobody like you. If he was talking to some of them ol' funny looking gals over town he'd be answering 'em just right. But he got to learn how to answer *you*. Now you ast *me* something and see how I answer you.

DAISY: Do you like me, Dave?

DAVE: *(Very properly in a falsetto voice)* Yes ma'am! Dat's de way to answer swell folks like you. Furthermore, less we prove which one of us love you do best right now. *(To* JIM*)* Jim, how much time would you do on de chain-gang for dis 'oman?

JIM: Twenty years and like it.

DAVE: See dat, Daisy? Dat nigger ain't willin' to do no time for you. I'd *beg* de judge to gimme life. *(Both* JIM *and* DAVE *laugh)*

DAISY: Y'all doin' all dis bookooin' out here on de railroad track but I bet y'all crazy 'bout Bootsie and Teets and a whole heap of other gals.

JIM: Cross my feet and hope to die! I'd ruther see all de other wimmen folks in de worl' dead than for you to have de tooth-ache.

DAVE: If I was dead and any other woman come near my coffin de undertaker would have to do his job all over . . . 'cause I'd git right up and walk off. Furthermore, Miss Daisy, ma'am, also ma'am, which would *you* ruther be a lark a flying or a dove a settin' . . . ma'am, also ma'am?

DAISY: 'Course I'd ruther be a dove.

JIM: Miss Daisy, ma'am, also ma'am . . . if you marry dis nigger over my head, I'm going to git me a green hickory club and season it over yo' head.

DAVE: Don't you be skeered, baby . . . papa kin take keer a *you*. *(To* JIM*)* Countin' from de finger *(Suiting the action to the word)* back to de thumb . . . start anything I got you some.

JIM: Aw, I don't want no more fight wid you, Dave.

DAVE: Who said anything about fighting? We just provin' who love Daisy de best. *(To* DAISY*)* Now, which one of us you think love you de best?

DAISY: Deed I don't know, Dave.

DAVE: Baby, I'd walk de water for you . . . and tote a mountain on my head while I'm walkin'.

JIM: Know what I'd do, honey babe? If you was a thousand miles from home and you didn't have no ready-made money and you had to walk all de way, walkin' till ye' feet start to rolling, just like a wheel, and I was riding way up in de sky, I'd step backwards offa dat aryplane just to walk home wid you.

DAISY: *(Falling on* JIM*'s neck)* Jim, when you talk to me like dat I just can't stand it. Less us git married right now.

JIM: Now you talkin' like a blue-back speller. Less go!

DAVE: *(Sadly)* You gointer leave me lak dis, Daisy?

DAISY: *(Sadly)* I likes you, too, Dave, I sho do. But I can't marry both of y'all at de same time.

JIM: Aw, come on, Daisy . . . sun's gettin' low. *(He starts off pulling* DAISY*)*

DAVE: Whut's I'm gointer do? *(Walking after them)*

JIM: Gwan back and dance . . . you make out you don't need me to play none.

DAVE: *(Almost tearfully)* Aw, Jim, shucks! Where y'all going? *(*DAISY *comes to an abrupt halt and stops* JIM*)*

DAISY: That's right, honey. Where *is* we goin' sho nuff?

JIM: *(Sadly)* Deed I don't know, baby. They just sentenced me to go . . . they didn't say where and I don't know.

DAISY: How we goin' nohow to go when we don't know where we goin'?

*(*JIM *looks at* DAVE *as if he expects some help but* DAVE *stands sadly silent.* JIM *takes a few steps forward as if to go on.* DAISY *makes a step or two, unwillingly, then looks behind her and stops.* DAVE *looks as if he will follow them.)*

DAISY: Jim! *(*HE *stops and turns)* Wait a minute! Whut we gointer do when we git there?

JIM: Where?

DAISY: Where we goin'?

JIM: I done tole you I don't know where it is.

DAISY: But how we gointer git something to eat and a place to stay?

JIM: Play and dance . . . just like I been doin'.

DAISY: You can't dance and Dave ain't gointer be ther.

JIM: *(Looks appealingly at* DAVE, *then away quickly)* Well, I can't help *dat,* can I?

DAISY: *(Brightly)* I tell you whut, Jim! Less us don't go no-where. They sentenced you to leave Eatonville and youse more than a mile from de city limits already. Youse in Mait-land now. Supposin' you come live on de white folks' place wid me after we git married. Eatonville ain't got nothin' to do wid you livin' in Maitland.

JIM: Dat'a a good idea, Daisy.

DAISY: *(Jumping into his arms)* And listen, honey, you don't have to be beholden to Dave nor nobody else. You can throw dat ole box away if you want to. I know ehre you can get a *swell* job.

JIM: *(Sheepishly)* Doin' whut? *(Looks lovingly at his guitar)*

DAISY: *(Almost dancing)* Yard man. All you have to do is wash windows, and sweep de sidewalk, and scrub off de steps and porch and hoe up de weeds and rake up de leaves and dig a few holes now and then with a spade . . . to plant some trees and things like that. It's a good steady job.

JIM: *(After a long deliberation)* You see, Daisy, de Mayor and corporation told me to go on off and I oughter go.

DAISY: Well, I'm not going tippin' down no railroad track like a Maltese cat. I wasn't brought up knockin' round from here to yonder.

JIM: Well, I wasn't brought up wid no spade in my hand . . . and ain't going to start it now.

DAISY: But sweetheart, we got to live, ain't we? We got to git hold of money before we kin do anything. I don't mean to stay in de white folks' kitchen all my days.

JIM: Yeah, all dat's true, but you couldn't buy a flea a waltzing jacket wid de money *I'm* going to make wid a hoe and spade.

DAISY: *(Getting tearful)* You don't want me. You don't love me.

JIM: Yes, I do, darling, I love you. Youse de one letting a spade come between us. (HE *caresses her)* I loves you and you only. You don't see *me* dragging a whole gang of farming tools into us business, do you?

DAISY: *(Stiffly)* Well, I ain't going to marry no man that ain't going to work and take care of me.

JIM: I don't mind working if de job ain't too heavy for me. I ain't going to bother wid nothin' in my hands heavier than dis box . . . and I totes it round my neck 'most of de time.

*(*DAISY *makes a despairing gesture as* JIM *takes a step or two away from her. She turns to* DAVE *finally.)*

DAISY: Well, I reckon you loves me the best anyhow. You wouldn't talk to me like Jim did, would you, Dave?

DAVE: Naw, I wouldn't say what he said a-tall.

DAISY: *(Cuddling up to him)* Whut would *you* say, honey?

DAVE: I'd say dat box was too heavy for me to fool wid. I wouldn't tote nothing heavier than my hat and I feel like I'm 'busing myself sometime totin' dat.

DAISY: *(Outraged)* Don't you mean to work none?

DAVE: Wouldn't hit a lick at a snake.

DAISY: I don't blame *you,* Dave *(Looks down at his feet)* cause toting dem feet of yourn is enough to break down your constitution.

JIM: *(Airily)* That's all right . . . dem foots done put plenty bread in our moufs.

DAVE: Not by they selves though . . . wid de help of dat box, Jim. When you gits having fits on dat box, boy, my foots has hysterics. Daisy, you marry Jim cause I don't want to come between y'all. He's my buddy.

JIM: Come to think of it, Dave, she was yourn first. You take and handle dat spade for her.

DAVE: You heard her say it is all I can do to lift up dese feets and put 'em down. Where I'm going to git any time to wrassle wid any hoes and shovels? You kin git round better'n me. You done won Daisy . . . I give in. I ain't going to bite no fren' of mine in de back.

DAISY: Both of you niggers can git yo' hat an' yo' heads and git on down de road. Neither one of y'all don't have to have me. I got a good job and plenty men beggin for yo' chance.

JIM: Dat's right, Daisy, you go git you one them mens whut don't mind smelling mules . . . and beating de white folks to de barn every morning. I don't wanta be bothered wid nothin' but dis box.

DAVE: And I can't strain wid nothin' but my feets.

(DAISY walks slowly away in the direction from which she came. Both watch her a little wistfully for a minute. The sun is setting.)

DAVE: Guess I better be gittin' on back . . . it's most dark. Where you goin', Jim?

JIM: I don't know, Dave. Down de road, I reckon.

DAVE: Whyncher come on back to town. 'Tain't no use you proguein' up and down de railroad track when you got a home.

JIM: They done lawed me way from it for hittin' you wid dat bone.

DAVE: Dat ain't nothin'. It was my head you hit. An' if I don't keer whut dem old ugly-rump niggers got to do wid it?

JIM: They might not let me come in town.

DAVE: *(Seizing JIM's arm and facing him back toward the town)* They better! Look here, Jim, if they try to keep you out dat town we'll go out to dat swamp and git us a mule bone a piece and come into town and boil dat stew down to a low gravy.

JIM: You mean dat, Dave? *(DAVE nods his head eagerly)* Us wasn't mad wid one 'nother nohow. *(Beligerently)* Come on, less go back to town. Dem mallet-heads better leave me be, too. *(Picks up a heavy stick)* I wish Lum would come tellin' me 'bout de law when I got all dis law in *my* hands. And de rest o' dem gator-faced jigs, if they ain't got a whole sto' o' mule bones and a good determination, they better not bring no mess up. Come on, boy.

(THEY *start back together toward town,* JIM *picking a dance tune on his guitar, and* DAVE *cutting steps on the ties beside him, singing, prancing and happily, they exit, right, as*

THE CURTAIN FALLS.)

THE *MULE BONE* CONTROVERSY

THE NARRATIVE ACCOUNTS

FROM *THE BIG SEA* BY LANGSTON HUGHES

During the winter Zora Hurston came to Westfield from one of her many trips into the deep South, and there began to arrange her folk material, stacks and stacks of it—some of which later appeared in *Mules and Men.* Together we also began to work on a play called *Mule Bone,* a Negro folk comedy, based on an amusing tale Miss Hurston had collected about a quarrel between two rival church factions. I plotted out and typed the play based on her story, while she authenticated and flavored the dialogue and added highly humorous details. We finished a first draft before she went South again, and from this draft I was to work out a final version.

Zora, a very gay and lively girl, was seriously hemmed in in village-like Westfield. But those backing her folk-lore project felt that she should remain quietly in a small town and not go galavanting gaily about New York while engaged in the serious task of preparing her manuscripts. So she was restless and moody, working in a nervous manner. And we were both distressed at the growing depression—hearing of more and more friends and relatives losing jobs and becoming desperate for lack of work . . .

Of course, I knew I had no tapeworm all the time, so I decided to go home to Cleveland and get in bed. My mother then lived in three rooms in a basement on Carnegie Avenue, with my step-father and my brother. Very kindly my mother gave me the only bed and they slept on the davenport. My brother stayed with some cousins, because we had only two sleeping rooms and a kitchen.

. . . By now my brother was no longer in school in New England. Work was scarce in Cleveland, and my mother and dad were not doing so well. We were all in a rather bad way. The doctor in Cleveland said it was my tonsils that were poisoning my system, so he took them out—and that took the last money I had. Strangely enough, I still wouldn't tell any of the doctors I was just upset and emotionally confused. I guess I enjoyed paying for attention. And certainly I felt better as soon as the last penny left from Park Avenue was gone.

But to cap the climax, while I was in Cleveland, I had my first literary quarrel—although, basically, it was not really a literary quarrel.

On the evening that I arrived in Cleveland, the Gilpin Players, America's oldest Negro theater group, were performing a new play and I went to see it, thinking it might ease my mind. After the performance I was talking with the director, Rowena Jelliffe, and she told me that she had just received an excellent Negro folk comedy by a talented young woman named Zora Hurston. I expressed interest, so she went on to tell me that it was about a quarrel between two rival church factions in the deep South, that it was a very amusing play, and that it was called *Mule Bone.* She said it had just been turned down by the Theatre Guild in New York, but that an agent had sent a rough draft to her with permission to try it out in Cleveland.

From her description and the title, I knew it was the same play Zora Hurston and I had worked on together. But it was not finished and it did not seem to me it should be produced in that form.

I tried to telephone Miss Hurston, but could not reach her. I wired her, but got no answer. I wrote her three letters, and finally she replied from New York. She said, yes, she had sent the play to *her* agent because she felt that if the play were ever produced I would only take my half of the money and spend it on a girl she didn't like. Besides, the story was her story, the dialogue her dialogue, and the play her play—even if I had put it together, and she didn't want me to have any part in it.

Girls are funny creatures! By now the Gilpin Players were worried and wished her permission in writing, which they tried to secure. An answer came from her agent, giving the Gilpins permission to continue. I agreed to make a final draft, so the play was put into rehearsal, pending a written agreement from Miss Hurston, who as yet had sent no business word. Finally, Miss Hurston wrote that she was driving out to Cleveland to see the rehearsals and would then sign the agreement. Shortly she arrived.

We had a long talk and she agreed that whatever her personal feelings were about other things, the production could go ahead.

But overnight she changed her mind—or, rather, before 12 P.M. She heard that the girl she did not like had been in town, so at midnight she called up Mrs. Jelliffe and said that never, under any circumstances, would she permit any of her work to be linked with mine, nor her name with mine, and that there could be no production of our play, *Mule Bone.* By that time the Gilpin Players had put a sizable amount of money into scenery and costumes for the play. So Mrs. Jelliffe requested a joint conference with me and Miss Hurston the following day. Nothing, she felt, could be settled over the phone at midnight.

Having recently had my tonsils out, I was forbidden by my doctor to leave bed, so the conference was called for my house. It was a cold and snowy day. Mr. and Mrs. Jelliffe arrived. Miss Hurston also came. But she would not talk about the play! Not at all. She would speak only of things that did not concern the drama in question, one way or another. She spoke passionately, long, and loud, until the Jelliffes begged to be excused. They went home. Miss Hurston then got the last word and left without saying good-bye to my mother, whom she had known for years. That made my mother angry, so she pursued Miss Hurston into the hall to give her a piece of her mind. I had to get up out of bed and restrain my mother. It was an exciting afternoon for a tonsillectomy patient.

That evening my fraternity brothers were giving a dance in my honor. I had informed them three days before that the doctor had forbidden me to leave my bed and that I could not come to any dance. But since it was all arranged, they went ahead with it just the same. In my honor, Miss Hurston, being a visiting celebrity, was invited to the party, since the brothers knew nothing of our literary quarrel. With a local young man, she went to the ball and told everyone how awful I was. Then she drove back to New York. As soon as I recovered my voice, I called up the local young man to tell him I meant to beat the hell out of him.

I never heard from Miss Hurston again. Unfortunately, our art was broken, and that was the end of what would have been a good play had it ever been finished—the first real Negro folk comedy—*Mule Bone.*

About that time, *Not Without Laughter* appeared and I received the Harmon Gold Award for Literature, given by the Federated Council of Churches—four hundred dollars and a gold medal. The week that I received the award, I wired Alain Locke, who knew the circumstances of our having written the play and had, I believe, seen a first draft. I asked him kindly to talk to Miss Hurston for me. Alain Locke wired back, YOU HAVE HARMON AWARD SO WHAT MORE DO YOU WANT. Exactly ten cooling words.

I could not go to New York to receive the award, so they sent it to me by mail—a medal and a check. I put the medal away in my trunk. With the four hundred dollars I went to Haiti.

I needed sun.

FROM *ZORA NEALE HURSTON: A LITERARY BIOGRAPHY* BY ROBERT E. HEMENWAY

"Mule Bone" has never been produced, and only its third act has ever been published. Fewer than ten copies of the play survive, all deposited in private papers. Still, despite the fact that it has been read in full by only a few, it is a notorious work, the center of a quarrel that transformed Hughes and Hurston from intimate friends to lifelong enemies. "Mule Bone" is the reason Langston Hughes, a kind, gentle, forgiving man, never forgave Hurston for what he considered theft and dishonesty. "Mule Bone" caused Zora Hurston, who had high hopes of making their collaborative efforts famous, to accuse her partner of stealing ideas and of sabotaging the play's production. "Mule Bone" explains why, after February 3, 1931, Zora Neale Hurston and Langston Hughes avoided each other for the rest of their lives.

The "Mule Bone" episode is not so important in itself, perhaps, but it provides an intimate glimpse of the kinds of pressures Hurston struggled to control all her life. The tale is worth focusing on because its true history has gone unreported, and also because it illuminates complex tensions in Hurston's life that arose from patronage and personality. These tensions illustrate why Zora Hurston's career would be at times controversial, at times puzzling, occasionally inconsistent.

The "Mule Bone" story is tangled, filled with bad behavior, shrill voices, and feigned innocence. When Hughes accused Hurston of claiming sole authorship of a play they had written together and of marketing it for the stage without consulting him, he acted from a legitimate sense of outrage. She had done both—whether out of misunderstanding, ambition, or malice, it is hard to say. Hughes's representation of the facts in *The Big Sea,* however—up to now the only public account of the dispute—oversimplifies an incredibly complicated affair. Hughes actually gave two versions of his side of things, one in his autobiography, another in correspondence with his lawyer. Hurston never gave a public account, and only a partial private one. The narrative that follows has been pieced together from a variety of sources, including the private correspondence of the principals.[1]

"Mule Bone" was written largely between March and June of 1930. Living near each other in rooming houses in New Jersey, seeing each other almost every day, Hughes and Hurston apparently talked about some of their plans for a "real Negro theatre." At a party in late February or early March, Hughes met Theresa Helburn of the Dramatists Guild; Helburn complained that practically all the plays about black people offered to the guild were serious problem dramas. Why didn't someone write a comedy—not a minstrel show, but a real comedy? Hughes took the idea back to Hurston, and they began to work, meeting at Zora's place in Westfield; they decided to build a three-act comedy around a folktale she had collected.

The tale was about two hunters who shot simultaneously at a wild turkey and then quarreled over who had killed it. In the ensuing fight, one hunter knocked the other unconscious with the hock bone of a mule found by happenstance during the struggle. The bone wielder was charged with assault and battery and brought to trial. When it was asserted that a mule bone could hardly be considered a lethal weapon, a minister read to the jury the biblical story of Samson's slaying three thousand Philistines with the jawbone of an ass. Pointing out that a mule is more dangerous the farther to the rear one goes, the minister concluded that a bone from the hind legs must be considered a very dangerous weapon indeed. The hunter was convicted and expelled from town.

How Hughes and Hurston shaped this story into a comic play—the division of responsibility, who wrote what—is unknown. Hughes claimed that he was to do the construction, plot, some characterization, and some dialogue, and that Hurston was to provide the authentic Florida color, give the dialogue a true southern flavor, and insert turns of phrase and "highly amusing details" from her collecting trips. By early April they were working together intensely, dictating to Louise Thompson. The three of them had a wonderful time, Zora sometimes reducing the others to helpless laughter as she acted out all the parts. In four weeks they completed drafts of the first and third acts and at least one scene of the second act. The turkey was dropped (over Hurston's objections) and a girl made the root of the argument. The combatants became members of different churches, and the trial became part of a sectarian struggle. In May, Hurston left Westfield. In June she returned to the South for the summer, taking with her notes and outlines for the trial scene of act 2; she was to complete this act over the summer, and they would polish it in the fall.

Hughes contended that he saw nothing unusual in this departure just when things were nearing completion, and he claimed to be surprised and disappointed when Hurston returned in September and brushed him off when asked about beginning work again. According to him, she canceled appointments, said she had no time, and by early December was no longer seeing him at all. However, this autumn coldness was consistent with her breaking off work in late spring when things were going smoothly; neither action had anything to do with the need for a trip south or the press of other business. She was angry over the growing friendship between Hughes and Louise Thompson, and she felt, rightly or wrongly, that Hughes was trying to make Thompson a part of their collaborative effort. Hurston broke off their partnership because she was angry over the way things were working out between them and their stenographer.

Her complaint, not voiced until later, was over Hughes's proposal that Thompson assume more than a stenographer's role in their effort, that perhaps she even be made business manager of any Broadway production. Hurston did not admit it, but this new partner was a considerable distraction to a creative collaboration looked forward to for years. She had already given up the racial opera they had talked about; Mrs. Mason* decided that Hughes could do it better with a composer, and she had sent him to Cuba to look for a new collaborator. Hughes later claimed that he attributed Hurston's behavior that fall to nerves and to the rush of getting her folklore collections organized for publication. It seems more likely that he knew what was bothering his co-worker and had concluded that it was best to let their long friendship cool.

The other factor complicating the Hughes-Hurston relationship at the time was Hughes's growing uneasiness with Mrs. Mason. During the fall and winter of 1930 Hughes began to feel guilty about eating caviar above Park Avenue while apple vendors hawked for survival on the street below. Hughes's poem "Advertisement for the Waldorf-Astoria" had addressed this feeling:

---

*Widow of the prominent physician Rufus Osgood Mason, Charlotte Louise Vandervere Quick Mason (1854–1946) was an influential philanthropist who invested more than $75,000 in the careers of young black artists such as Hughes and Hurston, as well as Aaron Douglas, Richmond Barthe, and Alain Locke. An opinionated patron, she involved herself in both the artistic and more personal aspects of her protégés' lives.

Have luncheon there this afternoon, all you jobless.
  Why not?
Dine with some of the men and women who got rich off
  of your Labor, who clip coupons with clean white
  fingers because your hands dug coal, drilled stone,
  sewed garments, poured steel to let other people
  draw dividends and live easy.

Mrs. Mason not only had clean white fingers, she also clipped coupons regularly. She was bound to disapprove of the poem, and Hughes probably knew it. Her disapproval led to his rethinking their relationship, with the result that in late December or early January he went off the payroll. There was a final traumatic scene at 399 Park [the home of Mrs. Mason], and the parting was bitter, Mrs. Mason accusing him of ingratitude and disloyalty. Hurston knew about Hughes's dissatisfaction and probably foresaw the breakup. It may be that she was trying to protect her own relationship with her patron, hoping that Mrs. Mason's unhappiness with Hughes would not rub off on her. She had apparently made her peace with Mrs. Mason and did not wish to sever the patronage arrangement until her field work was organized. If this sounds as though Hurston abandoned a friend, it is important to remember that Louise Thompson—in Zora's mind at least—had already come between them. Complicating it all was Thompson's support from Mrs. Mason while typing the play and her growing dissatisfaction with Mrs. Mason's interest in black people as primitives. Hurston herself was not entirely easy with this aspect of the Mason personality, but she knew how to play to Godmother's preferences. She once addressed Mrs. Mason as the "guardmother who sits in the twelfth heaven and shapes the destinies of the primitives." Thompson, who was very close to Zora before the "Mule Bone" blowup, remembers how, whenever Mrs. Mason sent an exotic dress for Zora to wear, Zora called

Park Avenue to report that it looked stunning on her; then she would hang up and turn to her companion, remarking with a laugh that she would not think of wearing such a thing.

Hughes's reaction to the breakup with Mrs. Mason was to become psychosomatically ill. He spent his remaining money on doctors and radiologists who could find nothing wrong with him. One New York physician, a specialist in diagnosing Oriental ailments, identified his as a Japanese tapeworm. When Hughes returned home to Cleveland to live with his mother in early January, 1931, a general practitioner attempted to solve his problems by removing his tonsils. As Hughes admitted, his real illness was in his wallet; he began recovering the moment the last of Mrs. Mason's money was gone.

Hughes's tonsillitis did not stop him from visiting Cleveland's Karamu House shortly after his return. A settlement playhouse run by Rowena and Alexander Jelliffe, Karamu was the home of a black acting company called the Gilpin Players, nationally known for the quality and vigor of their productions. When Rowena Jelliffe told Hughes on January 15 that she had just obtained the rights to a play called "Mule Bone," a comedy of "Negro life" by Zora Neale Hurston, he was mystified. When the script arrived and proved to be clearly the play they had worked on together, he was angry. And when he could get no satisfactory explanation from Hurston by phone call or letter, he was outraged. He immediately copied act 2 from the script received, added his own copies of acts 1 and 3, and sent the play off to be copyrighted in both their names. He also sent Hurston a registered letter threatening litigation.

What actually happened was that Hurston had given the play to Carl Van Vechten to read. Although the script was in a very unfinished form, he had, without her knowledge, sent it to Barrett Clark, a reader for the Theatre Guild. Clark was sure that the guild would reject it, but in his capacity as an employee of Samuel French, the theatrical producer, he had written Mrs. Jelliffe to ask if the Gilpin Players would be interested. When she said yes, he had sent the script on, indicating that a letter explaining rights to the play would follow.

Was Hurston thinking of marketing the play as her own? It seems likely, since the script read by the Theatre Guild carried only her name. Moreover, she, too, had submitted the play script for copyright, but in October of 1930, using her own second act, reinserting the turkey as the object of contention, and listing herself as the sole author. Still, she had not sent the play anywhere herself, and when she received an angry phone call from Hughes on January 16, she truthfully denied knowing anything about the play's being in an agent's hands or in Cleveland. Hughes found this hard to believe, and the phone conversation degenerated rapidly.

The Gilpin Players wanted very much to do the play. Mrs. Jelliffe was enthusiastic. Even though the script was in a rough state—the turkey had been reinserted, but the girl remained; there were two endings, with the suggestion that the performers take their pick—one of its authors was in Cleveland and available for rewriting. A number of phone calls followed, the upshot being that Barrett Clark promised Mrs. Jelliffe that he would try to obtain Hurston's permission for a production. On January 20, 1930, a wire came from French's saying that Hurston had refused to authorize the production and that the script should be returned at once. Within twenty-four hours, however, three wires came directly from Hurston authorizing the production and indicating that she would collaborate with Hughes on script changes. Within that same twenty-four-hour period. Hughes received a letter from Hurston, written on January 18, saying that no part of the play was his. Understandably confused, he contacted New York attorney Arthur Spingarn, one of the chief supporters of the NAACP, to protect his interests.

The letter that Hughes received from Hurston claiming he had no rights in the play was not vicious, although it undoubtedly angered him.[2] Hurston said that she wanted to have a heart-to-heart talk about the play, and finally expressed her resentment about Louise Thompson: "In the beginning, Langston, I was very eager to do the play with you. *ANY* thing you said would go over big with me. But scarcely had we gotten underway before you made three propositions that shook me to the foundation of myself. First: that three way split with Louise. Now Langston, nobody has in the history of the world given a typist an interest in a work for typing it. Nobody would think of it unless they were prejudiced in favor of the typist." According to Hurston, Hughes's second proposition was that Thompson be paid more than the usual typist's fee, and his third that she be made the business manager of the Broadway production. The effect, Hurston claimed, was to make her feel as though she were "among strangers, and the only thing to do was to go on away from there." (In a letter written two days later, she added a touch of melodrama to her exile: "I just went off to myself and tried to resolve to have no more friendships. Tears unceasing have poured down inside me.")

Having adopted the role of the betrayed partner, Hurston then told Hughes: "Now about the play itself. It was my story from beginning to end. It is my dialogue; my situations. But I am not concerned about that. Langston, with God as my judge, I don't care anything about the money it might make nor the glory. I'd be willing to give it all to you off-hand. But the idea of you, LANGSTON HUGHES, trying to use the tremendous influence that you knew you had with me that someone else might exploit me cut me to the quick." Then Hurston added her trump card, a veiled hint that although they both knew that her claim to the play was questionable, she had the money and power to back it up: "I told Godmother that I had done my play all by myself, and so I did, and for the reasons stated before."

Godmother's entry into the proceedings was not by happenstance. She apparently knew that Zora was now working alone on a play that had been written in collaboration, and she chose to back Zora in the dispute. In the spring of 1930 the authors' uncertainty over whether Mrs. Mason would approve of their theatrical venture had led directly to one of their first arguments over Louise Thompson. Neither Zora nor Langston had enough money to pay her for the typing, and Thompson offered to wait for payment until the play was produced. This seems generous, but Zora saw it as a ploy; she complained to Hughes, "She resisted pay and tried to put it on a sentiment and royalty basis. Establishing the record of being the first stenog. [rapher] to try to collect royalties." Finally they spoke to Mrs. Mason about the play and obtained her permission to work together with Thompson as their typist.

Hurston's report to Hughes that Godmother was on her side was probably designed to scare him. They had already had a nasty telephone conversation during which Hughes threatened to sue her, and she was replying in kind. He was just now beginning to find some peace of mind after the breakup with his patron, and it must have been unsettling to think that Mrs. Mason might express her resentment toward him by backing Hurston's claim of authorship—perhaps even accusing him of trying to steal folklore material from her. Hurston, who knew of the anguish in his departure, may have been more than a little designing; but then, she also felt wronged. She told Arna Bontemps years later that she had been jealous of Louise Thompson, that this was a key to the dispute. Exactly what Hurston meant is unclear; she also told Bontemps that she was not in love with Hughes.[3] In a letter to Hughes, dated January 20, 1931, Zora said, with some feeling: "Now get this straight, Langston. You are still dear to me. I don't care whom you love nor whom you marry, nor whom you bestow your worldly goods upon. I will never have any feeling about that part. I have always felt that if you had married anyone at all it would make no difference in our relationship. I *know* that no man on earth could change me towards you." She explained that she had gone off in June because "I couldn't hear myself saying unpleasant phrases to you." She had worked "the play out alone—carefully not using what was yours."

This claim to sole authorship melted away quickly when confronted by the good offices of Arthur Spingarn, when gentle persuasion brought the two friends back together again. Sorting out the sequence of events with help from Van Vechten, telling them they both were acting foolishly, Spingarn urged mutual apologies and a renewed attempt to polish the play; after all, it was a theatrical property that Van Vechten, at least, felt could be as great a popular success as *Green Pastures.* Things were smoothed over. Hurston consulted with her agent, Elizabeth Marbury, and although the preparation for the Cleveland production was tension filled, primarily because the signals from New York kept changing, it was finally agreed that Hurston would come to Cleveland by February 1 for last-minute work with Hughes. The first performance was scheduled for February 15.

Zora represented this accommodation to Godmother as a way for her to bring Langston to his senses and back into the Mason Holding Company. On January 20 she wrote Mrs. Mason that Hughes wanted to make up with his Godmother but was too emotional to come forth: "Personally I think that he has so much in him, that it is worth my swallowing and forgetting if by extending a friendly hand I can bring him back into the fold." She assured Mrs. Mason that Hughes "is ashamed of his attitude about the play," and that this enabled her to accept him once again as a co-author: "Godmother, I am so happy Langston has taken an honorable view of the thing, that I would give him part. I shant say that to him right now, but it takes all the sting out of the thing. The money didn't mean anything, Godmother, really."

Hurston arrived in Cleveland on the first of February and in a meeting with Hughes resolved their differences. They agreed to the Gilpin Players production—provided the players still wanted to do it. The players had held a conference the same evening and voted to discontinue; they were uncertain of Hurston's attitude, and the whole production had become problematical. When Mrs. Jelliffe and the leader of the players promised to reconsider, all seemed settled. "Mule Bone" could be performed in Cleveland and, if financial backing was obtained, taken to Broadway; eventually, they hoped, it would become a movie.

Overnight, however, Hurston learned that Louise Thompson had recently been in Cleveland to visit Hughes. Although Thompson's visit was part of some interracial seminars she was conducting and had nothing to do with the play, it is logical that Zora Hurston would think otherwise. She concluded that Hughes and Thompson were scheming to pirate her play, and her reaction was total anger. According to Hughes, she called Mrs. Jelliffe and berated her. She went the next afternoon to a conference at Hughes's house, where his tonsillitis had confined him to bed, and berated him, the Gilpin Players, and the Jelliffes. She even complained about the playground next door to the settlement house. She abused Hughes's mother and generally stormed and raged. Since Hughes is the only participant who left a reminiscence of this event, publicly or privately, we are dependent on his account, which obviously would not be favorable to Hurston; it is doubtful if she was quite as emphatic as his descriptions imply, or, if she was, that her behavior was without provocation. Nevertheless, Hurston's capacity for outrage was considerable, and in this instance she felt deeply wronged. She told friends in New York that she would tear Louise Thompson limb from limb the next time she saw her. Carl Van Vechten claimed that she once threw herself to the floor of his study in a tantrum over Hughes's betrayal. Needless to say, the production was called off. Hurston wired Mrs. Mason to tell of the betrayal, then left for New York, still angry, accusing Hughes of double-crossing her once again.[4]

Spingarn and Van Vechten did make some preliminary attempts to patch up the quarrel; Hurston became reconciled with Louise Thompson; and Zora and Hughes exchanged letters of a less hostile nature than their last meeting. Despite all this, "Mule Bone" was dead as a dramatic production. In March, 1931, in response to one of Spingarn's queries, Hurston replied acerbically, sending a copy of her letter to an approving Godmother:

> This is to deny your assertion that you have seen the original script. You have seen what your client *says* is the original script. You evidently forget that your client had my script out in Cleveland and I see did not hesitate to copy off some "emendations." The whole matter is absolutely without honor from start to finish and this latest evidence of trying to make a case by actual theft, "emendations" as you call them, makes me lose respect for the thin[g] altogether. From the very beginning it has been an attempt to build up a case by inference and construction rather than by fact. But all the liberal construction in the world cannot stand against certain things which I have in my possession.
>
> I think it would be lovely for your client to be a playwright but I'm afraid that I am too tight to make him one at my expense. You have written plays, why not do him one yourself? Or perhaps a nice box of apples and a well chosen corner. But never no play of mine.[5]

Hughes still had to assert his rights to the play as late as August, 1931, in conversations with Hurston's agent. In 1933 Hurston told Harold Jackman that she was thinking of revising "Mule Bone" again, and in January, 1934, she assured Van Vechten that a new version of the play was being prepared. But she more or less gave up hope for the play's production, as did Hughes. After Hurston's death he permitted the third act to be published in *Drama Critique,* but the play has never been performed or printed in full.[6]

Hughes's account of this whole episode in *The Big Sea* is discreet to the point of being self-serving. With his usual gallantry he chose not to mention Louise Thompson by name, and he nowhere suggests that a dispute over a typist was a central issue. He portrays Zora as a lively "girl," who was inhibited by village-like Westfield but made to stay there by "those backing her folklore project" who felt that it would be good for her to work quietly. He adds, "So she was restless and moody, working in a nervous manner. . . ." There are also factual errors in the *Big Sea* account, some probably resulting from slips of memory, some reflecting the interests of Hughes's case. Hughes leaves the impression that Mrs. Jelliffe had a copy of the script in hand when she first told him about it. Actually, he had to wait to see if it was the same script they had worked on together. He nowhere mentions that in the script sent to Cleveland, Hurston had somewhat rewritten all three acts. He denies that he talked with Hurston on the phone; yet he admitted privately that this was the first thing he did on January 16 when he saw the script. He does not mention that at one point he was willing to accept only a one-third interest in the play, granting that two-thirds of it was Hurston's work. He claims that Hurston's original folktale was about two rival church factions, but he told Arthur Spingarn that the tale was about two hunters and that the idea of making them representatives of the Baptist and Methodist faiths was his own. He also claims that there was a first draft finished before Hurston went south and that it was he who was supposed to work out a final version. He reports that Hurston wrote him that she gave the play to her agent—she gave it only to Van Vechten—because he would "only take my half of the money and spend it on a girl she didn't like." He concludes in *The Big Sea,* "Girls are funny creatures."

Apart from the factual errors in this account, Hughes's construction of events is subtly designed to make Zora Hurston appear a fickle woman, representative of her sex, nervous and moody in New Jersey, and, above all, a "funny creature." In short, he presents a chauvinistic interpretation of their collaboration. Hughes's greatest omission, however, is his failure to admit that both parties were thinking of Mrs. Mason sitting in her throne-like chair on Park Avenue. When he reports in *The Big Sea* his dismay over Alain Locke's siding with Hurston, he presents Locke as a man who is as mysteriously unfair as Hurston is unstable. But Hughes knew that Locke had heard the story of the play only from Mrs. Mason and Zora. Hughes's fear of Mrs. Mason's power was such that when Spingarn reported that Locke was backing Hurston, Hughes came to doubt even Spingarn. Convinced that his lawyer was siding with the money and power in New York, at one point he asked for the return of his private papers from Spingarn's files. Zora kept Mrs. Mason abreast of the entire matter by letter—including copies of her letters to Hughes; a common refrain runs throughout: "I'd love for Langston to face me in your presence," and "I wish it were possible for Locke to get him before you and then call me in and let him state his claims."

What one is left with, finally, is speculation about an honest misunderstanding exacerbated by the special pressures both writers experienced at the time. Although Louise Thompson served as a typist, she was also a talented, brilliant woman, in the beginning a good friend to both Hughes and Hurston. She undoubtedly made suggestions as they dictated, which Hughes, at least, appreciated. Hurston, seeing her as both a personal and an artistic rival, probably did not. On the other hand, she was primarily a typist, and Hurston had every right to resent Hughes's suggestions for her participation in the production. Yet one senses that Hughes's proposal probably arose as the two young writers grew excited about their play, imagined its Broadway production, and dreamed of its success. Envisioning fame and wealth for the authors, it seems perfectly plausible for Hughes to want the third person in the room not to feel left out. "And we'll make Louise business manager" seems a logical reaction, but one that a collaborator, already suspicious of that third person, might view skeptically. Since Louise Thompson had also been supported by Mrs. Mason while working with them on the play—and since both Hughes and Louise Thompson left Mrs. Mason in late 1930, shortly before the "Mule Bone" dispute, while Hurston stayed on—Mrs. Mason's presence had to have some effect on everyone's behavior. Arna Bontemps, working on a Hughes biography up to the time of his death, felt that Mrs. Mason was the key to the entire squabble and that Zora thought Louise Thompson might pose a threat to her relations with Mrs. Mason. Apparently the play arrived in Cleveland by pure happenstance, without Hurston's approval, making Hughes's initial willingness to accuse her of wrongdoing a bit unfair. Moreover, there is little question that most of the material in the play came from Hurston, including the basic characters and situation, which were Eatonville material. Still, though Hughes admitted that it was more hers than his, this does not justify her claim to sole authorship. At one point Hughes asked, with some exasperation, why she had not asked him to bow out of their work sessions if she was so convinced that the play was hers. Zora's reply was to accuse him of stealing from her for his first novel, *Not Without Laughter.*

None of this fully explains the behavior of all involved, and the circumstances surrounding the play will always remain a mystery. Hurston and Hughes were never entirely candid about their motives. One wonders if the dispute had something to do with Hurston's officially going off the payroll in March of 1931. Zora did ask Bontemps in 1939 to tell Langston that their quarrel was "the cross of her life," but the bitterness stayed with Hughes to the end. Although he tried hard to be fair to her in his autobiography, he could not easily forget the pain she had caused. Hurston never really forgave, either; when Hughes went to Cuba to regain his health and try to forget the whole episode, she remarked to Godmother: "I know Langston says he was going to Cuba, but I suspect that he is really gone to hunt up Eatonville to pretend that he knew about it all along."

The play is the thing, however, and "Mule Bone" is an interesting attempt to transcend black dramatic stereotypes. The play is set in Eatonville, the porch of Joe Clarke's store serving as the set for the first act, and the village lifestyle providing the key to the action. "Mule Bone" tries to convey the humanity of this experience from its comic side. It rejects the stock comic types of the minstrel tradition, replacing them with real human beings who get a good deal of fun out of life, but who unconsciously order their existence and give it special meaning with elaborate verbal rituals. The play's effect depends largely on the devices of verbal improvisation—sounding, rhyming, woofing—that are central to Afro-American folklore.

The major characters of the play are described by the authors as follows:

Jim Weston: Guitarist, Methodist, slightly arrogant, aggressive, somewhat self important, ready with his tongue.
Dave Carter: Dancer, Baptist, soft, happy-go-lucky character, slightly dumb. . . .

Daisy Taylor: Methodist, domestic servant, plump, dark and sexy, self-conscious of clothes and appeal, fickle.

Joe Clark: The Mayor, storekeeper and postmaster, arrogant, ignorant and powerful in a self-assertive way, large fat man; Methodist.[7]

The setting is the raised porch of Joe Clark's general store and the street in front. The porch is to stretch almost completely across the stage, with a plank bench at either end. At the center of the porch three steps lead up from the street. At the rear of the porch, in the center, is a door with Post Office painted to the left and General Store to the right. Soapboxes and small kegs are on the porch for townspeople to lounge on during the action. To one side is a large kerosene street lamp.

The time of the play is Saturday afternoon. "The villagers are gathered around the store. Several men sitting on boxes at edge of porch chewing sugar cane, spitting tobacco juice, arguing, some whittling, others eating peanuts. During the act the women all dressed up in starched dresses parade in and out of the store. People buying groceries, children playing in the street, etc. General noise of conversation, laughter and children shouting."

The first scene begins with a number of village men on the porch chewing their sugar cane and aimlessly talking. One of the regulars soon arrives carrying a hock bone of "Brazzle's ole yaller mule," an animal that is an Eatonville legend: "so skinny you could do a week's washin' on his ribs for a washboard, and hang 'em up on his hip bones to dry," so mean that he died on his back with his feet straight in the air, "too contra'y to lay down on his side like a mule orter and die decent." The bone was found down by the lake, where the village had gone to give the mule a mock burial only a few months earlier; its discovery produces a number of stories that illustrate the verbal talents of the porch sitters and the mulish nature of the animal. When the mule is finally buried as a conversation topic, Daisy Taylor enters the scene, much to the delight of the middle-aged men on the porch. She has a "mean walk on her," prompting one of them to say, "Yeah, man. She handles a lot of traffic! Oh, mama, throw it in de river . . . papa'll come git it." Joe Clark says that Daisy puts him in mind of "I God, a great big mango . . . a sweet smell, you know, with a strong flavor, but not something you could mash up like a strawberry. Something with body in it." The stage directions at this point are particularly interesting: the authors feel compelled to warn that the scene must be played to avoid sexual stereotypes. After Joe Clark's remarks there is to be "general laughter, but not obscene," and the actors are directed to comment admiringly but not lasciviously on Daisy's sexuality.

The play's two major conflicts are introduced, first, when the men remark on how Jim Weston and Dave Carter seem to be losing their friendship over Daisy, an unavoidable circumstance since "wimmen is something can't be divided equal," and second, when the Methodists and Baptists on the porch begin playfully to dispute each other. One Methodist says, "Y'all Baptist carry dis close-communion business too far. If a person ain't half-drownded in de lake and half et up by alligators, y'all think he ain't baptized, so you can't take communion wid him." In response, one of the Baptists tells a story about a Methodist minister's son who, because he can never get enough to eat, leaves home and goes to hell. He returns on a wintry day after seven years, and his father is overjoyed to have him back. The father invites him into the house where eight fellow Methodist pastors are sitting around the fireplace and eating. The minister asks his son how hell was, and his son replies, "It's just like it is here . . . you cain't git to de fire for de preachers."

The major conflict in act 1 is between Jim and Dave.

They enter as the best of friends, good-natured rivals for Daisy's affection. When one of the men on the porch suggests that Daisy may be after their money, Jim assures him that there will be no gold dug from him, since he "wouldn't give a poor consumpted cripple crab a crutch to cross the river Jordan." Dave agrees that this will not work with him either, for he "wouldn't give a dog a doughnut if he treed a terrapin." In their attempt to impress Daisy they sing for her:

> Got on the train
> Didn't have no fare,
> But I rode some,
> I rode some.
> Got on de train,
> Didn't have no fare,
> But I rode some,
> But I rode some,
> Got on de train,
> Didn't have no fare,
> Conductor asked me what I'm doing there
> But I rode some.
>
> Grabbed me by the neck,
> And led me to the door
> But I rode some,
> But I rode some.
> Grabbed me by the neck
> And led me to the door
> But I rode some,
> But I rode some.
> Grabbed me by the neck,
> And led me to the door,
> Rapped me cross the head with a Forty-Four,
> But I rode some!

The two men begin to argue over Daisy, and their rivalry becomes intense. A child calls out, "Fight, fight, you're no kin. Kill one'nother, won't be no sin." The argument comes to blows, and in the course of the fight Jim reaches down, picks up the mule bone, and knocks Dave out. This causes an uproar. Some of the townspeople exit to minister to the wounded Dave; the others arrest Jim and escort him to Joe Clark's barn, where he will be kept until trial on Monday. Daisy is left in stage center at the curtain, asking petulantly, "Now, who's gonna take me home?"

The setting for act 2 is the interior of the Macedonia Baptist church, where the trial will take place. The scene begins with the townspeople filing in to take their places on either one side of the church or the other, Jim's Methodist supporters on the right and Dave's Baptists on the left. The two groups begin to trade insults as they wait for the mayor and the principals to arrive. When these men do enter, it is suggested that the trial begin with a hymn, and the two congregations rise to sing simultaneously—the Baptists using "Onward Christian Soldiers" to try to drown out the Methodists' "All Hail the Power of Jesus' Name."

The legal niceties of the trial center around whether or not a crime was committed. Jim admits to hitting Dave but denies that it is a criminal offense. The Methodist minister argues persuasively on this point: "Naw, he ain't committed no 'ssault. He jus' lammed Dave over de head, dat's all. *(Triumphantly)* Yuh see y'all don't know whut yuh talkin 'bout. Now I done set in de court house an' heard de white folks law from mornin till night. . . . You got tuh have uh weepon to commit uh 'ssault. An' tain't in no white folks' law and tain't in dis Bible dat no mule bone is no weepon."

The Methodists are not to have the final word, for the Baptist minister then quotes Judges 18:18 about Samson's warfare. Since the jawbone killed three thousand, the hock bone, coming from the dangerous part of the animal, must be a lethal weapon; thus there was a crime. The Methodist minister still objects, but is squelched when Joe Clark tells him to be quiet: "You may be slick, but you kin stand another greasin'." Jim is banished from the town for two years as punishment. The mayor ends the trial, and the act, by announcing that those in the audience who are near blows must get off the church grounds before they start to fight, and they can't "use no knives, an' no guns, an' no mule bones. Court Dismissed."

The setting for act 3 is a high stretch of railroad track through a luxuriant Florida forest. It is near sundown. At the rise of the curtain

> there is no one on stage, but there is a tremendous noise and hubbub off-stage right. There are yells of derision and shouts of anger. Part of the mob is trying to keep Jim in town and part is driving him off. After a full minute of this, Jim enters with his guitar hanging around his neck and his coat over his shoulder. The sun is dropping low and red through the forest. He is looking back angrily and shouting at the mob. A missile is thrown after him. Jim drops his coat and guitar and picks up a piece of brick and makes threatening gestures of throwing it. He runs back the way he came, hurling the brick with all his might.

Jim's opening speech indicates how drastically the town's harmony has been disrupted: "I'm out o' yo' ole town. Now just let some of you ole half-pint Baptists let yo' wooden God an' cornstalk Jesus fool you into hittin' me. . . . I'm glad I'm out o yo ole town anyhow. I ain't never comin back no mo, neither. You ole ugly-rump niggers done ruint de town anyhow. Lawd, folks sho is deceitful. I never woulda thought people woulda acted like that."

Before long Daisy enters, claiming that she has been

worried about him. He does not believe her: "Ashes to ashes, dust to dust, show me a woman that a man can trust." She convinces him of her affection, however, and they have made up by the time Dave enters. The two men, sobered by the violence of their quarrel, become involved in a courting ritual designed to prove to Daisy who loves her most. Dave says to Daisy, "I love you harder than de thunder can bump a stump—if I don't—God's a gopher." Jim complains to Daisy, "You ain't never give me no chance to talk wid you right," and Daisy says, "Aw, you'all better stop dat. You know you don't mean it." Dave responds, "Who don't mean it. Lemme tell you somethin', mama, if you was mine, I wouldn't have you countin' no ties wid you pretty lil toes. Know whut I'd do. . . . I'd buy a whole passenger train and hire some mens to run it for you." Jim is not about to be outdone: "De wind may blow, de door may slam, Dat stuff you shooting ain't worth a dam. I'd buy you a great big ole ship—and then, baby, I'd buy you a ocean to sail yo ship on." Dave's reply is in kind: "A long train, a short caboose, Dat lie whut you shootin, ain't no use. . . . Miss Daisy, know what I'd do for you? . . . I'd come down de river ridin' a mud cat and leadin' a minnow." But Jim will not be topped: "Naw he ain't—he's just lyin'—he's a noble liar. Know whut I'd do if you was mine? . . . I'd make a panther wash you dishes and a gator chop yo wood for you." This verbal play goes on for some time. When Dave asks Jim how much time he would do for Daisy on the chain gang, Jim answers, "Twenty years and like it." Dave exults, "See dat, Daisy, Dat nigger ain't willin' to do no time for you. I'd beg de judge to gimme life."

Again, a significant stage direction interrupts the dialogue. By telling us that "both Jim and Dave laugh," Hurston and Hughes were trying to show the sense of verbal play and rhetorical improvisation characteristic of Eatonville generally, and Joe Clark's store-front porch specifically. To use a term from the professional folklorist, Hurston and Hughes were attempting to dramatize the "oral-aural worldview" of a black community that contrasts with the typographic-chirographic structure of white middle-class thought. The contest is a ritual, designed to defuse the violence implicit in the conflict, to channel the aggression into mental rather than physical terms. The manner in which the courting contest ends suggests its ritualistic nature: Dave says to Daisy, "Don't you be skeered, baby. Papa kin take keer o you [*To* JIM: *suiting the action to the word*] Countin' from de finger back to de thumb. . . . Start anything, I got you some." Jim is taken aback: "Aw, I don't want no more fight wid you, Dave." Dave replies, "Who said anything about fighting? We just provin' who love Daisy de best."

The courting rapidly ends when the men discover that Daisy expects that whoever she chooses will work for her white folks—washing windows, sweeping the sidewalk, hoeing, raking, and gardening. Although she has tentatively chosen Jim, the prospect of such employment causes her charms to diminish in his eyes. Dave has a similar reaction. The two men are reconciled, and Daisy is left without either of her lovers.

Daisy tells them, "Both of you niggers can git yo' hat on yo' heads and git on down de road. Neither one of y'all don't have to have me. I got a good job and plenty men beggin' for yo' chance." Jim heaves a sigh of relief: "Dat's right, Daisy, you go git you one them mens whut don't mind smellin' mules—and beatin' de white folks to de barn every mornin'. I don't wanta be bothered wid nothin' but dis box." Dave supports his buddy: "An' I can't strain wid nothin' but my feets." The good friends return to Eatonville, daring any townsman to deny them access to their community.

Although much could be said about this play, the most pertinent commentary has to do with authorial intention. Hughes claimed that they were trying to create "the first real Negro folk comedy"; what he meant, I think, was that the play could be contrasted with the black low-life comedy familiar to American theatergoers as the minstrel show. The minstrel stereotypes of the lazy, sensual, ignorant, laughing darky had been challenged by revue performers of the twenties such as Bert Williams; they had triumphed in spite of the tradition, on the basis of sheer talent rather than their stage roles. Hughes and Hurston, however, attempted to create a play that would be a part of what Larry Neal has called "a truly original Black literature," an attempt to portray the black folk in such a way as "to establish some new categories of perception; new ways of seeing a culture which had been caricatured by the white minstrel tradition, made hokey and sentimental by the nineteenth century local colorists, debased by the dialect poets, and finally made a 'primitive' aphrodisiac by the new sexualism of the twenties."[8] "Mule Bone" did not quite achieve this new mode of perception, but one wonders if its authors' continued collaboration might not have produced a breakthrough. The play that was originally titled "The Bone of Contention" turned out to be truer to its title than to its purposes.

One example will suffice to show the subtlety of the authors' attempt. The courting ritual in the final scene is a traditional mode of verbal lovemaking among southern rural black folk, very possibly African in origin. Some of the first recorded rituals appeared in 1895 in the *Southern Workman,* Hampton Institute's monthly magazine, written by a man remembering the tradition-bearer role that an old slave named Uncle Gilbert contributed to the quarters. Young slaves would go to Uncle Gilbert to learn "courtship's words and ways." The old man believed that to "git a gal wuth havin" a man 'mus' know how to talk fur her." Such talking involved a combination of testing the girl's availability, her willingness to be courted, her skill in solving riddles, and the suitor's ability to display verbal improvisation. Certain formulas and rhymes were set, others improvised at the moment. The slave's proof of his affection is similar to Dave's purchase of a passenger train or Jim's buying an ocean; yet the point is not the implausibility, but the imagination that thought of the example: "Kin' lady, ef I was to go up between de heavens and de' yearth an drop down a grain of wheat over ten acres of land an' plow it up wid a rooster fedder, would you marry me?" Courtship testimony from the folklorist in 1895—"Dear Miss, ef I was starvin' an' had jes one ginger cake, I would give you half, an' dat would be de bigges' half"—is similar to "Mule Bone" 's "If I was dead and any other woman came near my coffin de undertaker would have to do his job all over—'cause I'd git right up and walk off." A direct connection between act 3 of "Mule Bone" and traditional courting rituals is found in Dave's question to Daisy following one of his boasts: "Miss Daisy, ma'am, also ma'am, which would you ruther be—a lark a flyin' or a dove a-settin', ma'am, also ma'am?" In 1895 Portia Smiley reported the following as a part of courting rituals in Alabama: "Kin' lady, are yo' a standin' dove or a flyin lark? Would you decide to trot in double harness, and will you give de most excrutish pleasure of rollin' de wheels of de axil, accordin' to your understandin'?" In *Negro Folk Rhymes* (1922), Thomas W. Talley includes a similar exchange in the section on courtship rhymes:

> (He) Is you a flyin' lark or a settin' dove?
> (She) I'se a flyin' lark, my honey Love.
> (He) Is you a bird o' one fedder, or a bird o' two?
> (She) I'se a bird o' one fedder, w'en it comes to you.
> (He) Den, Mam:
>   I has desire, an' quick temptation,
>   To jine my fence to yo plantation.[9]

Hurston had collected such rituals and had sent some examples to Hughes. They were both aware that the genre was traditional, and they were consciously trying to represent for the stage the folkloric context. If successful, they would be able to undermine the minstrel image of the ignorant black man using long words he did not understand, the stereotyped conception of black verbal art. If done well, the verbal duel would prove the rhyming ability, the ingenious improvisation, and the general wit of black folk, who were anything but ignorant or inarticulate. A play like "Mule Bone" could challenge racist preconceptions by remaining true to the traditions of "lowly" black peasants; it could destroy stereotypes by entertaining a "cultured" audience with the functional comedy of the Eatonville community. The courtship rituals were behavioral manifestations of a unique aspect of Afro-American subculture, and "Mule Bone" could represent that behavior in a way never realized on the stage before. Contrary to Van Vechten's hope that "Mule Bone" might become another *Green Pastures,* the effect of the play was intended to be quite different. *Green Pastures,* a well-meaning play by a white author, was redeemed from comic stereotypes by black actors. As Du Bois pointed out, it was "de Lawd," Richard Harrison, who had "guided a genial comedy into a great and human drama."[10] "Mule Bone" was "Negro folk comedy" written by two black authors who designed the play around the traditional verbal behavior of black people. Its comedy came not so much from the authors' wit as from the skillful verbal communication of the folk. It never came to the stage because of the authors' quarreling over authorship. Yet in a sense it was written by neither Hurston nor Hughes. Much of the language in the play belonged to the race itself, making the argument over its ownership even more ironic.

The "Mule Bone" quarrel took place at the same time Hurston was working hard to prepare her field notes for public attention, and the play was influenced by an uncertainty about the best medium for popular consumption of Afro-American folklore. The presentation model offered by Boas and Locke was the scientific article—a most unliterary genre—in which the scholar subordinated personality in order to report factually on phenomena observed. The audience addressed was narrow and extraordinarily fickle, with a minimal capacity for an immediate effect on popular attitudes. Fretting scrutiny would follow the announcement of her findings, and even scholarly acceptance would be no guarantee of validity; as Hurston had seen with scientists like Odum and Johnson, truth was a culturally determined commodity. The adaptation of folklore for the stage in "real Negro theatre" was a possibility she had been drawn to for years. Yet the form necessarily compromised the authenticity of the lore; a hunter's quarrel had to become a lover's triangle to heighten dramatic conflict. The personal essay, published in forums accessible to the general public, had much to recommend it, but most mass-circulation magazines were controlled by whites, and if black material was accepted at all, it had to deal with the "race problem."

Hurston knew that her collections were unique and that she could write well enough to publish her findings in whatever form she chose. She spent considerable effort searching for the most appropriate medium. Songs and dances lost all life when confined to the written page. The communal participation in a tale-telling session disappeared when the folklorist intruded on the event. Yet a collector was not faceless. How did she report dispassionately on what she called the "boiled down juice of human living"? How did she camouflage a belief that "the greatest cultural wealth of the continent" was being ignored, and that she was the person who could save it from obscurity? Hurston used many presentational media in the next few years; all her efforts were characterized by an evangelical zeal for the form and substance of black folk art. Her missionary spirit was submerged in her scholarly attempts, left implicit in her career as a producer of folk drama, and proudly proclaimed in popular essays and *Mules and Men*.

Hurston came to speak for the esthetic consciousness of the "Negro farthest down," and her message was broadcast in many creative forms. "Mule Bone" was only one attempt to find an individual art commensurate with the native esthetics of her people.[11]

Notes

1. This chapter is based primarily on a file of letters and documents found in HUAL, including a twelve-page explanation of the entire "Mule Bone" episode written by Hughes and sent to Spingarn on Jan. 21, 1931; a complete version and other partial versions of "Mule Bone" in HUAL; LH, *The Big Sea* (New York: Hill and Wang, 1963), pp. 311–34; and my interview with LTP, June 22, 1976, in New York City. In reconstructing the episode from these materials and other published and unpublished sources, I have noted only those documents not in HUAL, and I have quoted directly only from Hurston's letters. My account comes chiefly from the following in HUAL: ZNH to LH, Jan. 18, Jan. 20 (two telegrams), Feb. 14, Mar. 18, 1931; ZNH to Mrs. Mason, Jan. 20, Mar. 25, Apr. 18, Aug. 14, 1931, Mar. 27, 1932; ZNH to AS, Mar. 25, 1931; ZNH to AL, Oct. 29, 1934; LH to ZNH, Jan. 16, 22, 27 (two letters); LH to AS, Jan. 21, 24, 26, 27, 30, Feb. 3, Mar. 6, 15, Aug. 14, 1931; LH to AL, Jan. 28, 1931; AL telegram to LH, Jan. 29, 1931; AS to LH, Jan. 24, 27, 28, Feb. 5, Mar. 5, 1931; LTP to LH, Jan. 28, 1931; Rowena Jelliffe to AS, Jan. 30, 1931; return receipt, registered mail, for LH to ZNH, Jan. 18, 1931; copyright notification for "Mule Bone," received Jan. 22, 1931.

2. This letter is not complete. Apparently Hughes kept the last page of the letter for personal reasons. As it has survived, the letter breaks off at this point: "I didn't intend to be evasive. With anyone else but you I could have said a plenty. Would have done so long ago but I have been thinking of you as my best friend for so long, and as I am not in love with anyone, that [rest of letter missing]."

3. Arna Bontemps to LH, Nov. 24, 1939 (JWJYale).

4. RH interview with LTP, June 22, 1976, New York City; Bruce Kellner (CVV's biographer) to RH, Sept. 1, 1972, quoting a letter from CVV to LH.

5. ZNH to AS, Mar. 25, 1931 (HUAL).

6. ZNH to Harold Jackman, Dec. 15, 1933; CVV, manuscript notes, "Introduction to the James Weldon Johnson Memorial Collection," p. 224; ZNH to CVV, Jan. 22, 1934 (JWJYale).

7. "Mule Bone: A Comedy of Negro Life," by LH and ZNH, mimeographed (HUAL).

8. Larry Neal, "A Profile: Zora Neale Hurston," *Southern Exposure,* 1 (Winter, 1974), 162.

9. Portia Smiley, "Folklore and Ethnography," *Southern Workman,* 24 (1895), 15; Frank D. Banks and Portia Smiley, "Old Time Courtship Conversation," ibid., pp. 14–15, 78, reprinted in *Mother Wit from the Laughing Barrel,* ed. Alan Dundes (Englewood Cliffs, N.J.: Prentice-Hall, 1973), pp. 251–57 (Dundes's notes to this article are especially valuable); Thomas W. Talley, *Negro Folk Rhymes* (New York: Macmillan, 1922), p. 135.

10. W. E. B. Du Bois, "Besides the Still Waters," *Crisis,* 38 (May, 1931), 169.

11. ZNH, "Folklore," typescript, Florida Federal Writers' Project, ca. 1938 (FHSP); ZNH to Thomas E. Jones, Oct. 12, 1934 (Fisk); ZNH, *Dust Tracks on a Road* (Philadelphia: J. B. Lippincott, 1942), p. 185.

FROM *THE LIFE OF LANGSTON HUGHES,* VOLUME I, BY ARNOLD RAMPERSAD

Back in Westfield, New Jersey, Hughes now had company. After a stay of over two years in the South (and a visit to the Bahamas) from which she had returned with a bonanza of notes on folklore, Zora Neale Hurston had moved into a roominghouse not far from his home at 514 Downer Street. Like Hughes, Hurston was there on their patron Mrs. Mason's orders. The two writers also would share the secretarial services of Louise Thompson, hired the previous September by Mrs. Mason to assist Hughes. As Thompson later recalled, Godmother had primed her for Hurston's coming: "She used to talk about Zora, about this wonderful child of nature who was so unspoiled, and what a marvellous person she was. And Zora did not disappoint me. She was a grand storyteller." Hughes himself, having found Westfield more than a little dull, also welcomed Hurston's vital, attractive presence. While she entertained him and Louise Thompson with tales of her escapades in the Florida wilds, imitating and parodying her folk subjects with almost uncanny theatrical gifts, he languidly awaited the arrival of proofs of his novel, *Not Without Laughter,* and copies of his *Four Lincoln Poets.*

Although Hurston had reported religiously from the South to Mrs. Mason and to Alain Locke, Hughes had emerged as her most dependable ally, a calm, strong force essential (so Hurston often protested) to her growth as an artist, especially in their proposed collaboration on a folk opera. "Langston, Langston," Zora had written from Eaton-ville, Florida, in March, 1928, "this is going to be big. . . . Remember I am new and we want to do this tremendous thing with all the fire that genius can bring. I need your hand." Wanting him closer, she urged Hughes to join her for a care-free ramble in the South, like their journey in the summer of 1927. She offered to share fifty-fifty with him, even forty-sixty, any profits that came from their collaboration, since he was "so much more practical than I." Although Hughes did not join her, Hurston kept up her adulation. "Without flattery . . . you are the brains of this argosy," she insisted, "all the ideas have come out of your head." Months later, she was still praising Hughes. "You are always helpful," she declared, "in fact you are the expedition." Excited over the prospect of an artists' colony in Eau Gallie, Florida, for Negroes ("NO niggers," she vowed), Hurston envisioned them living and working there in an ideal community shared by Wallace Thurman, Aaron Douglas, and other gifted members of the "Nig-gerati."

Much of this praise, in fact, was nothing more than flat-tery, one of the less attractive habits in Hurston's effulgent way of life. Sometimes out of necessity, perhaps more often out of her own deep-seated sense of vulnerability, Hurston tended to live by her wits—and successfully so. Once, she had moved into a Manhattan apartment "with no furniture at all and no money" (Hughes recalled with wonder), and "in a few days friends had given her everything, from decorative silver birds, perched atop the linen cabinet, down to a footstool." One day, on her way to the Manhattan subway, Hurston fished a nickel from a blind man's cup. "I need money worse than you today," she assured him. "Lend me this! Next time, I'll give it back." On the other hand, Hurston matched Hughes in his deep regard for black folk culture; also, she genuinely liked him. In turn, he looked out for her interests with God-mother. When Mrs. Mason grumbled about Zora's letters, he urged Hurston to write more often and in a different tone, and tipped her off about the kind of gift sure to please God-mother—wood carvings, driftwood, orange blossoms, and melons, like his own inspired gift of corn and evergreen branch ends (or a book such as Martha Beckwith's *Black Road-ways: A Study of Jamaican Folk Life,* which Hughes offered to Godmother as "Studies from Obeah Land"). Going further, he once warned Hurston to be more discreet with Alain Locke, who sometimes betrayed her confidences to God-mother. Unlike Hughes, Locke put no one before his lucrative relationship with Mrs. Mason; finding out that Godmother disliked his friend Wally Thurman, Locke offered to arrange a sneak attack on him in a publication. "The trouble with Locke," Hurston judged, "is that he is intellectually dishonest. He is too eager to be with the winner." Hughes, on the other hand, could be trusted to do his best to keep her in God-mother's good graces.

In Westfield together, Hughes and Hurston built on the goodwill developed in their correspondence; they were also frequently in New York at Louise Thompson's apartment at 435 Convent Avenue. Then, almost certainly from Locke, Godmother heard that there was too much playing and too little work going on in Westfield. Her displeasure was electric, and everyone felt the shock. Instead of upbraiding Hurston, Mrs. Mason snubbed her. When Hughes tried to soothe God-mother with a telephone call, he was brushed off by someone at her Park Avenue home obviously acting under instructions. Mainly on Hurston's behalf, he quickly drafted a calming letter. When Godmother relented, he sent a longer letter of apology—for what, he wasn't sure. He had been "terribly worried because Zora and I both felt that you had been dis-pleased, or hurt in some way about her work." Zora was "miserable," but he had been wrong to telephone and disturb

Godmother. "I do care for you," he wrote, "and when I hurt you through stupidity or error, I cannot bear it. . . . Whatever happened last week to make you unhappy must have been my fault—not Zora's. . . . But maybe I'm all wrong—all tangled up. You will forgive me if I do not understand. Perhaps it is all 'nerves' on my part. 'Emotional instability' or whatever they call it."

Although Godmother forgave him, Hughes understood that he was being watched. Mrs. Mason was angry that he had not plunged into work immediately after his return from Cuba, but the idea that she would tell him when and where to work chilled him. The novel was one thing; his writing in general was another. A short time later, he would write to Mrs. Mason about his instinctive reaction to her despotism. "So far in this world," he declared, "only my writing has been my own, to do when I wanted to do it, to finish only when I felt it was finished, to put it aside or discard it completely if I chose. . . . I have washed thousands of hotel dishes, cooked, scrubbed decks, worked 12 to 15 hours a day on a farm, swallowed my pride for the help of philanthropy and charity—but nobody ever said to me 'you must write now. You must finish that poem tomorrow. You must begin to create on the first of the month'." Godmother had gone too far.

For the moment, however, he kept his resentment to himself. Sometime in April, about a month after his return from Cuba, he began to work on a play with Hurston. Shelving their plans for a high-toned folk opera, in response to a casual complaint from Theresa Helburn of the Dramatists Guild that most scripts about black life were too grimly earnest, they decided to write a folk comedy. The basic plot came from a story, "The Bone of Contention," collected by Hurston, about two hunters who quarrel over the question of which one has shot a turkey. After one knocks out the other with the hockbone of a mule, he is tried on charges of assault and battery. Before an excitable crowd of black townsfolk, the example of Samson and the jawbone of an ass is invoked grandiloquently against the wielder of the mule bone, who is convicted and banished from the town. Uncertain how Godmother would react to such a project, Hughes and Hurston worked for a while without her permission. Hughes was responsible for "the plot, construction, and guiding the dialog toward the necessary situations and climaxes," he would recall; Hurston provided "the little story," gave the dialogue its Southern flavor and many of the 'wisecracks'." She had contributed a very brief play to *Fire!!* but did not feel very comfortable writing for the theater; with only the unfinished singing play about Haiti to his credit, Hughes nevertheless was more confident about his ability as a dramatist. Nevertheless, Hurston's contribution was almost certainly the greater to a play set in an all-black town in the backwoods South (she drew here on her childhood memories), with an abundance of tall tales, wicked quips, and farcical styles of which she was absolute master and Langston not much more than a sometime student. With Hughes and Louise Thompson laughing helplessly, she acted out male and female roles in a variety of voices. Whatever dramatic distinction the play would have, Hurston certainly brought to it. But "Mule Bone," as it was called, was at least as much a collaboration as, for example, that between Wallace Thurman and William Jourdan Rapp, who had tailored Thurman's *Harlem* into a Broadway property.

With Thompson typing almost as quickly as they invented, Hughes and Hurston made excellent progress. Then Zora seemed to grow tired of the project, becoming "restless and moody, working in a nervous manner." But, Langston reasoned, she had always been restless and moody. Moreover, while he was relatively unencumbered, Zora had to return to her massive folklore project and endure constant scrutiny from Locke and Mrs. Mason. Still, Hughes was very surprised when, with "Mule Bone" near completion but still in need of serious work, Hurston suddenly left New Jersey and moved to Manhattan. She was en route, she said, back to the South, but promised to work further on one act of "Mule Bone."

Hughes's disappointment at Hurston's departure from Westfield was completely overshadowed near the end of May, however, by the collapse of his friendship with Godmother. While the precise cause of the rupture would remain unclear even to Hughes, he took it to be a result of Godmother's displeasure over his unwillingness to return to work following his return from Cuba. Certainly the new quarrel involved a trip late in May to Washington, D.C.; when Godmother argued that he should stay home and write, Hughes rebelled against her authority and committed himself to go. This time, as if primed for destruction, the enraged Mrs. Mason went much further than she had gone before, much further than he ever imagined she would go in accusing him of ingratitude and disloyalty. "The way she talked to Langston," Louise Thompson would remember from Hughes's account later that day, "is the way a woman talks when she's keeping a pimp. 'I bought those clothes you are wearing! I took care of you! I gave you this! I gave you that!' " Godmother counted out precisely to Hughes his cost to her—$225 a month, of which $150 comprised his stipend and $75 half of Louise Thompson's time; in return, he was giving her—nothing!

Nine years later, in a reticent account of their relationship, in which Hughes never identified Mrs. Mason by name (she was still alive), he did not hide his extreme pain in their last meeting:

> I cannot write here about that last half-hour in the big bright drawing-room high above Park Avenue one morning, because when I think about it, even now, something happens in the pit of my stomach that makes me ill. That beautiful room, that had been so full of light and help and understanding for

me, suddenly became like a trap closing in, faster
and faster, the room darker and darker, until the
light went out with a sudden crash in the dark, and
everything became like that night in Kansas when
I had failed to see Jesus and had lied about it after-
wards. Or that morning in Mexico when I suddenly
hated my father.

Shattered by her words, his body betraying a neurotic
turmoil that made his muscles twitch involuntarily and his
fingers curl into bizarre shapes, he rode the train to Washington. Although he made his rounds in the city (in one place
going over a gift copy of Nicolás Guillén's newly arrived
pamphlet of poems, *Motivos de Son,* with a Cuban acquaint-
ance), Godmother dominated his mind. To Alain Locke,
Hughes poured out his hurt and confusion; listening carefully,
Locke softly tendered advice. Whatever he counselled, when
Langston finally wrote Godmother he begged her to release
him, "or rather to release yourself from the burdens of my
own lack of wisdom." Hughes flogged himself unsparingly.
"The fault is mine. The darkness is mine. The search is mine.
The Gods have given me the . . . light of your kindness and
I do not know how to follow." He offered to settle all financial
accounts ($200 in the bank, $37.94 elsewhere). Then they
could go back to the happier time when money did not come
between them: "The beauty of your gifts and the things of
your spirit are written in my heart—not in an account book."
"I should adore coming to see you when ever you will me to,"
he promised Godmother, "and I know you have loved the
better part of my self with the most beautiful love . . . a being
can know in this world."

To facilitate his financial break with Mrs. Mason he
turned to Carl Van Vechten, who lent him $200, then noted
Hughes's visit on May 26 in his diary: "His patron has failed
him & he borrows some money." . . .

. . . A new wave of illness overtook Hughes—a chronic toothache, tonsilitis, an upset stomach. With Godmother back in Manhattan after the summer, he moved cautiously. He sent her all the reviews of his novel from English and American papers; without enthusiasm, she acknowledged his letter, but advised him only to have his tonsils removed. Leaving Hedgerow near the end of October, he returned to Westfield in time to speak at an inter-racial conference at the recently opened Riverside Church in Manhattan, which the theologian Reinhold Niebuhr also addressed. At last, after several attempts, Hughes succeeded in reaching Zora Hurston, but when he begged her to resume work on their play, "Mule Bone," she was evasive, hesitated before settling on a meeting, then failed to keep their appointments. Still Hughes did not connect Hurston's behavior to his falling out with Godmother; Zora was notorious for unpunctuality even in Harlem. In fact, Hurston was looking for a dramatic stroke to sunder their link and affirm her total loyalty to Godmother. She made this desire clear in a letter to Mrs. Mason on November 25 from Asbury Park: "You love me. You have proved it. It is up to *me* now to let you see what my behavior of love looks like. So watch your sun-burnt child do some scuffling. That is the thing that I have lacked—the urge to push hard and insist on a hearing." She would be in town soon to see what "a certain person has to say to me." Her "scuffling," indeed, had already begun. . . .

. . . At last accepting as a fact that Godmother would not see him, Hughes planned to leave Westfield and the New York area—and without telling Mrs. Mason. After attending the usual parties in Manhattan, including one at Knopf's, he welcomed 1931 in Cleveland, to which his mother had just moved. Langston planned to stay at her home at 4800 Carnegie Avenue for only three weeks or so, then head south to Florida, with his trip financed from a check expected from Godmother early in January. But on January 10 Mrs. Mason informed him that no check would be sent—as "by mere accident it came to me that you had gone and where you were. Dear child, what am I to believe, what am I to think under these circumstances? Will the sap rise in the trees that the blossoms may come in the spring?"

Without money to visit Florida, Hughes settled in with his mother for a stay that would last three months. Cleveland was a changed city. Most astonishing of all was the spread of blacks in the decade since his graduation; from 22nd to 110th Street and beyond, mile after mile of once-white blocks now teemed with blacks. Central High School, where he had been one of a handful of colored students, was now more than fifty percent black. Returning in glory, he read his poems to the students and teachers; he also spoke to school officials in the wealthy district of Shaker Heights. Lecturing on modern writing, Hughes argued the superiority of new writers such as Hemingway, Sandburg, Millay, and Masters over virtually all the established names in American literature, excepting Whitman and Dickinson. He also visited his old friends Rowena and Russell Jelliffe, whose drama troupe, the Gilpin Players, had become probably the outstanding amateur black theatrical organization in the nation. Mrs. Jelliffe shared some good news with him. Always on the look-out for suitable new plays for blacks, she had just been offered a rich folk comedy, written by a young woman in New York, which the Gilpins would open on February 15. Within seconds, Langston recognized "Mule Bone," his collaboration with Zora Hurston. But his name was nowhere on the script sent by the reputable Samuel French play agency to the Gilpin Players.

On November 14 of the previous year, Hughes soon discovered, Hurston had delivered the play to Van Vechten for a reading. Admiring it, but without informing her, Van Vechten had sent "Mule Bone" to the Theatre Guild for consideration. An official of the Guild, Barrett Clark, certain that the Guild would not use "Mule Bone," had passed it on with high praise to the Gilpins in his capacity as an employee of the Samuel French agency. But why was Hughes's name not on the script? Only later would he discover that the previous October, while he was at Hedgerow, Zora Hurston had copyrighted "Mule Bone" exclusively in her name; she had then sent it to Van Vechten without mentioning Hughes's name. This was the start of the "scuffling" she had promised Godmother, and the main reason she had evaded Hughes in the fall.

Astonished, Hughes wrote Hurston at once for an explanation. By Friday, January 16, when she had not replied, he wrote Van Vechten for advice: "Would you do anything, or nothing, in the present situation, if you were me?" He was "amazed" by Zora; "is there something about the very word theater that turns people into thieves?" Friendly with both writers, Van Vechten advised only that Hughes had to do *something.* Hughes began gathering material and evidence; he also wrote Hurston threatening litigation.

On Saturday, January 17, Louise Thompson arrived in Cleveland. She was not there to see Langston or the Jelliffes but travelling as part of her job with the American Interracial Seminar, a non-partisan, non-propagandist group founded the previous fall with the goal of improving race relations. To the Jelliffes, Thompson backed Hughes's assertion of joint authorship. Then, later that day, Langston finally talked on the telephone to Hurston. Genuinely surprised to learn that the play was in Cleveland, she was not enthusiastic about an amateur production; on this point she had the support of Van Vechten, Fania Marinoff, Lawrence Langner, and other knowledgeable theater persons. As for the matter of authorship, it was too complicated to discuss on the telephone. She would write a letter to Hughes.

The next day, when Hurston went to see Van Vechten, she "cried and carried on no end," he wrote Hughes; years later he would remember her throwing herself to his library floor in an absolute "tantrum." But she moved more coolly on another front. Sending Hughes's complaining letters to Mrs. Mason, Hurston insisted that in "Mule Bone," "I am not using one single solitary bit in dialogue, plot nor situation from him and yet he tries to muscle in." On January 20, when Langston received her promised letter, Hurston denied his claim of co-authorship. But she also claimed grounds for grievance. Langston, she accused, had taken Louise Thompson's side against her in Westfield, bettering Louise's working hours and allowing her to be late for work; then, after Thompson had tried to cut in (so Hurston said) on future royalties of the play, he had proposed her as its business manager, when the play was produced. "By this time," Zora asserted, "I had come to feel that I hadn't much of a chance in that combination." She capped these charges with protestations of affection for him, but made it clear that her interest was not romantic. He could have anything he wanted. "Tears unceasing have poured down inside me," she wailed. But the play was her own: "I told Godmother that I had done my play all by myself, and so I did, and for the reasons stated above."

This was not Hurston's first expropriation of another person's material; in October, 1927, for example, she had published an essay that was, according to her biographer, "25 percent original research and the rest shameless plagiarism." But the theft of the play was probably secondary. Either mistaking or deliberately misrepresenting the relationship between Hughes and Thompson, she had characterized it as an affair to Godmother, who carefully noted Hurston's information that Langston and Louise often "went off to his rooms" while Zora toiled, then would return and say, "Let's see how much you got done then—that's fine *we're* getting along splendidly." Unquestionably, Hurston had wanted Thompson fired. Instead, Zora caused something she probably had not expected—that Mrs. Mason would summarily banish Langston. And, in banishing him, frighten Hurston into not only shunning his company but also denying that they had ever collaborated on "Mule Bone." Thus it became essential to Hurston to discredit both Hughes and Louise Thompson, although her main target was Thompson. "It is just as we know," she wrote Godmother, "Langston is weak. Weak as water. When he has a vile wretch to push him he gets vile. When he is under noble influences like yours, you know how fine he can be." Perhaps he should have another chance. "He is ashamed of his attitude about the play and apologized to me for it."

Although Hurston had acted like a lover spurned, there is no evidence either that an intimate relationship ever existed between herself and Hughes, or that Hurston even wanted one. And, according to Louise Thompson later, if Hurston spoke of an affair between Louise and Langston, "well, she's just lying. She's just lying. Because there was never any relationship between Langston and me other than as a brother. . . . If Langston had approached me in another way, I might have been receptive, but he never did. I accepted Langston on that plane, that we were the best of friends and comrades." (After knowing him most of his life, she would judge Hughes to have been "asexual"; as for suggestions that he was a homosexual, *"that* I felt was not true. I never had in any sense any intimation that he was that way.") Hurston's suspicion of Thompson seems to have been based on little more than a general sense of insecurity with a woman younger, prettier, more poised, and, although in a more orthodox way, as intelligent as Hurston herself.

Most interesting of all, in what was in effect an unusual emotional quadrangle, was Godmother's violent reaction to Zora's insinuations. Mrs. Mason behaved either like someone impossibly moral—or like a wronged, revengeful lover.

On January 20, the Samuel French agency wired the Jelliffes that Hurston had denied permission for their production. Langston then drew up an eleven-page letter to his law-yer, Arthur Spingarn, offering a compromise. Two-thirds of the royalties would go to Hurston, one-third to Hughes. But Zora had suddenly changed her position. Wiring her approval to the Jelliffes, she followed with two more affirmative tele-grams and promised to come to Cleveland at the end of the month. Weary but relieved, Hughes wrote Van Vechten that "the split is over."

Langston had other troubles. He spent the night of Janu-ary 21 in jail. With two black friends, he had left a car on busy Cedar Avenue to make a phone call. When they returned, a taxi driver accused them of denting the back of his cab. After two squad cars arrived, the police threatened the three with beatings unless they confessed. A paddy wagon took them to the station, where the owner of the car was roughed up and struck with clubs. But none "confessed"; they hadn't touched the cab. In jail overnight in a bitterly cold cell, with only a board to sleep on and no blanket, Hughes understood at last what Bessie Smith really meant in moaning of "Thirty days in jail / With ma back turned to de wall." In the morning they were released after signing "suspicious person" slips.

An even greater disappointment came later in the day. Hoping to publish his third book of verse with Knopf, Hughes had sent Van Vechten a collection of his poems, "The Singing Dark." But Van Vechten not only disparaged the title (people would call it, or Hughes, "The Singing Darkey")—the vol-ume would add nothing to Langston's reputation, since it contained no single poem as fine as "The Weary Blues" or "Mulatto." "I shouldn't wonder," Van Vechten said point-edly, "if you are pretty nearly through with poetry." Having sent the poems apologetically, knowing well that he had writ-ten nothing really significant since the appearance of *Fine Clothes to the Jew,* Hughes was hurt but not surprised by Van Vechten's judgment. Still, he revised the manuscript and sent it as "A House in the World" to Knopf, where it was quickly rejected. An editor, Bernard Smith, was "rather disappointed." The nonracial lyrics were "neither distinguished nor important"; all the best poems were in the section devoted to racial protest, but these were not enough. After the high quality of *Not Without Laughter,* the book would be "an act of retrogression."

The solitary bright note of the winter was the news that he had indeed been given the award for which Locke had nominated him—a prize of $400 and a gold medal for distinguished achievement among blacks in literature by the Harmon Foundation, established in 1922 to promote black participation in the fine arts; Cullen had won it in 1927, McKay in 1929. The largest single sum of money Hughes had ever possessed outright, the prize smelled now of freedom. Also encouraging, if also retrospective, was a request from Effie Lee Power, a white Cleveland librarian and a national adviser on children's books, for a selection of his poems suitable for younger people, who almost always responded keenly to Hughes's work. He sent her a selection that would be published by Knopf the following year (with an introduction by Power) as *The Dream Keeper.*

With "A House in the World" refused, Hughes needed the Gilpin production of "Mule Bone" to boost his morale. Thus he was glad to know that Zora Hurston planned to arrive in Cleveland on February 1, his twenty-ninth birthday. By this time, however, unknown to Hughes, she had a powerful ally against him—Alain Locke, who had just quietly and maliciously killed Louise Thompson's chances for a job with the economist Dr. Abram Harris at Howard University by describing her as indigent (as he let Godmother know). Assuring Mrs. Mason that he would back Hurston to the hilt against Hughes, Locke sadly reported the news of the Harmon award—"the tragedy is the credit will go to swell the false egotism that at present denies its own best insight." This "false egotism" was Hughes's attempts to alter his relationship with

Godmother, which Locke saw as endangering all her godchildren, especially himself.

Late on February 1, Hurston and Hughes met and apparently resolved their differences. Hurston, however, had nonchalantly missed a meeting she had promised to attend earlier that day with the Gilpin Players; fed up with the controversy, the group voted to cancel the play. Hurston was deeply offended. Russell and Rowena Jelliffe then decided to make a last attempt to salvage the production. Because Hughes was bedridden with influenza and tonsilitis, a meeting with Hurston was set for the afternoon of February 3 at his mother's home. Discovering, however, that Louise Thompson had been in Cleveland, Zora arrived at Hughes's home in an evil mood. "She made such a scene as you can not possibly imagine," he wrote Van Vechten the next day; "she pushed her hat back, bucked her eyes, ground her teeth, and shook manuscripts in my face particularly the third act which she claims she wrote alone by herself while Miss Thompson and I were off doing Spanish together. (And the way she said *Spanish* meant something else)." When Mrs. Jelliffe intervened, Hurston denounced her as a trickster, then ridiculed her sixteen years of community work in Cleveland. Throughout this tirade, the stricken Hughes did little more than gasp weakly; but when Hurston made to storm from the house, Carrie Clark suddenly leaped into the fray with some blistering words of her own. "Carrie was absolutely magnificent," Mrs. Jelliffe would recall; "for once she stood up for Langston and helped him. She let Zora have it in no uncertain terms. We were all very proud of her." But Hurston had achieved her goal. At 6:30 that evening she sent a triumphant telegram to Park Avenue: "DARLING GODMOTHER ARRIVED SAFELY HAVE PUT THE PERSON ON THE RUN PLAY STOPPED LOUISE THOMPSON HAD BEEN SENT FOR TO BOLSTER CASE I SMASHED THEM ALL BE HOME BY WEEKEND ALL MY LOVE ZORA."

"Do you think she is crazy, Carl?" Hughes inquired the next day of Van Vechten.

Knowing now what he was up against, Hughes made a deathbed appeal to Godmother. His appeal was denied. "What a sorrowful misguided way to have come!" Mrs. Mason mourned on February 12. "Has not the year spent tarnishing your wings proved that 'keeping accounts' had nothing to do with your failure to do creative writing? . . . Child, why build a labyrinth about yourself that causes you to wander in a miasma of untruth?"

Knocked into a relapse by her accusation of dishonesty, Hughes felt his whole body poisoned. He blamed his tonsils, but an astute doctor recommended the sun. After a week or so, Langston wrote a very brief note to "Dear Godmother": "When the sun shines again I will write you a long letter. Now, my thanks, and my love to you, as always."

Although he would never write this "long letter," Hughes could not say goodbye. When the Harmon medals came (there were actually two) he sent them like a child to her for her admiration. But she was like stone. "Langston," Mrs. Mason admonished him, alluding to the old woman of his novel, "do hurry to recognize the travail of Aunt Hagar to bring you face to face with yourself."

At 399 Park Avenue, Locke and Hurston hammered his coffin shut. When Hughes wired his favorite Harlem photographer, James L. Allen, for a set of portraits, Locke reported to Mrs. Mason that he evidently was preparing "a signed author's portrait racket." Hughes wrote a friend in Florida about a possible visit; Locke saw "a mad careening before a big fall." As for Langston's hopes to go to the Caribbean, "isn't that shameful—or rather shameless," Locke asked. "Well—he'll have a long rope—but eventually it will pull taut." To the Labarees at Lincoln, who heard of Hughes's illness, Locke intimated that he was having a nervous breakdown. To someone Langston challenged about the unauthorized use of his work, Locke apologized for Hughes's "real mean-ness." Against Van Vechten, who still befriended both Hurston and Hughes, Locke cried out to Mrs. Mason: "Why can't he die! Nothing seems to kill him." Not to be outdone, Hurston elbowed Locke out of the way to kneel behind God-mother. "Dear Godmother, the guard-mother who sits in the Twelfth Heaven and shapes the destiny of the primitives," one March letter began. And later: "Knowing you is like Sir Perci-val's glimpse of the holy grail. Next to Mahatma Gandhi, you are the most spiritual person on earth." Hurston stuck by her charges of Langston's corruption. "I can't conceive of such lying and falsehood," she sighed; "but then there are many things in earth and sky that I don't know about." A year later, more amusingly: "Honest Godmother it requires all my self-restraint to keep from tearing the gin-hound to pieces. If I followed my emotions I'd take a weapon and go around the ham-bone looking for meat." And to Arthur Spingarn, Lang-ston's lawyer, Zora suggested that he should write a play for his client, if Hughes wanted one so badly. "Or perhaps a nice box of apples and a well chosen corner. But never no play of mine."

By this time, Hurston perhaps had internalized the con-viction that Hughes had had no part in the play; how she was able to do so is a mystery, perhaps a part of her imaginative genius itself. Whether she ever regretted her deception is unclear. Eight years later, Arna Bontemps would report to Hughes that she was "a changed woman, still her old humor-ous self, but more level and poised. She told me that the cross of her life is the fact that there has been a gulf between you and her. She said she wakes up at night crying about it even yet." Certainly Hurston had matured as a writer; in the inter-vening years she would publish two novels, including her masterpiece, *Their Eyes Were Watching God,* about a black woman's experience first of a near-perfect love, then of the more profound satisfaction of a noble, feminist self-reliance.

Hurston's desire for a reconciliation with Hughes was probably wrecked by his droll, teasing treatment in *The Big Sea* of her quixotic behavior during the controversy; two years later, when Hurston published her own autobiography, *Dust Tracks on a Road,* she left out Hughes altogether. After "Mule Bone," the two writers apparently met only once. But, incredibly, when Hurston needed help during the most humiliating episode of her life, in which she faced prosecution on a sordid (but unfounded) morals charge, she would turn for a testament to her good character to—Langston Hughes.

Her self-deception, in any case, was in its way not much more bizarre than Hughes's pathetic enslavement by Mrs. Mason, which Louise Thompson, for one, could never understand. "He got sick," she would remember. "When I got over it, I got mad!" Mrs. Mason was "an old witch" whose behavior made Thompson "hate the power of money," the idea "that someone because they have money can do to you as they wish and talk to you as they want to. How *dare* they!" The reason for the difference between Langston's reaction to Mrs. Mason and her own, she guessed, was her mother's unceasing love of her and Langston's mother's neglect of him as a child. "Now I am ready to die," "Mother" Thompson had said when Louise graduated from college. "I can't imagine Carrie saying anything like that about Langston," Thompson judged flatly. The episode was as decisive as any other in urging her into an association for life with communism, just as it would drive Hughes almost as far to the left for many years, and in other ways affect the entire course of the rest of his life.

Nor was Hurston's self-deception less excusable than Mrs. Mason's abuse of her wealth, race, age, and intelligence in so torturing the lives of her blacks. In her case, the mitigating factors were that she exhibited a mental power so volatile, and cherished notions about Africa so novel for her class and race, that her inability to control herself was perhaps finally excusable. Only Locke's behavior was almost entirely reprehensible. For all his great learning he was a slippery character, too fond of intrigue and of the pleasures that Mrs. Mason's money assured. The tawdry "Mule Bone" affair rang down the curtain on one long era of Hughes's life. And in pitting black brother against sister, artist against artist, it marked just as conveniently the end of a cultural age. The highly sensitive Locke unconsciously caught a sense of this death of golden innocence in one of his reports to Godmother. "I hear almost no news now from New York," he confessed to her near the end of March; "a younger crowd of 'Newer Negroes' are dancing in the candle flame. The older ones are nursing their singed wings."

Notes

page 189 "She used to talk about Zora": Louise Thompson Patterson to author, interview, May 23, 1984.

pg 190 "Langston, Langston . . . this is going to be big": Zora Neale Hurston to LH, Mar. 8, 1928, LHP.

"so much more practical": Zora Neale Hurston to LH, May 1, 1928, LHP.

"Without flattery . . . you are the brains": Zora Neale Hurston to LH, July 10, 1928, LHP.

"You are always helpful": Zora Neale Hurston to LH, Apr. 30, 1929, LHP.

"NO niggers," she vowed: Zora Neale Hurston to LH, May 31, 1929, LHP.

"with no furniture at all": LH, *The Big Sea,* p. 239.

"I need money worse than you": LH, *The Big Sea,* p. 240.

page 191 "Studies from Obeah Land": In presentation copy, Aug. 12, 1929; courtesy of Thomas H. Wirth.

"The trouble with Locke": Zora Neale Hurston to LH, n.d., LHP.

"terribly worried because Zora and I": LH to Mrs. R. O. Mason, draft, n.d., LHP.

page 192 "So far in this world": LH to Mrs. R. O. Mason, draft, June 6 [1930], LHP.

page 193 "the plot, construction, and guiding the dialog": LH to Carl Van Vechten, Jan. 16, 1931, CVVP, Yale.

"restless and moody, working": LH, *The Big Sea,* p. 320.

page 194 "The way she talked to Langston": Louise Thompson Patterson to author, interview.

"I cannot write here": LH, *The Big Sea,* p. 325.

page 195 "or rather to release yourself": LH to Mrs. R. O. Mason, draft, n.d., LHP.

"His patron has failed him": Carl Van Vechten, Diary (May 26, 1930), CVVP, NYPL.

page 196 "You love me. You have proved": Zora Neale Hurston to Mrs. R. O. Mason, Nov. 25, 1930, ALLP, MSRC.

page 197 "by mere accident it came to me": Mrs. R. O. Mason to LH, Jan. 10, 1931, LHP.

page 198 "Would you do anything": LH to Carl Van Vechten, Jan. 16, 1931, CVVP, Yale.

"cried and carried on": Carl Van Vechten to LH, Jan. 20, 1931, LHP.

page 199 in an absolute "tantrum": Carl Van Vechten to LH, Aug. 17, 1942, LHP.

"I am not using one single solitary": Zora Neale Hurston to Mrs. R. O. Mason, Jan. 20, 1931, ALLP, MSRC.

"By this time . . . I had come to feel": Zora Neale Hurston to LH, n.d., LHP.

"25 percent original research": Robert E. Hemenway, *Zora Neale Hurston: A Literary Biography* (Urbana, Ill.: Univ. of Illinois, 1977), p. 96.

"went off to his rooms": Entry, Jan. 22, 1931, in Mrs. Mason's notebook, "1928 [*sic*] Data as we close 399 [Park Avenue]"; ALLP, MSRC.

page 200 "It is just as we know": Zora Neale Hurston to Mrs. R. O. Mason, Jan. 20, 1931, ALLP, MSRC.

"well, she's just lying": Louise Thompson Patterson to author, interview.

page 201 "the split is over": LH to Carl Van Vechten, Jan. 22, 1931, CVVP, Yale.

"Thirty days in jail": *Ibid.*

"I shouldn't wonder if you are": Carl Van Vechten to LH, Jan. 19, 1931, LHP.

page 202 An editor . . . was "rather disappointed": Alfred A. Knopf Inc. (Bernard Smith) to LH, Mar. 2, 1931, LHP.

"The tragedy is the credit will go": Alain Locke to Mrs. R. O. Mason, Jan. 29, 1931, ALLP, MSRC.

page 203 "She made such a scene": LH to Carl Van Vechten, Feb. 4, 1931, CVVP, Yale.

"Carrie was absolutely magnificent": Rowena Woodham Jelliffe to author, interview, Dec. 7, 1980.

"DARLING GODMOTHER ARRIVED SAFELY": Zora Neale Hurston to Mrs. R. O. Mason, Feb. 3, 1931, ALLP, MSRC.

page 204 "Do you think she is crazy": LH to Carl Van Vechten, Feb. 4, 1931, CVVP, Yale.

"What a sorrowful misguided way": Mrs. R. O. Mason to LH, Feb. 12, 1931, LHP.

"When the sun shines again": LH to Mrs. R. O. Mason, draft, Feb. 22, 1931, LHP.

"Langston . . . do hurry to recognize": Mrs. R. O. Mason to LH, Mar. 1, 1931, LHP.

"a signed author's portrait racket": Alain Locke to Mrs. R. O. Mason, Mar. 5, 1931, ALLP, MSRC.

"a mad careening": *Ibid.*

"isn't that shameful": Alain Locke to Mrs. R. O. Mason, Mar. 20, 1931, ALLP, MSRC.

page 205 Hughes's "real mean-ness": Alain Locke to Mrs. R. O. Mason, Apr. 16, 1931, ALLP, MSRC.

"Why can't he die!": Alain Locke to Mrs. R. O. Mason, Mar. 29, 1931, ALLP, MSRC.

"Dear Godmother, the guard-mother": Zora Neale Hurston to Mrs. R. O. Mason, Mar. 10, 1931, ALLP, MSRC.

"Knowing you is like Sir Percival's glimpse": Zora Neale Hurston to Mrs. R. O. Mason, Sept. 28, 1932, ALLP, MSRC.

"I can't conceive of such lying": Zora Neale Hurston to Mrs. R. O. Mason, Mar. 25, 1931, ALLP, MSRC.

"Honest Godmother it requires all my self-restraint": Zora Neale Hurston to Mrs. R. O. Mason, May 17, 1932, ALLP, MSRC.

"Or perhaps a nice box of apples": Zora Neale Hurston to Arthur B. Spingarn, Mar. 27, 1931, ABSP, MSRC.

she was "a changed woman": Arna Bontemps to LH, Nov. 24, 1939, LHP. In Charles H. Nichols, ed., *Arna Bontemps-Langston Hughes Letters: 1925–1967* (New York: Dodd, Mead, 1980), p. 44

page 206 "He got sick": Louise Thompson Patterson to author, interview.

page 207 "I hear almost no news": Alain Locke to Mrs. R. O. Mason, Mar. 29, 1931, ALLP, MSRC.

THE CORRESPONDENCE

HUGHES TO HURSTON   January 16, 1931
[incomplete]

I'd also immensely like to know your attitude about our collaboration on the play. You were so strange and evasive the last
time I saw you that I didn't know what you were about.
    Would you mind explaining it all to me?

                                        Sincerely,
                                        LH

43 W. 66th St.
New York City
January 18, 1931

DEAR LANGSTON,

I had written you a letter last week, but I have moved and in my distraction I put it in the desk drawer and found it again yesterday.

Now Langston, let us have a heart to heart chat about this play business. Please believe that what I am saying is absolutely sincere. I mean every word, so that you can bank upon it.

In the beginning, Langston, I was very eager to do the play with you. ANYthing you said would go over big with me. But scarcely had we gotten under way before you made three propositions that shook me to the foundation of myself. First: That three-way split with Louise. Now Langston, nobody has in the history of the world given a typist an interest in a work for typing it. Nobody would think of it unless they were prejudiced in favor of the typist. Not that I care what you give of yourself and your things. As Kossula says, dat don't reaches me. But I do object to having my work hi-jacked. There is no other word for it. I don't see how, even if in your magnificent gallantry you had offered it, she could have accepted it. But next day she voiced the matter herself when the subject of her pay came up. I offered to pay her five dollars a day and she said to you, trying to look hurt, "Pay me, Langston! No, I don't want a thing now, but when it goes over, then you all can take care of me then." So then I saw that the thin[g] had been agreed upon between you. First I was astounded that such a suggestion should have come from you, and next I was just plain hurt.

Then your argument that if we paid her money, that it ought to be something fancy. I still don't follow your reasoning. First you give <u>me</u> no credit for intelligence at all. Knowing the current prices for typists, you must despise my mental processes to have broached the subject at all. You know what you said, so I don't need to go into that.

Then when these had failed you come forward with the Louise-for-business-manager plan. That struck me as merely funny. With all the experienced and capable agents on Broadway, <u>I</u> should put my business in the hands of some one who knows less about the subject than I.

From all these things I could not but get the idea that your efforts were bent on turning everything into a benefit for somebody else. I say again, I have nothing to do with what you do with your own things, but I choose to bestow mine where I will. Therefore, I felt that I was among strangers, and the only thing to do was to go on away from there.

Now about the play itself. It was my story from beginning to end. It is my dialogue; my situations. But I am not concerned about that. Langston, with God as my judge, I don't care anything about the money it might make nor the glory. I'd be willing to give it all to you off-hand. But the idea of <u>you</u>, LANGSTON HUGHES, trying to use the tremendous influence that you knew you had with me that some one else might exploit me cut me to the quick. I am only human, you know. I'll be willing to bet that if you told Mrs. Mason what you did exactly, she would agree with me.

I told Godmother that I had done my play all by myself, and so I did, and for the reasons stated before. Perhaps you know that a firm is bound by the contracts of any of its members. Therefore, with what had been proposed in mind, I realized that I could expect you to be promising many things that wouldn't do me a bit of good. That and that only is my reason for going it alone. I haven't gone happily. Just felt obliged to. I didn't intend to be evasive. With anyone else but you I could have said a plenty. Would have done so long ago but I have been thinking of you as my best friend for so long, and as I am not in love with anyone, that naturally made you the nearest person to me on earth, and the things I had in mind seemed too awful to say to you, I just couldn't say them. I tried for a long time to bring the subject up with you, but I just couldn't. I just kept trying to make a joke of it to myself, but somehow the sentences in my mind wouldn't laugh themselves off. So now, it is all said.

I am sorry that you are having intestine trouble. That is what has harrassed [*sic*] me for a long time. I am glad that you are home with your mother so that you can get your stomach right. I have discovered that New York and ambition and the nervous condition that accompanies it are hard on stomachs.

Now, Langston, I have not wanted to grab things for myself. I don't want to thrust you forth or anything like that. It was just self-preservation. Suppose I had proposed such an arrangement with say, Harry Block as the beneficiary. No matter who it was, you would have acted to save yourself.

I didnt quite understand the wire from the Gilpin Players. I know no Mr. French and so I wondered what the reference meant. I don't know what you meant by it either. I should like to see the play worked out so that the things that read well but don't act well can be eliminated. I'd like to be there to offer explanations as to folk habits, etc. But I don't know how it could be arranged just now. At any rate I wonder if the producing of it would do much good. I wish to think it over. Let me hear from you about it.

With all good wishes, I am sincerely yours,

ZORA

P.S. First act recently rewritten. Synopsis of "Papa Passes" done for the first time.

You say over the phone 'my version of the play'. Are not both copies my version? I don't think that you can point out any situations or dialogue that are yours. You made some suggestions, but they are not incorporated in the play.

HUGHES TO HURSTON   4800 Carnegie Ave.,
                                            Cleveland, Ohio.
                                            January 19, 1931.

DEAR ZORA,

I'm sorry the Guild turned down Mule-Bone—but I'm also sorry it won't to them in such a shape, and in such a way. . . . This is the Cleveland situation: The Gilpin Players here are probably the best Little Theatre Negro group in the country, and for ten years have been producing plays successfully. Each year they do a downtown season. In the past they have used such plays as Roseanne, In Abraham's Bosom, etc. They do try-out plays for New York producers also, and have been offered try-outs of plays the Guild was considering. New York scouts and agents attend their openings. This year they are to open downtown at the Theatre of Nations under the auspices of The Cleveland Plain Dealer, leading white paper out here, which would mean a great deal of assured publicity right there. Then later they will move to the Ohio, one of the leading legitimate downtown theatres here. All of which means an assured two-weeks run. This would in no way hurt a New York production. In fact, it would help it, because if the play is well-received out here, New York managers will be sure to bid for it—and I think that is our best bet, now that the Guild is out of the running. I hope you will agree for it to be done here, as I think it will mean much to us both. . . . I was in touch by phone today, through Mrs. Jelliffe, manager of the Gilpin Players, with Barrett Clark, the reader who handled your play. He thinks it will be swell when whipped into shape. Mrs. Jelliffe explained the entire situation to him, and he also promised to get in direct touch with you about it. I have also written two letters to Carl, since the play seems to have reached the agent and eventually Cleveland through him. . . . Since the Gilpin Players must open on the 15th of February, some work from you by wire at once would be appreciated. I haven't your letter yet. . . . As you know, the comedy reached here entirely without my knowledge, but since it did get here, and since the Players are anxious to do it, I would be interested in seeing it go through. They would be glad to have you come out for rehearsals and the opening if you cared to do so. . . . In any case, I do not think it would be a bad beginning for our first play, and for the first Negro folk-comedy ever written. . . . Let's not be niggers about the thing, and fall out before we've even gotten started. Please wire me.

Sincerely,
L.H.

VAN VECHTEN TO HUGHES
150 West Fifty-fifth Street
New York City
[January 19, 1931]

DEAR LANGSTON,

I read <u>The Singing Dark</u> some days ago, but have not had time to write you about it. It may not subtract anything from your reputation, but it certainly will not add to it. It contains no outstanding poem like The Weary Blues or Mulatto. On the other hand it contains a great many poems based on ideas that have been better expressed by others. I shouldn't wonder if you are pretty nearly through with poetry. However, I found many of the poems admirable and some of them of almost a mystic originality—almost all of those in the section entitled

Passing Love. And I think the book would gain in force and charm if it were reduced in volume. My choice for rejection (on the grounds of banality, etc.) would be the following: Walls, Old Lincoln Theatre, Barrel House (which I remember I never liked), Bodies, To a New Dancer (If you disagree about his one, Look up Karsavina: I do not think she is dead), African Dancer in Paris, For a Woman with Cancer, Burial, To Certain Intellectuals, Brothers, Terminal, Search. Indeed, I find the entire last section (The Singing Dark) weak. Of course, everybody will call the book The Singing Darkey! What shall I do with the ms.?

Zora's performance is not very pretty, but I am not surprised. I have seen some other strange behavior there. I do not know what you can do. Even if she has entirely rewritten the play in a version of her own, she had no moral right to do so without getting your permission. However, perhaps you had better <u>try</u> to do something. I think the play is fresh and amusing and authentic and <u>if properly produced</u> will be a success. Several members of the Guild liked it enormously. So, perhaps you had better put yourself on record by telling a few people what you have just told me so that if the play makes money you can claim part of it. After all, you have standing as a writer and Zora has not and people will believe you. If the Gilpin Players are going to do it, you might threaten suit unless your rights as co-author are recognized and unless you are financially reimbursed. This is not advice. This is all suggestion. If you have a lawyer friend, you might talk it over with him. Perhaps Chestnutt might be useful right here. I think also the stenographer might be a good witness.

George Schuyler's <u>Black No More</u> is in the house, but I haven't read it. I shall certainly read <u>God Sends Sunday,</u> as soon as possible.

If you want <u>Mule Bone</u> to succeed: i.e. if you establish your rights, it is my idea that it should be done with a certain stylized exaggeration in costume and gesture (violent colors, with sunflower and watermelon backgrounds, like a Currier and Ives print) and with lots of music. This should be suggested rather than sung. What I mean is a couple o' bars here, a couple there, with some banjo strummings and a mouthorgan or two.

With Nora Holt and Donald I attended a superb drag in Harlem the other night, and then we went <u>everywhere</u>. Harlem is better than ever and wilder, and more English, and more everything, I guess. I love it! . . . I went to a party at Cora La Redd's that is probably the best party I ever went to. It was given for Harold Jackman (whom she had met the night before). So I gave a party for Harold myself, and had Billie Cain and Alma Smith and Al Moore and a few Ofays and this was rather good too . . . Eddie Wassermann went to Cuba and wanted some addresses, but this was before I heard from you and I didn't know where to reach you.

With 17 royal purple dachshunds (housebroken) with polished silver legs!

CARLO

<u>over</u>
<u>over</u>

!!!

[*handwritten on the back of the letter:*]

I have just dug out the letter Zora wrote me when she sent me the play on November 14. In it she says: "Langston and I started out together on the idea of the story I used to tell you about Eatonville, but being so much apart from rush of business I started all over again while in Mobile and this is the result of my work alone." Of course she should have written you to this effect.

HUGHES TO VAN VECHTEN   4800 Carnegie Ave.,
[incomplete]   Cleveland, Ohio,
                                     January 19, 1931.

DEAR CARLO,

Forgive me for worrying you to death—but once more the
Mule-Bone. Last night I talked to Zora by phone. She said she
knew nothing about French handling her play, or how it got
to Cleveland. I told her how it got here, and that it came in
a terribly tangled up version with two first-act endings, and
two different third acts—one our collaborated version we did
together, another evidently her new version—seemingly leaving it up to the producer to decide which endings and which
acts he wanted. I told her the director here, Mrs. Jelliffe,
couldn't make head or tail of it as sent from French but, liking
the version I have here (the one we did together) she wishing
to put it on, and would Zora be willing that she do it, using
the script we had originally planned? Zora would not answer
yes or *no,* but kept stalling over the phone and asking what
good it would do her to produce it in Cleveland. Then I asked
Zora was she attempting to sell the play alone under her
name? She replied that at first she hadn't intended to, "but,
well—I'm writing you a letter." What she'll say in that letter,
I don't know. . . . Anyway, this morning Mrs. Jelliffe phoned
Barrett Clark, representative for French and also, I understand, reader for the Guild. She explained the whole matter
to him, asking at the same time what he could do so that she
could go ahead with her production, as time is getting very
short. Barrett Clark said that he had gotten the manuscript
through your having first sent it in to the Guild and, feeling
that the Guild would refuse it, he had, some weeks ago offered
it to the Gilpin Players here; that he didn't know Zora Hurston but that he would get in touch with her at once and see
if he could persuade her to allow the Cleveland production to

go through, and under our joint names, (since he had not been aware before that I had any thing to do with the play.) He is to wire Mrs. Jelliffe after he has talked with Zora. . . . Now, Carlo, the situation regarding the production here is this: The Gilpin Players, probably the best Little Theatre Negro group in the country, must open downtown with this play on February 15th, so you see how pushed for time they are. The play came to them through French quite without my knowledge, and bearing only Zora's name, but in such a confused form that I don't see how the Guild or anybody else read it. The Jelliffes are friends of mine and swell people, and realizing the predicament they are in for time, (and also being interested myself in seeing a trial production of the comedy) I am willing to overlook Zora's seeming attempt to get rid of the play without my knowledge, and to do my best to patch up the script using the two acts that I have, and the script of the second act from French which I had worked on with Zora before she went South, and thus enable the Gilpins to put it on out here and to begin rehearsals at once, doing the play under Zora and my names, as she and I had originally intended. This is what I tried to make Zora see over the phone last night but New York to Cleveland calls are expensive and I couldn't talk all night. The Gilpins plan a two-week season for this play, opening under the auspices of the Cleveland Plain Dealer's Theatre of Nations downtown (which means a great deal of publicity through the Plain Dealer) and later moving to the Ohio one of the big legitimate downtown houses here, as they have done in past seasons with Roseanne, In Abraham's Bosom, and other plays, and with great success. This is their first Negro comedy downtown, and they feel that it would go over big, which would be fine for both Zora and I from the standpoint of both publicity and royalties. The Gilpin Players are in a sense a semi-professional group and have been offered try-outs by the Guild and other New York managers before, and a production here would mean that

representatives of the New York people would see it—which
is important to us too, since the Guild has turned it down,
from all I can discover. . . . So Carlo, would you, please, get
in touch with Zora and try to make her see all this. I am not
at all angry about her actions, because she always has been
strange in lots of ways, but I do hate to see a good Folk-play
go to waste, because for some reason I do not know, she no
longer wants to work with me. Tell her the Gilpins would be
happy to have her come out for rehearsals and the opening,
if she wants to. . . . This morning I got some legal advice on
the matter and with all the proof I have: a file of notes in my
own handwriting, pages of construction and situations, car-
bons of the first draft, and the testimony of the stenographer
who worked with us for three or four weeks, Zora can certainly do nothing at all with <u>Mule-Bone</u> without my permission. Why she should have set out to do so is beyond me.
. . . Of course, I know that you knew nothing of all this until
I wrote you, and I hope it won't be putting you to a great deal
of trouble, but would you do what you can to get it untangled,
and explain to Lawrence Langner or some of the Guild people
how sorry I am that such an unfinished version ever reached
them. . . . Since time is so pressing for the Gilpins, if you could
send me a night letter or something about Zora's attitude, I'd
appreciate it immensely. . . . Snowballs . . .

HUGHES TO HURSTON   4800 Carnegie Ave.,
                                    Cleveland, Ohio,
                                    January 20, 1931.

DEAR ZORA,

You know very well why paying Louise later was suggested
when we first began working on the play. You also know why
that suggestion lost its meaning and no longer held after we

disclosed the fact that we were doing the play. You know that
Louise has been paid for her work and that she has, of course,
no other interest in the play. You know also that after we
disclosed our working together on the comedy, the idea that
Louise was to have anything to do with the handling of it was
also cancelled, and I myself made a personal appointment with
Theresa Helburn of the Theatre Guild last June about the
play, and that I said whenever it was ready I would take it to
the Guild myself, and that if they turned it down then we
would get a reputable Broadway agent. So don't be absurd
about Louise—because you know better than that. . . . Certainly you know, at least, that never in any way did I attempt
to deceive you, and that every idea that came to mind was
disscussed with you, and Louise as well, since all three of us
were engaged in working at the same place and time. So I
didn't expect you to do the silent and uncalled-for thing that
you did. However, I am quite willing to go back to our original bassis of collaboration, to do what I can to get the play in
shape for presentation out here, and to work with you at any
time or anywhere in the future that will be to the benifit of the
play Mule-Bone. I think it would be a great shame for the first
Negro comedy to go to pieces on account of selfish or foolish
disagreement among us. If you want the larger share of the
royalties which the play may earn, we can make a legal aggree-
ment defining our shares, and you can take the biggest, (if
that's your main trouble.) In any case, if you make any further
attempts to dispose of any script based upon the play which we
did together and now called Mule-Bone, it will be a matter for
my lawyers and The Authors' Guild, to both of whom I have
written full details. . . . I have also gotten legal advice here in
Cleveland. . . . It would be much happier for all of us, if you
would stick to our original agreement — because the play is
ours, neither yours nor mine, and I feel it is too good to be
lost. The Gilpin Players cordially invite you to Cleveland, and
I'd be very happy to see you and to work with you here if you

come, and at the same time to prepare a script for New York sale that would at least be clean and readable. What do you mean that, "I made suggestions, but they are not incorporated in the play," when one of the two versions that the agent sent here is exactly the same third set that you and I did together, and to which I gave you a carbon in New York in November. It looks to me like the <u>same</u> carbon? You're an awfully amusing person, Zora.

Sincerely,
L.H.

HURSTON TO HUGHES   43 W. 66th St.
                                     New York City.
                                     January 20, 1931.

DEAR LANGSTON,

Gee, I was glad to get your letter!

I don't feel bad about the Guild refusing my offering, for I have learned that they thought well of it, and more things besides merit entered into the refusal. That is why Clark took it over to French's office—because he felt that it would not be hard to place, and that is why he gave it to Mrs(?) Jeliffe. However, it may be rotten as heck.

Now, I suppose that both of us got worked up unnecessarily. I have explained myself so that I see no need to rehash it. I know that you are nervously constituted like me and so the less emotion the better. I am busy smoothing out my lovely brow at present and returning to normal. I am in fault in the end and you were in fault in the beginning. I shall freely acknowledge my share at anytime and place. Somehow I don't mind re-versing myself, especially when it moves me towards pleasanter relationship. Perhaps I am just a coward who loves to laugh at life better than I do to cry with it. But when I <u>do</u> get to crying, boy, I can roll a mean tear.

I shall write Godmother a letter leaving you in a white light. Not that you have been slandered, but she dotes so on our rock-bottom sincerity that she would be upset to know of a spat, however trivial it might turn out for us.

Hope to see you in Cleveland in a few days. Until then,

Most sincerely,
ZORA

P.S. How dare you use the word "nigger" to me. You know I don't use such a nasty word. I'm a refined lady and such a word simply upsets my conglomeration. What do you think I was doing in Washington all that time if not getting cultured. I got my foot in society just as well as the rest. Treat me refined.

VAN VECHTEN TO HUGHES 150 West Fifty-fifth Street
New York City
[January 20, 1931]

DEAR LANGSTON,

Zora came to see me yesterday and cried and carried on no end about how fond she was of you, and how she wouldn't have had this misunderstanding for the world. And she said she had written you six typewritten pages and talked to you over long distance and said she was going to write to you again. So I hope you are straightened out with her by now.

And she doesn't want the play done in Cleveland, and here I think she is wise. A semi-amateur production of this play will kill it completely. It needs the most careful and sympathetic production and casting and if it gets it, I think should duplicate the success of <u>The Green Pastures.</u> And sooner or later I think it is quite certain to be produced.

Please keep my name out of any further conferences you may have with Zora about the matter. It wouldn't help any and I'd rather not become involved.

145 red crocodiles with golden tongues to you!

CARLO

HUGHES MEMORANDUM   January 20, 1931

JAN. 20—4:PM

Miss Hurston is invited by phone to come out for rehearsals after she says that her reason for not wishing the play to be done here is because she feels no one else understands it but her. The telephone conversation is conducted by Mr. Dubin of the <u>Cleveland Plain Dealer</u>, (as they are anxious to see the play done here).

HURSTON TO JELLIFFE [*via wire*]   January 20, 1931

To Rowena Jelliffe—Sent 5:32

Okay

   Zora H.

To Rowena Jelliffe—Sent 7:04

Mr. Clark at French feels badly over complications thru unauthorized sending script but says you can be trusted for integrity of script material copyright not one word must be altered except by me script not to leave your hands N.Y. agent not available now but decision tomorrow.

HURSTON TO MASON   January 20, 1931

DARLING GODMOTHER,

   You will note that Langston makes no claim of authorship. In the letter, over the phone and thru his friends, he attempts to set up the claim that he is due something because I didn't tell him to get out. You can't talk about a work with a person and then do it alone unless you pay them.

   Now I noted in his Not Without Laughter that he used several bits that I had given him. Now I am not using one single solitary bit in dialogue, plot nor situation from him and yet he tries to muscle in. I am enclosing the letter I wrote him and spoke to you about. I have since sent him a practical duplicate of it.

   I wish it were possible for Locke to get him before you

and then call me in and let him state his claims.

But my nigger mess aside, I hope that you are well as can be expected and that your dear C. is the same. My heart goes out to Mrs. Biddle in her bad hour. She is being crushed like grapes in the press, but she has been singled out by the gods to bear heavenly fire to men. So she must suffer. Like Prometheus. Perhaps the grapes cry out under the press until a voice whispers, "Hush! The gods are making wine." Blessed and cursed is the bearer of heavenly fire.

The man is still haggling over the car. He wants me to pay for having the carbon ground and I am not going to do it. The price is too low anyway. Having made that sacrificing price, he concludes that I am lacking in a sense of values. But I won't give another inch.

All my love to you, Godmother. I told Langston that you knew that I had written the play. Take good care of your precious life.

Devotedly,
ZORA.

HURSTON TO MASON   43 W. 66th St.
                                    New York City
                                    January 20, 1931.

DEAREST GODMOTHER,

Things are happening hot and fast. Now it has developed that Langston did not start the bidding for the play to Cleveland. You know that Mr. MacGowan is connected with the Guild. So the play has been read there. It seems that they really want this company to try out the play. It has tried out other plays that the Guild was interested in. So it looks both to be a better proposition, and better for Langston than it did at first glance. It came to his notice after it had been mentioned to the head of the organization out there.

AND BEHOLD! It begins to look like Langston has at last gotten one eye open. He seems to have gone to Cleveland to escape certain entanglements. He is staying on there indefinitely. He is a little pathetic in his wish to make up with you. He told me that in a registered letter I have just received, but someone else called me up to say that he is wretched and sick because he feels that he has fallen in the esteem of many folks, including me. He is fed up on New York for the time being. I thought he had a very hang-dog look the last time I saw him. He is highly emotional, and I can see how realization of how he looks to others would affect him, that is why he stays ill. At any rate, he wrote me a pathetic letter. It is just as we know, Langston is weak. Weak as water. When he has a vile wretch to push him he gets vile. When he is under noble influences like yours, you know how fine he can be. Personally, I think that he has so much in him, that it is worth my swallowing and forgetting if by extending a friendly hand I can bring him back into the fold. I think we are in a spot now to make a grand slam.

I hurry to send these lines to you, because I don't want to be unjust to anyone ever. Especially Langston. I did not get my facts about the play from him, however. I got them from the agency downtown that is connected with the Guild.

I shall write Langston at once. I am sure that if he felt that he could get your confidence again he would work hard to earn it. He is ashamed of his attitude about the play and apologized to me for it. Isn't that like the Langston of old? He says he feels so badly about going down to certain friends of his the way he did. I know just what happened. After he had spent a night or two in town and had been fed and flattered, he was told what a sucker he was not to fight for his rights. I was held up to him as a double-crossing monster. Plenty sighs went up over the fickleness of friends, etc. After all, Langston, you are so fine and generous and the crass world robs you. I think it is just magnificent of you to love Zora the way you do, but you poor dear, nobody ever seems to love <u>you</u>. Lie down, let mama fix you some cocoa. Maybe you ought to have a cocktail. I'll run right out and fix you one. Umph! Umph! I forgot that all the liquor was gone. Better let me run get some. Now where is my purse? Oh, you'll get some? NO! I couldn't let you do that. You are so good to us. Well, if you will, but remember next time I do the buying. I wouldn't take advantage of you like others. Etc. By the third cocktail and the tenth ton of flattery, the Galahad goes forth to defend his rights, and tell that flat-foot sea buzzard of a Zora just where she gets off. "And while you are about it, dear, free yourself from the strings of these people who give you a few pennies just to dominate you."

Godmother, I am so happy that Langston has taken an honorable view of the thing, that I would give him part. I shan't say that to him right now, but it takes all the sting out of things. The money didn't mean anything, Godmother really. You know how I felt.

So Mr. [Barrett] Clark, one of the Guild people, thinks that I ought to go to Cleveland and work the thing out. I don't know, but it looks like a build-up for New York production. He says that it, the play, is so exotic that they would like to see how it works up.

Please see me with your inner vision, waving a fan gaily.

Lovingly,
ZORA.

HUGHES TO SPINGARN

4800 Carnegie Ave.,
Cleveland, Ohio,
January 21, 1931.

Mr. Arthur Spingarn,
19 West 44th Street,
New York, N. Y.

DEAR ARTHUR SPINGARN,

I am very happy that you are willing to do what you can for me in safeguarding my interest in a play of which I am half author. The play is now called Mule-Bone, and it was done by Miss Zora Hurston and myself in collaboration, largely by the dictation method to Miss Louise Thompson, our stenographer at the time. Miss Hurston, it appears, has recently attempted to dispose of the play under her name alone, and without my knowledge and permission. Here is the whole story:

Sometime last spring, I believe in late February or March Taylor Gordon gave a party, and there I met Theresa Helburn of the Theatre Guild. We had quite a talk about the theatre, and Negro plays. Among other things Miss Helburn said that practically all the plays by or about Negroes offered to the Guild were serious problem dramas, and that they would like very much to have a comedy. She suggested that I write one. At that time Zora Hurston was living in Westfield, N.J. working on a marvellous collection of folk-material that she had brought back with her from the South. A few days later, when I saw her, I repeated Miss Helburn's suggestion and proposed to Miss Hurston that we do a comedy together. She readily agreed, and in a short time we went to work, using as a basis a folk-tale that Miss Hurston had about one man who hit another in the head with a mule-bone in a quarrel over a turkey. There was a trial in the church and the culprit was proven guilty by the minister grabbing the Bible and reading about Samson and the Philistines, saying that if Samson could kill ten thousand Philistines with the jaw-bone of an ass, a mule-bone was much worse—and therefore this man should be run out of town, which he was. I suggested using this tale as our beginning. . . . It was agreed that I would do the construction, plot, whatever characterization I could, and guide the dialog. Miss Hurston was to put in the authentic Florida color, give the dialog a true Southern flavor, and insert many excellent turns of phrase and "wise-cracks" which she had in her mind and among her collections. In conversation, I suggested that we make the two men friends for years, one a guitarist, the other a dancer, who made their living by playing for the white folks who came to Florida from up North in the winter, that they meet a girl, a fickle high-brown just come down from New York with a white family as maid, that these two boys both try to "make" the girl, that their life-long friendship begins to go apart, that they finally fight over her in front of the village store, and one hits the other in the head with the mule-bone. One is knocked out, the other locked up, and the girl is left standing alone in the excitement, saying, "Now who's gonna take me home?" as the curtain falls for the first act. . . . Act 2: The trial in the Baptist church. I said make one boy a Methodist and the other a Baptist and let the whole town split over the trial into two religious camps. Let the trial be a loud and noisy rumpus between the Baptists and the Methodists, and finally end in the folk-story manner, with the minister, the Bible, and the man being run out of town. . . . Act 3: On a lonesome stretch of railroad line outside of town. The boy sits down and strums his guitar, his former buddy follows him, anxious now to make up, but unwilling to let on he is. They are about to patch up their differences, when the girl comes along anxious to get back one or the other of her lovers. There is a proposing contest, (Miss Hurston's suggestion) and each fellow tries to out-do the other with the girl,

but more or less in a burlesque-serious manner. She accepts
one of them, and then says that she will get him a job with her
white folks. At the mention of the word <u>work</u> he backs out and
turns her over to his buddy. The other boy doesn't want her
either when he learns that he has to take care of her, so they
both shy off, again leaving the girl forlorn. She goes off down
the track in a huff, while both boys, friends again now, start
singing and dancing their way back to town. Final curtain.
. . . That's the gist of the story we decided to do together,
largely worked out and constructed by myself, and the whole
action outlined in my own handwriting. We sent for Miss
Thompson who came from New York, sometimes commut-
ing, sometimes staying over night with Miss Hurston, and in
late March or April we three went to work by dictation to the
stenographer, on the play. It moved along beautifully for
some three or four weeks, during which time we completed
drafts of the entire first and third acts, and a Scene 1 (short
street scene before the trial) for the second act. About that
time Miss Hurston had to leave Westfield, and later went back
South for the summer, taking all the notes, outlines, etc. with
her for the trial scene, with the understanding that she would
finish a draft of that act down South while she was away. I did
not see her again untill November in New York. In the meantime I had spent some weeks at the Hedgerow Theatre near
Philadelphia, and while there had gotten some advice and
help from Jasper Deeter on the first act. He did not read the
third act which I also had with me, but from what he saw, he
thought the thing would work out to be a swell comedy.
. . . When I came back to New York in November and
attempted to work with Miss Hurston, saying that we should
put the play together and type out the final version, she gave
me an appointment for work, but when I came, was not at
home. Other appointments followed, but always she either
was not home or had to go out at once as soon as I arrived;
had no copies of the play in the house to work on; said she was

terribly busy and terribly nervous and couldn't work anyway; said she thought we ought to put the turkey back in the story and cut down on the girl-interest; finally gave me a copy of what she had done in the South, but demanded it back almost at once before I could make a copy of it for myself; said she had to go back South again almost at once; was not home for the last appointment that she gave me—and I have not seen her since. (That I believe was early December.) I thought her behavior strange, but since we have always been such good friends, and had had no disagreements about our work on the play together or anything else, I put down her actions to a rush of other work, and perhaps nerves. So I put the play aside and thought no more of it, except that we would finish it when she next came back to New York. . . . Imagine then my surprise when, some three weeks ago, attending a performance at the Little Theatre of the Gilpin Players here in Cleveland, I learned from Rowena Jelliffe, their manager, that they thought they were about to get the rights to do a swell Negro comedy called Mule-Bone, which Samuel French had offered them for their annual downtown production! Miss Zora Hurston was the author! . . . I was, of course, completely amazed, and told Mrs. Jelliffe that it was a play of which I knew a great deal. She then went on to tell me that they had not yet received the script because it was being considered by the Theatre Guild, but that Barrett Clark felt that the Guild would refuse it, and rather assured them here that the script would be forthcoming in a few days. So the Gilpins more or less went on the assumption that they would have it in time for production on the coming February 15th. In the meantime I at once sent for my copies of the play which I had left in Westfield. I also wrote Zora Hurston for an explanation. She did not answer. Last Friday, Jan. 16, Mrs. Jelliffe received from Samuel French a manuscript of Mule-Bone, saying that a letter regarding rights would follow later. Up to that point I had done nothing except to write Miss Hurston, because I was not entirely sure it was our play. I thought there might be some mistake. But as soon as I saw the manuscript (bearing only Zora Hurston's name) I knew at once that it was what we had worked on together. It came here in very bad shape, as if hastily put together, and there is little wonder that the Guild refused it. It was in about the same shape as when we stopped work on it last spring (an unfinished second draft version) except that Miss Hurston had inserted the turkey, caused the fight to take place off-stage, thus changing the ending of the first act (and weakening her climax), and had also written a second slightly different ending which she sent along with the note attached that maybe it was better than the other. The second act sent here was the one of which I had no copy and which she herself put together in the South (with the aid of my notes, except that here again talk of the turkey appears). Of the third act two versions were sent, one the original that we did together last spring, the other a new version, based on and very much like the original. (An awful way to send out a manuscript, evidently leaving the producer his choice of acts and endings. In fact the whole thing is perfectly amazing. Maybe she has lost her mind!) But anyway—Mrs. Jelliffe immediately saw that the play French sent her and the one that I had (the first and third acts and complete out-line notes) were the same. She liked my version of the first act much the best (because it does have order and climax in construction, whereas Miss Hurston's insertion of the turkey threw the whole thing out of gear, as she simply put it in to an act that had not been written for it.) I at once got in touch with Miss Hurston by long distance phone to New York. She denied knowing anything about the play being in the hands of an agent, or that it had reached Cleveland; would give me no answer when I asked her if she were trying to sell the play herself, but said she would write me. Mrs. Jelliffe also got in touch with Barrett Clark, representative for French with whom she always deals, told him the whole story, said that she wanted to produce the play, had very little time as rehearsals would have to start this week, and asked him over the phone what to do about it. He said he would try to get in touch with Miss Hurston. He also said that the play came to him in this way: Carl Van Vechten sent it to the Guild; Barrett Clark is a reader for the Guild, and also on the staff for French; the Guild turned down the play; he sent it to the Gilpin Players here, but he himself had never been in touch with the author or authors. However, he would do what he could to persuade Miss Hurston to allow the original collaborated version of the play to be done here. . . . On Jan. 20 a wire came from French saying Miss Hurston refused to authorize the production and to return the script at once. That, Mrs. Jelliffe did yesterday. But since then three wires have come from Miss Hurston after the Plain Dealer people talked with her by phone which seemingly authorize production here, and which indicate that she will again collaborate with me, so the Jelliffe's are going ahead today with the whole show, and have asked me to revise the second act so that it again comforms with the original play. Their lawyer here assures them that Miss Hurston's wires constitute a contract, and that the players will be safe now in going ahead with rehearsals. But if anything else should happen to delay or hinder the production, their downtown season would be ruined, as they must open on Feb. 15th. . . . When first I tried to phone you yesterday, I had just received a letter from Miss Hurston saying that no part of the play was mine, so I thought you had better do something at once about it, but when I finally reached you on the phone, two of the agreeable telegrams had arrived. Nevertheless, I think you had better know all this, and I hereby give you full authority to act as my personal representative in protecting my rights and interest in the play Mule-Bone. . . . It's all a very strange mess, and it's lucky for me that I happened to come home to my mother in Cleveland when I did, otherwise I probably would have known nothing of this until the play went on here. Mrs. Jelliffe

first heard of it from French's on December 17, so it must have
been in the hands of an agent or the Guild at the very time
when I was trying to work on it and make a final draft with
Miss Hurston. At that time, I spoke of her strange behavior
to your sister, Mrs. Amy Spingarn the day when she did her
pencil drawing of me. Perhaps she can repeat to you what I
told her then. . . . As to proofs of my statements: First, there
is the stenographer, Miss Louise Thompson, 435 Convent
Avenue, New York, who knows of the play and who worked
with us from the very beginning last spring taking dictation
and copying and recopying parts of it many times in the presence of both Miss Hurston and myself. Second, I have now in
my possession in my own handwriting several pages of construction and characterization notes from which the present
play was built, as well as a carbon of the first draft of the first
act, containing insertions and corrections in mine and Miss
Hurston's handwriting in pencil on this carbon. I have also
clean copies of the first and third acts which I told Miss Hurston I would take to Hedgerow for Jasper Deeter's advice.
Third, Jasper Deeter saw and read aloud to a part of his
company the entire first act, which is practically the same as the
act which Miss Hurston sent out as her own. Fourth, the day
that Carl Van Vechten sailed for Europe last spring Miss Hurston and I went to bid him goodbye, and at that time told him
we were doing a folk-comedy together—so he knew that we
were working jointly on something. (Although I in no way
blame him for the present situation, since he had no way of
knowing that the play which Miss Hurston took to him alone
was the one we did together.) Fifth, Miss Hurston's former
landlady in Westfield, my landlady there, the boarding house
keeper where Miss Hurston, Miss Thompson, and myself frequently ate, and others, all knew we were doing a play together. Sixth, a few of my friends, like Mrs. Spingarn, knew
of it, either that spring or in the fall. But both Miss Hurston
and myself had agreed to say very little about it until we had

finished—so that no one would be likely to get hold of our ideas. <u>Seventh</u>, I probably have in Westfield letters from Miss Hurston in the South last summer in which she mentions, or replies to questions of mine, how she is progressing on the second act which she had taken with her to finish up. . . . So with all that against her, I can't imagine why she would attempt to sell the play which we did together without any knowledge or consent on my part. . . . There are these details which you should know. The version which arrived here from French bore no copyright notice, so I immediately copied from it the second act which I had not possessed since last spring, except for a few hours loan in New York, and together with the original first and third acts that I ordered sent me from Westfield, I mailed the comedy off to be copyrighted on Monday (Jan. 19) in my name, but giving both our names as the authors. If she has already copyrighted the play in her name alone something must be done about that. . . . I have been as decent as possible about the matter, writing Miss Hurston only in the nicest way, and making no attempt to create a row about it, but trying to find out what's going on. I have not been successful, so if you could kindly check up on the whole business for me at once, I would appreciate it immensely. I have written Carl Van Vechten several letters asking his advice and giving him the same story I have set down here. Perhaps it would be wise for you to phone him about it, since he is a friend of both Miss Hurston and myself, and since it seems that he gave the play to someone connected with the Guild, and in that way it reached French. Then, too, perhaps you could get the whole story of its attempted sale from Barrett Clark who handled it for both the Guild and Samuel French, Inc. Jack Walsh at French's also seems to have had some knowledge of the business, as the correspondance shows which I am sending you. Undoubtedly you know where to find all these people except Miss Hurston. Her address is 43 West 66th Street, and her telephone is Endicott 2-2441. (I do not know whether you will care to get in touch with her at once or not, but please do what you think is wise in regard to the whole matter) [*handwritten in margin:* Better talk to her if possible as to royalties—as explained below. I am writing her that you will represent me in New York now.] In all my letters to Miss Hurston I have said that I was perfectly willing to continue our colaboration, willing to work with her on the script for the production here, and to do everything I could for the future sale and success of "Mule-Bone." I am not particularly angry about what has happened, only puzzled, and I do not wish any legal entanglements, or to make things unneccessary unpleasant for her. We have always been good friends for the past six or eight years, since I first came to New York. But I do not want to see what may be a splendid play, and the first Negro folk-comedy to be written by Negroes, be torn apart before it has even gotten started. Carl Van Vechten writes me that several members of the Guild liked it very much, and that it is a sparkling and original play that, if properly produced, might be as successful as the *Green Pastures.* So you see what a shame it is for this sort of thing to come up. I hope Miss Hurston will see fit to continue our work together on this play so that it might be an artistic success. She has an amazing fund of folklore, wit, and knowledge of Southern life, and is marvellous at dialect and Southern turns of speech, but she has almost no sense of construction, (as the version which she tried to do herself shows) and little sense of continuity or form. She is a delightful person in many ways, and I think you would enjoy meeting her, if you don't already know her. Carl, Harry Block, T. R. Smith, Taylor Gordon, or most anybody could introduce you.

This is the situation here: I would never have thought of a Cleveland production myself, but since it was practically underway when I first heard of it, and since the Jelliffe's are old friends of mine from high school days, (marvellous white couple who have lived for fourteen years in the heart of the

Negro section here working and playing with the people, establishing art classes, clubs, a camp, and their fine theatre group, the Gilpin Players) and since they have been very kind and helpful in the present situation, I am perfectly willing to see them put the play on here, as Miss Hurston's agent seemed to think desirable when he sent out her script. And since it is to be produced under the auspices of the Cleveland Plain Dealer at the Theatre of Nations, and later move to the Ohio, for a week's run, a large legitimate playhouse downtown here, it will give Miss Hurston and I an excellent opportunity to study its faults, and if it is fairly successful here it will be a great help toward an opening in New York, as New York managers usually have representatives here in town, since Cleveland is a great try-out town for Broadway productions. . . . A production here would probably do us all good. Miss Hurston seems to have agreed to it by wire. But Mrs. Jelliffe has no contracts or anything of the sort, so far, from either of us. And Barrett Clark denies by phone that French is really her agent. She has my personal word that I agree to the production, and with that and Miss Hurston's wire, she is going ahead. She wants, of course, as soon as possible something signed and down on paper. So far, with Miss Hurston there has been no talk of royalties. I am writing her today about them. The royalties in the case of the Gilpin Players use of Roseanne for 14 performances amounted to $267.50, in the case of In Abraham's Bosom, $350.00 for 23 performances, but the size of the theatres varied in each case. Mrs. Jelliffe is willing to pay us as high a rate of royalty as has been paid on any other play. The Players are a non-comercial group, the money they make going toward the buying of a permanent scholarship for Negro students at the Cleveland School of Art and toward the improvement of their own little theatre made from an old pool hall on Central Avenue. Royalties are decided between the authors and the group, through Mrs. Jelliffe and the Ex. Com.

Could you get from Miss Hurston some sort of agreement allowing me to act as her representative here for a tentative agreement on royalties for a two weeks run of the play Mule-Bone, all terms, of course, to be finally approved by her? . . . Again, I wish to make a personal agreement with Miss Hurston as to the division of royalties between us. Since from her letter to me she evidently feels that she is more author of the play than I am,—to keep the colaboration from going to pieces and to save an interesting play, I have written her that I was quite willing to accept the lesser share of the royalties we might make. She may have <u>two-thirds</u> of the joint royalties if she feels that she should, I will accept <u>one-third</u>—as a permanent agreement for all future productions of the play, should she not wish to split half and half. You may tell her that for me, and if you can get a signed agreement to that effect, I will also add my signature. I do not know how one goes about such matters, and since I am not in New York now, would you kindly advise me what to do, if you cannot attend to the royalty matters yourself? . . . I am enclosing copies of most of the correspondance. . . . I believe that is all. I am deeply grateful to you for helping me in this matter. I'm dead broke right now, but book royalties are due soon, and if <u>Mule-Bone</u> ever goes on in NEW YORK it may make something, so I trust I will be able to meet whatever fee you may charge. You may write or wire me at the above address at any time, or phone Endicott 9028. Mrs. Rowena Jelliffe may be reached at the Playhouse Settlement, 2239 East 38th St. Cleveland, or by phone Henderson 7798. . . . Thank you so much.

> Sincerely,
> LANGSTON HUGHES

HUGHES TO HURSTON   4800 Carnegie Avenue,
[incomplete]   Cleveland, Ohio,
                           January 22, 1931.

ZORA, MY DARLING,

Brazzle's mule is one ungodly beast. He's done a mean piece
of kicking lately, but I trust once more that the ghost of his
dead carcass is ready to repose in piece! We're all sorry! Last
night in jail with my back turned to the wall, I thought deeply
on the subject—because with a cousin of mine, I was mixed
up in a traffic run-in with a taxi driver who claimed we'd hit
his car—so I've just this morning come out of jail! . . . Well,
we're all glad you will come out here soon. I've told the
Jelliffe's what a grand person you are—even the New York
folk-tale about you and the blind man's tin cup. You see what
a famous person you are already, that folk-tales are made up
about you while you're still in your youth—not even dead yet.
. . . There's a matter of business to be taken up at once
regarding the production here. Since French is out of the
picture, there is no one to deal with except the authors direct
(which means we get all the royalties anyhow), but Mrs. Jelliffe wishes at once some signed right to the play from us as
to the royalties we will accept, etc. They are quite willing to
pay us the same rate they paid on Roseanne, their highest
royalty play so far. The royalty seems to vary with the size of
the theatre. In the case of Roseanne: 7 Little Theatre performances and Ohio Theatre performances netted to the author
$267.50. In the case of In Abraham's Bosom: 23 perform-
ances brought the author $350.00. Mrs. Jelliffe wishes that I
meet the Executive Comm. of the Players on the matter as
soon as possible. Would you be willing that I act as your
representative at this meeting to decide on our royalty rates
for the production here? The tentative decision which I might
accept due of course to your final O.K. and to have your

signature . . . Someone must merely act as a representative here for our interest. I have asked Mr. Arthur Spingarn to do that for me in New York, and I have asked him to see if he can formulate a personal agreement between you and myself as to division of royalties between us, either a temporary agreement for the Cleveland run, or a permanent one for whatever productions of the play there might be anytime in the future, (preferably I think a permanent one to cover all future income, since that would save everybody's time. If you feel that the major part of <u>Mule-Bone</u> is yours, I am quite willing that you have two-thirds of all incomes, myself accepting one-third, and have so informed Mr. Spingarn. His address is 19 West 44th Street. Maybe you know him. If not, you'll find him a very nice fellow, and I am sure, perfectly square. You might call him up and make an appointment. Or perhaps he will call you, but since this should be done soon, I hope you will get in touch with him. He has full authority to act as my personal representative. . . . I hope nothing will come out of this matter to worry Godmother. As you know, I had nothing to do with initiating this Cleveland production, so please get her straight on that point. The dated correspondance with French shows that the play had been offered here some weeks before I even thought of coming out this way. . . . I'm glad things seem to be straight again now. I hate mixups. Everybody's happy—so O.K. . . . It'll be great to see you. Maybe you'll like this big old dirty town. I hope so. There's a low-down night club that almost equals the Sugar Cane. . . .

HUGHES TO SPINGARN   4800 Carnegie Ave.,
                                      Cleveland, Ohio,
                                      January 24, 1931.

Mr. Arthur Spingarn,
19 West 44th Street,
New York, N. Y.

DEAR MR. SPINGARN,

Miss Hurston is expected here by February first to help the
Gilpin Players with their production, and she has written me
a very nice letter, so I guess everything is O.K. . . . I have your
note in response to my phone call, and I trust that you have
my letter by now in which I tell you all about the case, and a
second envelope containing copies of letters, wires, etc., in
regard to it. I posted them to you Wednesday. . . . Here are
the royalty terms which the Gilpin Players offer for the production of Mule-Bone here, and which I have sent today to
Miss Hurston: The Gilpins, a working people's Little Theatre,
pay on all their plays what is known as "amateur royalties".
They are quite willing to pay us as high a rate as they have ever
paid on any other production. What they suggest now is as
follows: (This does not include the week they expect to do at
the Ohio Theatre—that being a professional legitimate house,
the arrangement is made through the management there, and
cannot be made until later, so Miss Hurston will probably be
here by that time.) But for the downtown opening under Plain
Dealer Theatre of Nations auspices, (one Art Scholarship performance, and probably one Saturday night extra performance) and for five nights at their own Kamaru Theatre on
Central Avenue, with possibly three to six other performances
for special groups like the city librarians or the Art Museum

patrons who may buy out the house for their own private evenings, they offer either of the following propositions:

Plain Dealer performances (some 750 seats)
. . . .$50.00 per performance
Kamaru performances (120 seats). . . . .$20.00 " "

Or:

Plain Dealer performances. . .5% of profits per performance
Kamaru performances. . . .20% "   "   "   "

The first proposition would give the authors $150 for six performances, the minimum number to be given (exclusive of the Ohio). The second proposition would be a little less, (and a great deal less if the houses did not sell out) so I think we would be safer in taking the flat-rate proposition, which is agreeable to me, if it suits Miss Hurston. I have asked her to get in touch with you about the matter. So far the Gilpins have no signed agreement with anybody about the play (at the moment they are considering Miss Hurston's wires as constituting a contract) and if French is no longer acting as Miss Hurston's agent (or is he?) they must deal directly with us, and they wish to have something tangible as soon as possible, so I trust you can do something toward settling this royalty business. I hope so. . . . With best wishes to you,

Sincerely,
LANGSTON

SPINGARN TO HUGHES   January 24th, 1931
                                                        19 West 44th Street
                                                        New York City

Mr. Langston Hughes,
4800 Carnegie Avenue,
Cleveland, Ohio.

DEAR LANGSTON:—

As soon as I received your letter of Jan. 21st, I spoke to
Carl Van Vechten and he suggested that I ring up Miss Hurston directly. Miss Hurston made an appointment for Friday,
which she was unable to keep on account of ill health, and I
saw her this morning at my office. In the meanwhile, Carl has
told me that he had heard from French that the script to
"Mule-Bone" had been returned to them, so I do not know
just what the status of the play is in Cleveland.

Miss Hurston insists that the account you gave me of
your collaboration in the play is grossly exaggerated and that
virtually all of the play was written by her. She says that you
should not have been surprised when the script arrived in
Cleveland with her name thereon as the sole author, as she
showed you this script last Fall with her name on it as sole
author and that you made no comment at the time, except to
say, couldn't there be two versions, so if we could not sell the
one, perhaps we could sell the other.

Miss Hurston says she is not so much concerned about
the matter of royalties, but feels that you have been unfair and
unjust in the matter. She feels that she cannot decide whether
or not the play should go on in Cleveland without consulting
her agent, Miss Elizabeth Marbury, who she expects to see this
afternoon. She has promised to let me know on Monday what

the decision is. As soon as I receive it, I shall communicate with you.

As to the royalties you should receive for your participation in the play, Miss Hurston thinks, and I agree with her, that this matter can be much better adjusted if you two meet face to face. Perhaps if the play goes on, she will go out to Cleveland and you can then talk it over, but if the play does not go on, when you come to New York you can then talk it over; preferably in the presence of some friend, either Carl Van Vechten or myself, or perhaps both. In the meanwhile, Miss Hurston will not take any action which will jeopardize your rights.

I may add that your letter of the 19th to Miss Hurston threatening litigation aroused her ire, and she has shown me a copy of the letter which she wrote to you and which I frankly told her was foolish, as I think your letter to her, which I have not seen, was probably also. Litigation is the last thing either of you should think of if it can possibly be avoided, not only for your own sakes, but for the sake of the group.

This letter is dictated in my office in Miss Hurston's presence.

> Faithfully yours,
> ARTHUR B. SPINGARN

HUGHES TO SPINGARN   4800 Carnegie Avenue,
                                  Cleveland, Ohio,
                                  January 26, 1931.

DEAR ARTHUR SPINGARN,

I regret very muich that Miss Hurston still does not wish to acknowledge our collaboration. I suggest that you get in touch with the young lady who acted as our stenographer, and who took by dictation from us jointly practically the entire first and third acts, Miss Louise Thompson, 435 Convent Avenue, New York. During the working day she can be reached by phone at the office of Mr. Herring, who is in charge of the Caribbean Seminar, and the inter-racial seminar tours. His office is, I believe in East 19th Street. I am sure the address can be gotten from the N.A.A.C.P. or from Mrs. Thompson.

I am enclosing a carbon of my letter to Miss Hurston on January 20th, also her letter to me of the same date, the two letters having crossed one another. This letter of mine was written after three others over a period of some two weeks had been sent, none of them receiving a sensible response, nor could I get a definite answer by phone. Then it was that I turned the whole matter over to you, and wrote Miss Hurston that I was doing so, since I had no one else in New York to talk to her for me. Then when her letter arrived (the one enclosed) and the wires to the Jelliffe's saying <u>Okay</u> and <u>Proceed</u> I thought the whole thing was about settled, except for a royalty arrangement, and I wrote you January 24th saying so. This morning Mrs. Jelliffe received a letter from Elisabeth Marbury [*handwritten in the margin:* Could you discover what Mrs. Marbury believes herself to be negotiating for—the production of a play by Miss Hurston, or one by Miss Hurston and myself?] asking if she were willing to pay half of Miss Hurston's fare to Cleveland in lieu of royalties for the production of <u>her</u> play. The letter said nothing regarding the play as being ours, nor did it in any way mention my name. It was just as if the negotiations were being conducted entirely for a play by Miss Hurston alone—so again I do not know where matters stand, either in regard to the Cleveland production or to the authorship of the play. I am writing Miss Marbury now merely to say that I am part author, and that full details can be gotten from you.

*   *   *

Last night I mailed you a script of the first act of the play and will mail you the rest as soon as the Gilpins have made their copies. They are proceeding with the production on the strength of Miss Hurston's wires and my own verbal permission, which their lawyer interprets as our joint consent. As you know, the whole matter of this Cleveland production came through Barrett Clark and Samuel French, Inc., and I had nothing to do with it, nor knew of its likelihood, untill I arrived here just a short time before the script itself came from Barrett Clark, so Miss Hurston can in no way hold me responsible for beginning this business here. Then my consent to do the play here always, thereafter, hinged jointly with her own—if the Jelliffe's were able to get it. They felt that they had it after Mr. Dubin of the <u>Cleveland Plain Dealer</u> talked to her by phone, and they received her first wire OKAY, and a second the following day saying PROCEED GOOD LUCK.

Surely you are right—nobody wants litigation.

Sincerely,
LANGSTON

Enclosed with the above letter, Langston Hughes sent the following handwritten note as an introduction to Zora Neale Hurston's letter to him of January 18, 1931:

Miss Hurston's letter to me—Jan. 18th.

_____

Please return

_____

The first three pages are largely concerned with a personal matter over which Miss Hurston seems to be angry, and which she deliberately mistakes and exaggerates and offers for an excuse of her recent actions. The most definite statement about the play is in the Postscript!

HUGHES TO HURSTON
[incomplete]

4800 Carnegie Ave.,
Cleveland, Ohio,
January 27, 1931

DEAR ZO,

Everybody's happy about your announced coming. Lillian Smith's friends are all anxious to see you, and I believe it is being arranged for you to stop where Lillian used to stay. Mother is sorry our place is not large enough to have you stay with us. . . . Last night there was a reading of the first act, and it seemed to take pretty well with the company. They are mostly working people, and not many high-hats, as their theatre is located in the heart of the low-down colored district right on Central Avenue. And the Jelliffes are swell people. I think you'll like most of the group and I'm sure they'll like you. I told them the basis for the play is your folk material and home-town background, and said that all the color and wit belonged to you. . . . About royalties: The Gilpins, a Little Theatre, pay on all their plays what is known as "amateur royalties"—you can find out from French about the other plays they have rented from them—and as I told you, they are quite willing to pay us as high a rate as they have paid on any other production. What they offer immediately is as follows: (This does not include the week they expect to do at the Ohio Theatre. This being a professional legitimate house, the arrangement is made through the management there, and cannot be made until they have looked at the production, so you

will be here by that time.) But for the downtown opening
under <u>Plain Dealer</u> Theatre of Nations auspices, (one Art
Scholarship Performance, and probably one Saturday night
extra performance) and for five nights at their own Kamaru
Theatre on Central Avenue, with possibly three to six other
performances for special groups like the Library Club or the
Art Museum Group who may buy out the house for their own
evenings, they offer either of the following propositions:

<u>Plain Dealer</u> performances. . .$50.00 per perform-
ance
Kamaru performances. . . . .$20.00 per perform-
ance

Or:

<u>Plain Dealer</u> performances. . .5% of profits per perform-
ance

Kamaru performances. . . .20% of profits per "

The first proposition would net us $150.00 for six perform-
ances, (the minimum performances to be given). The second
proposition would be a little less for us (and a great deal less
if the house did not sell out). The Theatre of Nations seats
about 750 people, the Kamaru 120 people. . . . I think we
would be safer in taking the flat-rate proposition, which would
mean that we would get ours at all performances that might
be given, regardless of how the seats sold. Wire me if either
of these is agreeable to you. Besides this, of course, your fare
one way is to be paid, you will be housed with some member
of the company, (probably Lillian's friends) I believe, so that
your expenses here will not be large. . . . I am outlining these
two propositions to Mr. Spingarn, so if you decide to accept
one or the other at once without further correspondence, you
may get in touch with him and he will know about the legal

forms for you and I to comply with. Let me know when you're coming out. There is a grand [illegible] dramatic minister here that folks are crazy about . . . [illegible to end]

SPINGARN TO HUGHES   19 West 44th Street
                                      New York City
                                      January 27th, 1931

Mr. Langston Hughes,
4800 Carnegie Avenue,
Cleveland, Ohio.

DEAR LANGSTON:—

I received your letter of Jan. 24th yesterday afternoon when I returned from Court and to-day I spoke to Miss Hurston over the telephone. She tells me that her agent, Elizabeth Marbury, insists, if she is to handle the matter, that her office take charge of all arrangements as to royalties, etc., and that as she (Miss Hurston) knows nothing about these matters, she is leaving those arrangements to Miss Marbury's office. She says that she is writing to you directly and that she is going out to Cleveland, where you can discuss the whole situation face to face and in a friendly manner. I am sure that she is at bottom very friendly disposed toward you and that she really has been more hurt by what she thinks is an ungenerous attitude on your part than by anything else, but I believe and sincerely hope that when you see her, you will be able to straighten out the situation satisfactorily.

Last Sunday night Alain Locke came in to see me about the matter and told me a long story, the upshot of which was that he believed Miss Hurston was right and that you were wrong in the matter. I told him, naturally, that I would have to suspend judgment until I saw you and talked over the situation. The typed script which you sent me reached me this morning.

In conclusion, let me send you my warmest congratulations on your well deserved award of the Harmon prize. I, in common with everybody who has read your book, cannot help being gratified at the admirable judgment of the Harmon committee.

As always,

> Sincerely yours,
> ARTHUR B. SPINGARN

HUGHES TO SPINGARN   4800 Carnegie Avenue,
                                      Cleveland, Ohio,
                                      January 27, 1931.

DEAR MR. SPINGARN,

I have received this morning a card from the Register of Copyrights granting me a copyright in my name for "The Mule-Bone, A Comedy of Negro Life in Three Acts, by Langston Hughes and Zora Hurston of the United States." Evidently, then, Miss Hurston had neglected to copyright the play before sending it out. As I told you, no copyright notice was attached to it when it arrived here from Barrett Clark, therefore I immediately sent it off to Washington to the Register of Copyrights. Knowing the thievery of the New York Theatre, that seemed to me the best immediate protection for both of us. . . . This morning a wire came to Mrs. Jelliffe from Miss Hurston saying that all future communications should be addressed her through her agent at the office of Elisabeth Marbury. Today the Gilpin Players are sending a contract form for the production of "Mule-Bone" here to that office.

The play has been cast and the first rehearsal is tonight. . . . Do you think, from reading the first act which I sent you, that the comedy seems amusing enough to merit all this rumpus? Miss Hurston and I wanted to make of it a play full of the real folk quality, keeping it pure comedy.

Sincerely,
LANGSTON

THOMPSON TO   The American Interracial Seminar
HUGHES   112 East 19th Street, New York
                  Algonquin 4-9365
                  January 28, 1931

DEAR LANG:

You have certainly had your time with Zora! However, I would not be startled at anything now—so shoot the works. No one has called me regarding it, but you count on me as a very able witness should it be necessary.

Congratulations on the Harmon award. I suppose you have guessed that that is why I wanted to know about you, Hannah had asked me, but also had pressed silence upon me. I am glad particularly because of the $400, as I don't think you need the recognition. How about a little party!?!

I have been sick ever since I returned home with a cold and have only today come to the office. I had to be fashionable you know, as everybody is doing it.

I'll give Mary your message. She had a party of her friends Monday night and felt she had a fine evening.

Kindly remember me to your Mother and all the others. Tell her I certainly thank her for taking care of me during my day in Cleveland.

I haven't been anywhere since I have been back as I have

been sick all the time. So I don't know any news to tell.

Success to the play and all matters pertaining thereto. It has truly become a bone of contention, hasn't it. The only thing I can say is that Zora is crazy, but unfortunately maliciously so.

Always,
Lou

Hughes to Locke   January 28, 1931

Wire to Alain Locke, Jan. 28, 1931, 6:30 p.m.

Just received letter Arthur Spingarn please put me straight on Zoras attitude and your knowledge of matter by return wire collect I am afraid I don't understand

Langston

Phone End. 9028.

SPINGARN TO HUGHES   19 West 44th Street
                                     New York City
                                     January 28th, 1931

Mr. Langston Hughes,
4800 Carnegie Ave.
Cleveland, Ohio.

DEAR LANGSTON:—

    I have your letter of the 26th and also your letter of the
27th.
    I did not question Miss Hurston on the subject, but she
volunteered the information that she had the play copyrighted
last October. My advice continues to be the same as in my last
letter to you; that you and she can best straighten the matter
out when you see each other face to face.
    I certainly think the comedy can be made into a real
success; if not in its present form, at least after it has been
worked over a bit.

                      Very sincerely yours,
                      ARTHUR B. SPINGARN

HUGHES TO SPINGARN   4800 Carnegie Ave.,
                                     Cleveland, Ohio
                                     January 30, 1931

DEAR ARTHUR SPINGARN,

    Thanks for your letters. Am in bed with the grippe, so
I haven't been so quick with an answer. I do not understand
Dr. Locke's zeal in upholding Miss Hurston's position—ex-

cept that they are both employed by the same patron. Miss
Hurston has probably claimed <u>Mule Bone</u> as entirely her own
before Dr. Locke and their patron; and Dr. Locke, knowing
only one side of the story, chooses to back Miss Hurston. So
far as I can recall, I have never spoken to Dr. Locke about our
comedy, nor was I aware, until I heard it from you, that he
ever knew Miss Hurston and I had worked on a play together.
I wired him asking for an explanation of his statements to you.
His answer was: "<u>Congratulations on the Harmon award but
what more do you want</u>.". . . . Isn't that annoying? . . .
Yesterday Mrs. Jelliffe received a letter from Mr. Paul Banks,
one of the Gilpin players at present visiting in New York for
some few weeks or so. Mr. Banks had just called on Miss
Hurston. He quotes her as saying that I have been stupidly
untruthful about the play; that she has convinced you that I am
wrong; that you are very much disillusioned about me and that
you will no longer represent me in New York; and that she
has Dr. Locke on her side. Further, that she will shortly leave
for Cleveland, but that she absolutely refuses to associate my
name with the production.

Of course, all this excited Mrs. Jelliffe anew. She tried to
reach both you and Miss Hurston yesterday by phone but
failed—so she tells me today that she has written you. The play
is in rehearsal here and has been announced by <u>The Plain
Dealer</u> as a Negro comedy by myself and Miss Hurston. Miss
Hurston, as I told you, authorized the production by her two
wires <u>Okay</u> and <u>Proceed Good Luck</u>. Now Mrs. Jelliffe does
not know what might happen from her present attitude as
expressed to Mr. Banks. Miss Hurston has never ordered the
production stopped here—but seemingly after I told her I had
put the matter in your hands she became angry and decided
to go back to her strange and stubborn policy of not admitting
our collaboration. Mrs. Jelliffe feels that she had better get
expert legal advice here to prevent anything happening at this
late date which would disrupt and spoil their downtown sea-

son, for that reason she asks me to get from you all correspondence of which I kept no copies! i.e. Miss Hurston's two letters to me, and anything else you may have, marked in red "<u>Please return</u>." So would you kindly send letters so marked back to me. . . . Also if you can aid me by giving Mrs. Jelliffe some expert advice about her touring it here when you answer her letter, I would appreciate it immensely, since I know nothing more to do or say about it myself. The check for Miss Hurston's fare to Cleveland has been sent to her—so maybe the face to face conference can be held soon. I hope so—as this strange and unpleasant business is beginning to get on my nerves. Judging from Mr. Banks's letter, New Yorkers are beginning to think that I am the robber instead of the robbed! Well, sir!! What next?

Sincerely,
LANGSTON

P.S. Would the copyright office be likely to copyright the same play twice by mistake? Is it possible to discover whether or not Miss Hurston did copyright <u>Mule Bone</u> last October by asking the question of the Register of Copyrights? If the play has been copyrighted twice, once by Miss Hurston with herself as sole author, again by myself this month with both of us as authors, what bearing would that have on the situation here regarding the impending Gilpin production—should it come to a matter of injunctions, etc. from Miss Hurston or her agents? The play was once tentatively called "The Bone of Contention"—and that's what it really has become. Miss Hurston has evidently decided to bluff her way through on the false stand that she has taken. Or else she is ashamed to back down before her New York friends. I'm sorry about the whole matter.

P.S. Am sending the II & III acts of the comedy as prepared for the Gilpin's production using the I and III acts done in collaboration last spring, and the II act revised form the version Miss Hurston did last summer in the south with the use of my spring notes for its construction, and following my outline as to scenes and action, except that in her version <u>the turkey</u> incident was used instead of <u>the girl</u>. This had to be removed to conform with our original two acts. This is really a 2nd draft version of our collaborated play. I had wanted to work it over once more with Miss Hurston before we tried to sell it, or even tried it out here.

JELLIFFE TO SPINGARN   The Neighborhood Association
2239 East 38th Street
Cleveland, Ohio
January 30, 1931

Mr. Arthur Spingarn,
19 West 44th Street,
New York, N. Y.

DEAR MR. SPINGARN:

There has, as you know, been a deal of controversy over a play by Zora Hurston and Langston Hughes called <u>Mule Bone</u>. I am necessarily involved in it, in as much as I am to produce and direct the play.

It seems to me that Miss Hurston has behaved very strangely. I know from Louise Thompson, who worked with them on the typing of the play that Langston Hughes did the construction of the play and that it was understood between them from the beginning that they were to be co-authors of the play. Moreover, I have seen and examined in detail the work-notes for the entire play in Mr. Hughes's own handwriting. I can see, comparing his script with hers that she has made changes in an attempt perhaps to claim that she has re-written the play. But there's no question that it is the same play—and the changes are feeble.

Believing as I do, that Langston Hughes has rights in the matter, I will not produce it under her name alone. I think she has treated him very badly.

In one connection, Miss Hurston acknowledged his collaboration. Now, apparently, she repudiates it. One telegram says, "O.K.—Zora Hurston."—this in reply to a request to do the play, her name being used as co-author with that of Langston Hughes. Two hours later, I got another one calling it all off. The next morning, I have another one saying "Proceed. Good luck. Zora Hurston".

I am wondering whether she is not really too unreliable a person to deal with.

I have sent to her agent a confirmation of the agreement reached thru the telegrams to be signed, naming royalty terms, offering one-half rail fare here, and using her name jointly with that of Langston Hughes. Under the circumstances, I feel I cannot risk beginning the production until it is returned to me signed. And the date is near at hand.

Do you represent Langston Hughes in this affair? Do you believe that he has rights in the play?

Can Miss Hurston be dealt with? Can she or can she not be depended upon to keep a contract?

Would you care to have Louise Thompson's angle on the affair? Her address is 112 East 19th Street, New York City, in care of The American Inter-racial Seminar. Hubert Herring is Director of this organization. I know Miss Thompson and believe implicitly in her integrity.

> Very truly yours,
> ROWENA WOODHAM
> JELLIFFE, DIRECTOR,
> THE GILPIN PLAYERS.

RWJ:A

HUGHES TO SPINGARN   4800 Carnegie Avenue,
                                      Cleveland, Ohio.
                                      February 3, 1931.

DEAR MR. SPINGARN,

Miss Hurston arrived in Cleveland, she says, on Sunday evening. Anyway she notified Mrs. Jelliffe of her presence here on Monday, and we all had a conference together at the Playhouse on Monday afternoon. On Sunday evening, however, because they had had no word from Miss Hurston, and the agreement which they had sent her and her agent had not been returned, the Gilpin Players voted to no longer continue with the production, due to the uncertainty of her attitude. However, when Miss Hurston showed up on Monday, Mrs. Jelliffe felt that the group would perhaps reconsider their action and continue with the play, so she asked Mr. Elmer Cheeks, president of the Players to also come to the conference. We met at four o'clock. Miss Hurston and I had a talk together alone first to straighten out our difficulties, so that we could then confer in unity with the representatives of the Gilpin Players. . . . In her talk with me, Miss Hurston's main grievance seemed to be Miss Thompson. She seemed to feel that by taking the play alone and go[ing] off with it she was thus protecting me and herself from what she chose to call "a gold digger." I told her that she and I both knew Miss Thompson had been paid for her typing last spring and she could have no further claim on the play in any way, of course. I asked her why she did not tell me of her ill feeling in the fall when I tried to resume work with her, and she said she could not bear to tell me. As to the play itself, Miss Hurston agreed that I had had some part in it's making, and she said she would sign an agreement to work together again jointly with me. She felt however that my part in the making of the play had been a very small one, and that her name should be first on the playbills, etc. I said that I had never claimed the play as even half mine, and in talking about it, had always said that the wit and color were in the main hers—but that I did not see how one could make a mathematical division of construction and characterization as opposed to dialect and wisecracks, the latter being clothing for the former. Miss Hurston insisted that the play which had been sent to Cleveland under her name had been a "new" play, anyhow, and that "there wasn't an idea of mine left in it." (That, of course, is untrue, as Mrs. Jelliffe could tell you. As I told you the play which came here was the same which we had outlined and planned and two-thirds finished together except for a rewritten ending to the first act, another secondary ending sent attached with a note saying either could be used, and the introduction of the turkey. One third act was the very same as we had done together. The rewritten third act, also sent, leaving it to the choice of the producer as to which would be used evidently, was built on the same construction lines . . . [type illegible] like type, leaving the similarity obvious.) Miss Hurston was very nice at this first conference, though, and we agreed that it was all over and settled and that we would sign together for a Gilpin production, should they re-decide to do it. We then called in Mrs. Jelliffe and Mr. Cheeks and told them of our agreement

and decision. They said they would call a meeting of the
Players the following night (today, Tuesday). Zora said she
was glad it all came out all right and that she would wire Carl
at once and that I should wire you so that nobody in New
York would any longer be in doubt about the matter. . . . That
was last night! This morning early Miss Hurston called Mrs.
Jelliffe by phone and began to abuse her, accusing her of
acting on my word and in my behalf before she had gotten in
touch with her, etc., Mrs. Jelliffe said she could hardly discuss
the matter by phone that way, so it was agreed that we all get
together again. This afternoon at five, then, at my house (because the doctor forbade me to go out as I've been down with
tonsils for a week) Miss Hurston, Mrs. Jelliffe, a Mr. Banks
whom Miss Hurston brought with her, and myself got together again. Miss Hurston was in a most angry and emotional
mood. She began to berate Mrs. Jelliffe as being a dishonor-
able person saying that she didn't know what was going on
here (when the facts are that she was informed by myself in
two letters which remained unanswered for some ten days, as
did Mrs. Jelliffe's wire to her when she failed to get any
definite answer from French). Statements in any way disprov-
ing her wild assertions were absolutely disregarded. She im-
plied that I was trying to steal the play from her. Kept bringing
Miss Thompson into the conversation as a bad woman—and
in general made a noisy and most undignified scene. She did,
however, in the presence of Mrs. Jelliffe, admit that we had
started the play together, and that certain characterizations
such as making the two boys, one a dancer, the other a guitarist, work for the tourists, etc. were originally my ideas, and
that one line in the first act had been mine—but that she had
cut that out! . . . The whole thing was most absurd, like a scene
in a play itself. Mr. Jelliffe stopped by to take his wife home
for dinner, and hearing what was being said, asked her to no
longer remain to be further insulted. Miss Hurston even insulted the city playground attached to the Playhouse Settle-

ment by saying that it was so muddy and dirty that it made her sick to look at it when she had arrived yesterday for the first conference. You can see from that how crazy and irrational the afternoon was. Miss Hurston said that something she had heard during the night before make her seek another understanding, as she hadn't come out to Cleveland to be made a fool of; she said she didn't want the play to be done here now; that whatever I had put in the hands of my lawyer could stay there; and without even saying goodbye, she pushed her hat on the back of her head and walked out. . . . So there is our face to face ending! Of course there are a hundred other remarks and sayings that were passed here that would take a dozen more pages to put down, but you have here the gist of what went on. (For one: Mr. Cheeks as President of the Players might have been more tactful in his handling of the situation. One of the first things he said to Miss Hurston was that in ten years they had done plays by Paul Green, O'Neill, and various other big people, and they'd never had the difficulties with any one in regard to the permission to do or not do a play as they had had with Miss Hurston!) And today's scene, of course, made tonight's meeting of the Players to reconsider the play, useless. . . . I also learn that she has said some unpleasant things about me and the play in New York to people whom I trust are friends—so it appears that she has chosen to be as malicious and untrue about the matter as my silence will allow her to be, making her version of the story a public matter. In any case, the whole thing has come to the ears of some of the colored newspaper reporters here. One of them has promised to print nothing about the matter, but no telling about some of the others may do. It's turned out to be a most unpleasant mess here certainly, as the Gilpins will now probably lose their downtown date and the money to pay on the Art School scholarship. . . . As for myself, I see nothing to do except to ask you to inform Elisabeth Marbury of my claims as co-author of the play. (Raymond Crossett, I believe, is the man who personally handles Miss Hurston's manuscripts there.) I have writen their office some days ago but have had no answer. I trust they will not attempt to sell the play until this is settled. If the play should ever be published or produced without my knowledge or consent, I feel that I have just proof, and ample grounds, on which to take action against the publishers or producers, as well as Miss Hurston—and after the disgraceful way in which she has acted, I certainly would wish to do so. . . . However, if she at any time again wishes to acknowledge our collaboration, or to work with me on the finishing of the play, I am perfectly willing to complete the play with her as regards the final polishing up and putting in shape which I feel that it needs. . . . At the moment I regret the loss of what I had considered her friendship, and the loss (I hope only temporarily) of what might have been an amusing comedy—but which really turned out to be A Bone Of Contention. . . . In the light of the face to face failure, I would appreciate your further advice on the matter. Aside from word to Marbury, I see nothing to do but let it all drop until Miss Hurston herself in some way brings it to life again. But I'd like to know what you think, too.

Sincerely,
[Langston Hughes]

SPINGARN TO HUGHES   19 West 44th Street
                                      New York City
                                      Feb. 3rd, 1931

Mr. Langston Hughes,
4800 Carnegie Ave.
Cleveland, Ohio.

DEAR LANGSTON:—

Your letter of Jan. 30th has just reached me and I am
returning herewith the papers previously sent to me and
which you ask for.

I did not tell Miss Hurston that I would not represent you
here in New York. What I did tell her was, that up to the
present I was acting, not as your lawyer but as your friend, in
an attempt to bring about an amicable adjustment and that, of
course, nothing she told me in my office would be used by me
in a legal capacity. This was, of course, the only ethical thing
to do, for if I were seeing her in a legal capacity, it would only
be proper that she be accompanied by her lawyer when she
saw me, but it had been my hope that in this matter the law
would not be resorted to.

I told Miss Hurston that I believed you were a strictly
honest person and that I resented your being described as
otherwise. When she gave me her detailed description of your
collaboration and other circumstances attending it, I told her,
as I wrote you and Mrs. Jelliffe, that I was not in a position to
controvert her statements without having a personal interview
with you, but that I felt your differences were largely tempera-
mental and emotional, and that I firmly believed that when she
got there you could adjust the matter between yourselves.

I also told Miss Hurston that no one would produce the
play without the consent of both of you and urged this as a

reason for a speedy settlement. She said that unless the matter could be settled "honestly" she would prefer to tear up the play. I told her this was foolish and that you doubtless could come to some accord. Likewise, when Dr. Locke came to see me, I made no comment further than to say that if the story told me were true, it was unfortunate, but that I was not in a position to pass on the matter without hearing your version.

As to the copyright, it is not unusual for the Copyright Office to copyright any material that is regularly presented to it. You can write to the Copyright office directly and ascertain the date on which Miss Hurston obtained her copyright.

By this time, you have seen Miss Hurston and I trust that my original belief that you could settle the matter amicably between you has been justified.

Believe me, as always,

Faithfully yours,
ARTHUR B. SPINGARN

Enclosures.

SPINGARN TO HUGHES

19 West 44th Street
New York City
February 5th, 1931

Mr. Langston Hughes,
4800 Carnegie Avenue,
Cleveland, Ohio.

DEAR LANGSTON:—

Your letter of February 3rd has just reached me and I am terribly sorry that the conference ended as it did.

The thing is particularly unfortunate, because unless you and Miss Hurston can come to some arrangement, the labors of both of you on the play will come to nought. On Miss Hurston's own statements at the Cleveland conference, you have some interests in the play and under the law, neither of you can dispose of the full rights to the play without the consent of the other. There are no steps for you to take now, inasmuch as the play is not going to be produced.

If you should ever learn of a production being contemplated, you would then be in a position to obtain an injunction. I understand from your letter that you have already notified Miss Marbury of your interest in the play, so there would be no point to my repeating the notice. I assume that you have kept a copy of the notice that you sent to her.

Perhaps when Miss Hurston has a chance to think further over this matter, you may again get together and collaborate on the manuscript and turn it into a really fine play. I sincerely hope this will come to pass.

In the meanwhile, with most cordial greetings, believe me to be, as always,

Faithfully yours,
ARTHUR B. SPINGARN

HURSTON TO HUGHES   43 W. 66th St.
                                     New York City
                                     February 14, 1931.

DEAR LANGSTON,

Arrived safely back in New York. Stopped in Westfield and got two books of mine that I needed. Asked Mrs. Peoples to tell you that I had taken them.

In case that my letter to Mrs. Jeliffe mis-carries, tell her that I just found the check this afternoon. My nephew put part of the mail on my desk, and put the rest in the dresser drawer so I just found it, and am returning it to her. That is, I enclosed it in the letter I wrote her. In view of the fact that we did no business, I don't know whether I am due it. In addition it was incorrectly made out.

Sorry that you are having so much throat trouble. You are late on that again as you were on the intestinal trouble. I have wrassled with my throat for ages. Helene Johnson is in the hospital now having her tonsils out and I think I shall do the same before warm weather.

>Lots of luck.
>Sincerely,
>ZORA NEALE HURSTON

SPINGARN TO HUGHES   March 5th, 1931

Mr. Langston Hughes
4800 Carnegie Ave.
Cleveland, Ohio.

DEAR LANGSTON:—

Miss Hurston was in to see me this morning. She tells me that there is no possible chance of her ever collaborating with you on the play and that she wants to eliminate all parts of the play in which you claim collaboration, and make a new play in which you will have no interest, and she wants a release from you of your rights in this play.

I told Miss Hurston that Walter White had informed me that you were coming to New York shortly and that I could not take the matter up with you by correspondence, but that when you came to New York, I would talk it over with you.

Will you please let me know by return mail what your plans are and when you expect to come to New York. I do not mean by this that you should come to New York on this account, but that you should let me know immediately when you expect to be here, so that I can inform Miss Hurston of the time when she may expect to hear your reaction from me.

In the meanwhile, with personal greetings, believe me to be, as always,

Sincerely yours,
ARTHUR B. SPINGARN

HUGHES TO SPINGARN   4800 Carnegie Ave.,
                                      Cleveland, Ohio,
                                      March 6, 1931

DEAR ARTHUR SPINGARN,

I hope to be in New York about March fifteenth. I will get in touch with you as soon as I arrive. I think it would be just as well to let Miss Hurston have the play, don't you? Or at least her part of it.

The copyright office informs us that Miss Hurston has not copyrighted the play (as she claimed she did in October). So I hold the only copyright. How would we dispose of that?

Thank you for writing me.

Sincerely,
LANGSTON HUGHES

HUGHES TO SPINGARN   4800 Carnegie Ave.,
                                       Cleveland Ohio,
                                       March 15, 1931

DEAR ARTHUR SPINGARN,

I cannot be in New York until next Monday, the 23rd.
Have just had my tonsils out this week, so the doctor forbids
my leaving until the end of next week. . . . I've finished a play
of my own and want to ask your advice about a reliable agent
when I see you. . . . With all good wishes,

                                       Sincerely,
                                       LANGSTON

HURSTON TO HUGHES   43 W. 66th St.
                                       New York City
                                       March 18, 1931

DEAR LANGSTON,

I got your clipping today. Thanks. I read it. I dont know
whether you sent it to me so that I might know that this sort
of thing happens to lots of folks, or whether some part of it
appeared to you to fit the case.

At any rate, it was kind of you to want to help me. I am
glad to hear that your throat is well. I have yet to undergo
what you have just passed thru. I am feeling fine and well, but
that throat is just waiting to spring on me again. I am calm
again and went to a party and had a nice time. Hard at work
on the African thing and plan to have it all done by next week.

Then I shall re-write the conjure book. I have a good scheme for doing it now.

Sincerely,
ZORA

HURSTON TO SPINGARN   43 W. 66 St.
New York City
March 25, 1931.

MY DEAR MR. SPINGARN,

This is to deny your assertion that you have seen the original script. You have seen what your client <u>says</u> is the original script. You evidently forget that your client had my script out in Cleveland and I see did not hesitate to copy off some "emendations." The whole matter is absolutely without honor from start to finish and this latest evidence of trying to make a case by actual theft, "emendations" as you call them, makes me lose respect for the thing altogether. From the very beginning it has been an attempt to build up a case by inference and construction rather than by fact. But all the liberal construction in the world cannot stand against certain things which I have in my possession.

I think it would be lovely for your client to be a playwright but I'm afraid that I am too tight to make him one at my expense. You have written plays, why not do him one yourself? Or perhaps a nice box of apples and a well chosen corner. But never no play of mine.

Most emphatically yours,
ZORA NEALE HURSTON

Hurston to Mason

43 West 66 St.
New York City
March 25, 1931.

Darling Godmother,

My work is coming along well. I have taken a great deal of pains to rewrite certain passages and feel satisfied for the moment with the introduction. I have done over two entire chapters and now I am within a few paragraphs of the end of the whole thing. Then for the final typing.

I found at the library an actual account of the raid as Kossula said that it happened. Also the tribe name. It was not on the maps because the entire tribe was wiped out by the Dahomey troops. The king who conquered them preserved carefully the skull of Kossula's king as a most worthy foe.

Harry's not being able to help me makes it unnecessary to give him anything at present. I would want to offer him part of my allowance as a gift if and when he does something for me. He says that he cannot do anything until I have done it over myself.

I find that Langston is in town and that he copied whole hunks out of my play in Cleveland and NOW tries to say that while he didn't write the thing in the beginning, he made all those "emendations" on the play last Fall. I can't conceive of such lying and falsehood. But then there are many things in earth and sky that I don't know about.

All my love Godmother. I am very well and I have even learned to live above Langston's vileness. So I am happy.

Love and love and love, and many prayers for your own good health and happiness. I am making a supreme effort at this time to make you happy and strengthen your faith in my creative ability.

Devotedly,
ZORA

I'd love for Langston to face me in your presence.

HURSTON TO MASON   April 18, 1931

DARLING GODMOTHER,

At last "Barracoon" is ready for your eyes. I pray so earnestly that I have done something that can come somewhere near your expectations.

The pictures at the museum were magnificent. I am sending you the catalog so that you may know what the subjects are. The exhibit lasts until April 20th or thru that date.

I have been working on the Conjure book this week. It's getting easier now. I wrote Alain too. He is very busy I know but I hope for an answer.

Godmother darling, you don't know how the thought of you comforts me these devilish days. Sometimes what is inside me breaks out and destroys me for hours. Usually I am calm, but sometimes I need a refuge to run to. So I light a candle in your name and wait for you to send the peace.

The dress looks magnificent on me so I bought a hat to go with it. I am so grateful to you that you remember me always and try to drag me up to the light.

I saw Alta Douglas last week and she asked of you. This is the first time that she has said anything about you. She says she wants to write you but she knows you are not well.

I know that Langston says he was going to Cuba, but I

suspect that he is really gone to hunt up Eatonville to pretend that he knew about it all along.

When I look back on the three and a half years that I have known you, Godmother, I am amazed. I see all my terrible weakness and failures, my stark stupidity and lack of vision and I am amazed that your love and confidence has carried over. That is why I am plugging away so diligently now, so that your faith will have something to live on. I know that your perfect understanding of me will read all the volumes that are compressed in this paragraph.

I fear that the tonsils will have to come out soon. They stay sore and lower my vitality too much. I am only half of me at least a third of the time.

With a prayer for a greater understanding on my part, a continued love from you and some achievements from my person to nourish you, I am

Your own
ZORA

HUGHES TO SPINGARN   181 West 135th St.,
New York, New York,
August 14, 1931.

Mr. Arthur Spingarn,
19 West 44th Street,
New York, New York.

DEAR ARTHUR SPINGARN,

Yesterday morning, August 13, I went with my aunt, Mrs. Toy Harper, 2 East 127th Street, to the office of Elizabeth Marbury, where I had a talk with Raymond Crossett regarding the comedy <u>Mule Bone</u> by Zora Hurston and myself. I told Mr. Crossett that I had written his office last spring stating that I was co-author with Miss Hurston of the play, and that they had not answered my letter. Mr. Crossett said it was never received by the Marbury office. I then proceeded to tell him the facts of the collaboration. He said my story left him cold. That I had no rights in the play. That he had absolute faith in Miss Hurston. That he would continue to handle the play. That I could get all the lawyers I choose. That they had one of the best law-firms in town, (which he named). And that he just loved fights. He further stated that he had laid the whole case before the Dramatists Guild, and that he was well protected there. . . . When I left his office, I went to the Dramatists Guild, where I am a member, and was informed that they had never heard of the case there, and had never talked with Crossett about it! They said Miss Hurston is not a member of the Guild. And they advised me to write them a letter setting forth the details. I am doing so today. . . . I am also writing the Marbury office again, this time registered mail, so that they cannot deny receiving my letter. The play has been for some weeks in the hands of Wallace Thurman, whom the Marbury office asked to revise it. Yesterday Mr. Thurman told me he was returning the manuscript, having done no work on it, as he did not wish to be involved in a controversy. . . . I am enclosing a carbon of my letter to the Marbury office today.

Sincerely,
LANGSTON HUGHES

HURSTON TO MASON   43 W. 66th St.
                                   New York City
                                   August 14, 1931

DARLING MY GODMOTHER,

You have been with me every day in the spirit and I have felt you there. My silence has neither been negligence nor illness. Things have been in such a fluid condition from day to day that there was not a statement I could safely make, except to acknowledge your gift to me. For about 15 days the revue "Fast and Furious" looked <u>bad</u>. Financial difficulties. One day it would look hopeful, the next very black. Yesterday the producer got the money and the house all settled. Somehow my inner self tells me that even now something is not well. Perhaps he and I shall disagree about changes in my material. Godmother, they take all the life and soul out of everything and make it fit what their idea of Broadway should be like. It's sickening at times.

Langston is back in town. I received an announcement that he was to lecture on the West Indies, or his travels, to be exact, under the auspices of the "Crisis." He went down to my agent's with a long line of most malicious lies in an effort to prejudice them against me. He took along some woman whom he introduced as his aunt to help him talk. All he got for his trouble was to be called a vicious liar to his face, a sneak and a weakling. The woman was asked what she was doing there and to keep her mouth shut or get out of the office. He was made out a liar on five different counts, and told to do anything that he wished, for there was able legal backing behind me. So he finally slunk out telling Mr. Crossett that he was collaborating on a play with Wallace Thurman and he would like for the Marbury office to handle it. Mr. Crossett told him that he handled Thurman's affairs, but that the office would positively refuse to touch anything that he had anything to do with as he had shown himself to be a person of no honor. Nobody had to convict him of being a liar. He convicted himself. With his own letter of Oct. 6, before Mr. Crossett in which he asks me to send him the second act of the play, he tells Mr. Crossett that he had written the play himself in January and I had stolen it and made a copy of his play and submitted it to the Guild. Then of course, Mr. C. showed him my copyright card of Oct. 29, 1930 and he all but fainted, for he thought he had played a sharp trick by making a copy while it was in Cleveland and getting copyrighted.

He tried to tell the agent these things which you had told me he was saying—that it was a personal affair and that I had taken his play because I was jealous of Louise. The agent of course cut him short and told him that he [had] no interest in anything except the authorship of the play, and that his place was an office and not a cleaning house for Harlem gossip. He wanted him to point out what he had done on the play. He [Hughes] said that he had taken a page and a half of my notes—all that there was of my story—and built it into seventy magnificent pages of a play. Whereupon he was again told that he was a stupid liar. He told him (I mean L. told C.) that I was a person of a most violent disposition and had called him and his Cleveland friends liars and crooks, etc. Mr. C. again reminded him that he was only interested in the business and commented that if his tactics were the same in Cleveland as they were in his office, I was more than justified and much too mild, really. So much for that. It no longer even annoys me. Give a calf enough rope—

Had a card from Alain. He gave me a nice bawling out. I loved it. It was the first time he had noticed me and I was so glad he had calmed down enough to speak to me at all. I shall write him c/o Cook's Place, Madelaine, Paris.

Now about the money, Godmother, darling. By the time for you to send me my next allowance, I shall be receiving money from the theatre. I should love to keep up our original arrangement. I'd like to send you all monies and have you then give me an allowance as usual. If you say, "Now that you are earning money, go for yourself," I'll feel alone in the world again. And Godmother, that would be too awful.

What would happen if I were to jump in our car and come up to talk with you?

Thanks and thanks Godmother, darling. I love you truly.

Devotedly,
ZORA

HURSTON TO LOCKE

The Young Womens
Christian Association
of Chicago
South Parkway Branch
and Residence
4559 South Parkway
October 29, 1934

Dr. Alain Leroy Locke,
1326 R. Street,
Washington, D.C.

DEAR ALAIN:

I have written godmother for the permission to dedicate the new book.

Did I tell you in the last letter that it is being illustrated by Baldridge? It would have been off the press in November but for that. It will be out in January now.

Instead of feeling less need of godmother and more independent as success approaches me, I need her more and feel her great goodness to me more deeply. If I am acclaimed by the world, and make a million in money, I would feel still that she was responsible for it. I have not written often because I did not get answers and thought she did not want to hear from me. Just did not understand. She shall have a weekly letter from me—from now on.

I do hope that you come to Chicago, within the next few days. I wish that you could be here for my concert on the 23rd of November. I would like very much to have you tell the audience what godmother has meant to Negro literature and art. She is where she can do no more, but before she passes I think there ought to be some acknowledgment to the world, from at least one of the people that she has saved or tried to save, and what she has meant to America.

There will be three performances, two evening performances on the 23rd and 24th of November and a matinee on the 24th.

I am beginning my third book as soon as the concert is over.

My play "Mule Bone" has been asked for by the Little Theatre in New York. Same director as for "Run Little Chillun." I am wondering whether to send it there or to produce it myself here. I have a very good opening. Since all funds for the play and everything else can be had right here, I am wondering if I could not do a better job of interpreting Negro material than any white director ever could.

Most sincerely,
ZORA NEALE HURSTON

October
Twenty-ninth
1 9 3 4
ZNH/mp

VAN VECHTEN TO HUGHES

James Weldon Johnson
Memorial Committee
Sixty-nine Fifth Avenue
New York, NY
[August 17, 1942]

Dear Langston, I've been away for a few days and when I come back I find your letter. . . . While away I have read a book called The Sabbath Has No End, by John Weld (ofay) a story of slave days on a plantation where the slaves were "well treated." Without much trouble, Mr. Weld shows you that it was impossible to treat slaves well and gives many intricate reasons in the course of his story. In many ways a vivid and extraordinary story. . . . I've also been reading many Negro letters for Yale, including the correspondence re Mule Bone which includes letters from YOU and Zora and Barrett H. Clark and Lawrence Langner and Theresa Helburn. It's a pretty complete tale and your letter regarding Zora's tantrum in your mother's room in Cleveland is wonderful. She had a tantrum in my library at 150 West 55 Street too and threw herself on the floor and screamed and yelled! Bit the dust in fact. You woulda loved it, had it not concerned you. . . . Something very important has happened, perhaps for the first time. *LIFE* in the August 17 issue has a couple of pages concerning the fire that destroyed part of the managery of the Ringling Brothers and it gives the name of the incendiary, but it does not say he is a Negro or print his picture! On my return I find a bundle (for Yale) a mile high from Walter White, another full of music from William Dawson, another smaller package from Verna Arvey and many letters promising help. Arna writes that he has already seen Georgette's manuscript and talked it over with her about a year ago. WHY will people behave in this fashion? She said she had never heard of him. Obviously I can't trust Miss Harvey on the next go-round. . . . Mr. Knollenberg has just given the Yale Collection some terrific letters, including items of Lincoln, Frederick Douglass, and Harriet Beecher Stowe. And Ray Stannard Baker has given us a tremendous amount of important material. . . . I had already planned to write Mrs. Rapp but thought I would wait till Mr. Rapp had been dead a minute. . . . I guess people would walk into your life even if you didn't write poems, but perhaps the poems makes 'em walk in quicker. . . . MY LAST copy of Theatre Arts went to Noel, as you requested. Somebody told me the magazine was out of print, but I'll see what I can do. You shall have a copy if there is one! My reserved copy, of course, went to Yale. . . . I'm afraid Kenneth F. is somewhere in the catalogue as Miss Taggard's spouse. If so, this information came from You, you rascal! I haven't been to Fat Man in the Bronx though Eddie and his blonde wife asked me to the housewarming at their Love Nest. . . . It was too hot and too late a party, so I didn't go. Tita, Gate; is This Is The Army! And I have photographed the three leading Negroes. . . . In the Pennsylvania station last night there wasn't a single porter. Lugged a 90 pound bag (full of letters and books) about a mile in pitch blackness (the roof is glass and they keep the lights out). Your slow eating habits will be a distinct disadvantage to you in a boarding house where you are expected to talk. Better take vitamins. . . . The Everleigh Club in Chicago also had a fountain in the living room. Some of the best families used to fall in. Affection to you and FM even sends a kiss, after your "Tell Fania I love her!"

Monday (I'm off to the Canteen SOON)

CARLO!

ABOUT THE EDITORS

George Houston Bass (1938–1990), one of this country's leading authorities on Afro-American art and literature, was professor of Theatre Arts and Afro-American Studies at Brown University, and was founder and artistic director of Brown's Rites and Reason Theatre. He studied at Fisk (New York) and Yale Universities. Under his leadership, Rites and Reason Theatre won a citation from the New England Theatre Conference, and the Monarch Award from the National Council for Culture and Arts. Bass is the author of several plays including *Providence Garden Blues, Black Masque, Malacoff Blue,* and *Brer Rabbit Whole,* and Dr. Bass's research on the aesthetics of African-American performance tradition has appeared in many scholarly publications. He was editor of *The Langston Hughes Review,* the official publication of the Langston Hughes Society, published by Brown University's Afro-American Studies Program.

Henry Louis Gates, Jr., received his Ph.D. from the University of Cambridge in 1979. Duke University's John Spencer

Bassett Professor of English and Literature, he has also taught at Yale and Cornell Universities. His interests are in African and African-American literature and criticism. He is the general editor of *The Norton Anthology of Afro-American Literature,* and the editor of Oxford's thirty-volume series, *The Schomburg Library of Nineteenth-Century Black Women Writers.* His publications include *Figures in Black: Words, Signs, and the Racial Self* (Oxford, 1987) and *The Signifying Monkey: A Theory of Afro-American Literary Criticism* (Oxford, 1988), which won the American Book Award.